W9-CWR-407

GHOSTLY
PARALLELS

GHOSTLY PARALLELS

ROBERT PENN WARREN AND
THE LYRIC POETIC SEQUENCE

RANDOLPH PAUL
RUNYON

The University of Tennessee Press / Knoxville

Copyright © 2006 by The University of Tennessee Press / Knoxville.
All Rights Reserved. Manufactured in the United States of America.
First Edition.

Frontispiece: Antefix with Gorgoneion (Medusa head), mid-fourth century BCE, southern
Italy. Gift of Walter I. Farmer, 1978. Courtesy of Miami University Art Museum.

Part of chapter 6 originally appeared in *Style* 36.2 (Summer 2002); part of chapter 7 in
RPW: An Annual of Robert Penn Warren Studies Vol. 1 (2001), and the *Southern Review*
38.4 (Autumn 2002). I am grateful to their editors for permission to republish here.

Selections from *The Collected Poems of Robert Penn Warren* copyright © 1997 by the
Estate of Robert Penn Warren. Reprinted by permission of William Morris Agency, Inc.,
on behalf of the author.

This book is printed on acid-free paper.

Library of Congress Cataloging-in-Publication Data

Runyon, Randolph, 1947-
  Ghostly parallels : Robert Penn Warren and the lyric poetic sequence / Randolph Paul
Runyon.— 1st ed.
    p. cm.
Includes bibliographical references (p.   ) and index.
ISBN 1-57233-465-7 (acid-free paper)
1. Warren, Robert Penn, 1905—Criticism and interpretation.   2. Perseus (Greek
mythology) in literature. I. Title.
PS3545.A748Z86425 2006
811'.54—dc22   2005035884

CONTENTS

INTRODUCTION

America's most eminent man of letters in his later years, and one of the greatest writers of the American South, Robert Penn Warren has increasingly come to be appreciated as a poet, and primarily so, though his significance as a novelist, critic, and essayist will always be recognized.[1] Harold Bloom writes that while the novels *All the King's Men* and *World Enough and Time* will endure, "I believe that Warren's name will be more associated with his *Collected Poems*." They are "Warren's center, and his lasting glory."[2] *Ghostly Parallels: Robert Penn Warren and the Lyric Poetic Sequence* focuses on an important part of that center, the poetic sequences of his early and middle career: *Thirty-Six Poems* (1935), *Eleven Poems on the Same Theme* (1942), *Promises* (1957), *You, Emperors, and Others* (1960), *Tale of Time* (1966), *Incarnations* (1968), *Or Else* (1974), and *Can I See Arcturus from Where I Stand?* (1976). As I did in *The Braided Dream: Robert Penn Warren's Late Poetry*, a study of his last four sequences (*Now and Then, Being Here, Rumor Verified*, and *Altitudes and Extensions*), I will show here how Warren delighted in constructing poetic collections in which each poem is enriched by the context of the poems surrounding it.

Other readers have noted the high degree of coherence Warren's sequences display. In a letter to Warren, Cleanth Brooks described "Island of Summer" in *Incarnations* as a "chain" in which "there is not a weak link," and remarked upon "the impact of the whole group taken as one beautifully interlaced and very rich, massive, long poem."[3] Victor Strandberg writes of "interlocking continuity" in the Rosanna poems in *Promises*.[4] Dave Smith writes that "Warren has constructed the poems of *Or Else* as reflectors, baffles, mirrors, and back-lights" and alludes to the "juxtaposition and oblique continuities" evident there.[5] A. L. Clements writes of Warren's poetry that "not only grouping and repeated subjects and thematic concerns but also full sequences with the recurrence of certain words and images conduce to the sense of continuity of integration."[6] "We are compelled from one poem to another," writes Daniel Hoffman, "by unpredictable loopings of thought."[7] Robert Koppelman urges us to bear in mind that "any one of Warren's poems needs to be read in relation to others, especially those appearing in juxtaposition within each collection, in order to best appreciate how the individual poem or image functions in the complex 'web' or 'mysterious logic' of both Warren's poetry and his fundamental epistemology."[8] According to John Burt, "Warren's characteristic form" is "the sequence of lyrics connected by an unwritten story that allows each poem's insistence on the fixity of the moment it presents to be conditioned by the necessity of turning to the next part of the sequence, another moment of fixity whose relations with the last one are not always obvious."[9]

As Strandberg wrote of "interlocking continuity" in *Promises,* Warren himself was intrigued by the "cunning interlockings" he saw in the poetry of John Crowe Ransom, under whom he had studied poetry at Vanderbilt. In a 1968 essay, Warren notes how, in Ransom's sequence *Two Gentlemen in Bonds,* "one poem seems to lead, as it were, to another." In one pair of neighboring poems, the conversation carried on by twittering birds repeats that of the human protagonists; two others maintain "a teasing relationship" with each other; another pair "come together and thematically supplement each other"; and one poem is followed by another "which seems so different, but is . . . a repetition, in another range, of the same theme."[10] In reading Ransom's poems, Warren provides a way of reading his own, for these are just the kinds of continuities, repetitions, and coherence his own sequences display.

Indeed, Warren does find a certain similarity between his approach and Ransom's: "I myself, in trying to write poetry, and in thinking about poetry, was torn between the Pound-Eliot strain and another possibility, shadowy to me and undefined, which, though not like Ransom's poetry, then seemed nearer to it, in some way, than to anything else" (305). In Warren's essay, it becomes apparent that what his poetry has that makes it closer to Ransom's than to anything else is a certain "oscillating mechanism" he finds to be characteristic of Ransom's style. The phrase came from Ransom himself, who once told Warren that "he was rather inclined to think that man was, naturally, born as a kind of 'oscillating mechanism'" (305). He said this after Warren showed him an earlier essay he had written on him[11] in which he spoke of a "dissociation of sensibility" characteristic of the modern world and compared him in this regard to Pound, Eliot, and Faulkner. Ransom's point was that there was nothing particularly modern about this malaise, but that it had always been part of the human condition. After that conversation, "I kept remembering the phrase 'oscillating mechanism.' So that was what he saw as the underlying fact of his poems, the source of his style!" (306). Looking back, he finds the earlier essay "fumbling" and inadequate: "I was trying to find a mere pattern of ideas when I should rather have been trying to find a characteristic movement of mind—of being" (305). He had been looking for what Ransom's poetry was about when he should have been looking at what it does. We would be well advised to do the same, to read Warren's poetry for what it does. And what it does is oscillate, because in his sequences, words, images, and situations recurring from one poem to the next force our attention to oscillate back and forth between the two poems. The recurring words oscillate, too—for example, the words "the last red" in "Literal Dream" and "After the Dinner Party," two contiguous poems in *Altitudes and Extensions*:

> I woke at the call of nature. It was near day.
> Patient I sat, staring through the
> Wet pane at sparse drops that struck
> The last red dogwood leaves. It was as though
> I could hear the plop there. See the leaf quiver. ("Literal Dream" 543)[12]

> You two sit at the table late, each, now and then,
> Twirling a near-empty wine glass to watch the last red
> Liquid climb up the crystalline spin to the last moment when
> Centrifugality fails: with nothing now said. ("After the Dinner Party" 544)

The raindrops that struck the last red dogwood leaves are meant, within "Literal Dream," to recall some other drops that fall earlier in the poem: "The stain on her neat ceiling gathered to a / Point. / Which hung forever. / Dropped" (543). As a note after the title makes explicit, the speaker in the poem is dreaming of the scene in Hardy's *Tess of the d'Urbervilles* in which blood drips from the ceiling. The drops in the dream are red; the raindrops on the red dogwood leaves combine liquidity with the color in a different way. In "After the Dinner Party," we encounter another red liquid, and it too is falling, as centrifugality gives way to gravity. Our eyes oscillate from one "the last red" to the other, from one red liquid to the other, from the blood to the wine, as we try to figure out why each poem speaks, despite different themes and contexts, of the same things. And despite the considerable changes that occurred in Warren's poetry in other regards, particularly after the decade-long break between the *Selected Poems* of 1943 and *Promises,* this sequentially echoing structure remains nearly constant. I say "nearly" because it appears to be absent from the *Selected Poems* of 1943, in which Warren rearranged the *Eleven Poems* and most of the *Thirty-Six Poems* into something resembling the chronological order of their composition, mixing in "The Ballad of Billie Potts," "Variation: Ode to Fear," and "Mexico Is a Foreign Country: Five Studies in Naturalism."

Another constant is evoked by the "call of nature" that awakens the speaker in "Literal Dream." This discreet allusion to the need to urinate is, in the larger picture, part of a complex network of images that can be found throughout Warren's poems and novels in which the writer sees himself as Perseus, conceived in the golden shower in which Zeus made love to Danae. The same Perseus confronted the dread Medusa and slew her by means of a mirror image. I will argue that Danae and Medusa stand for positive and negative aspects of the mother in Warren's personal mythology. Warren, most notably in the opening pages of his last novel, *A Place to Come To,* but also in the sequentially combining poems "Tale of Time" and "Homage to Emerson," suggests an equivalence between urine and sperm that is a way of accounting for the golden shower in the myth. Evidence of the myth is there from the beginning of his sequences, in the first poem of *Thirty-Six Poems,* "The Return: An Elegy." There he alludes to sexual guilt through the disguise of infantile bed wetting ("make me a child again just for tonight / good lord he's wet the bed come bring a light"). His poetry is charged with hidden sexuality, disguised in such seemingly innocent images as childhood mishaps and flowers—such as the "dark and swollen orchid of this sorrow" he would pluck and lay upon his mother's breast if he could in that same poem.

The railroad journey the poet undertakes in order to return to his dying mother in that poem supplies my title: "I come I come / Whirl out of space through time O wheels / Pursue down backward time the ghostly parallels." The parallels are the rails, ghostly in the darkness, that lead him back. But the phrase could also be taken to allude to the way the poems of Warren's sequences are invariably both the parallel and the ghost of the poems that precede them. To read them is to be drawn continually back.

PROLOGUE

THE PERSEUS MYTH IN
APOLLODORUS AND OVID

When Acrisius inquired of the oracle . . . the god said that his daugh-
ter would give birth to a son who would kill him. Fearing that, Acrisius
built a brazen chamber . . . and there guarded Danae. However . . .
Zeus had intercourse with her in the shape of a stream of gold which
poured through the roof into Danae's lap. When Acrisius afterwards
learned that she had got a child Perseus, he would not believe that she
had been seduced by Zeus, and putting his daughter with the child in
a chest, he cast it into the sea. The chest was washed ashore on Seriphus,
and Dictys took up the boy and reared him.

    . . . [Of the three Gorgons] Medusa alone was mortal; . . . Perseus
was sent to fetch her head. But the Gorgons had heads twined about
with the scales of dragons, and great tusks like swine's, and brazen
hands, and golden wings . . . and they turned to stone such as beheld
them. So Perseus stood over them as they slept, and while Athena
guided his hand and he looked with averted gaze on a brazen shield,
in which he beheld the image of the Gorgon, he beheaded her. When
her head was cut off, there sprang from the Gorgon the winged horse
Pegasus. . . . Perseus put the head of Medusa in the wallet.

    . . . [Perseus] found the king's daughter Andromeda set out to be
the prey of a sea monster. . . . When Perseus beheld her, he loved her.
[He] slew the monster and released Andromeda. However, Phineus,
. . . to whom Andromeda had been first betrothed, plotted against
him; but Perseus discovered the plot, and by showing the Gorgon
turned him and his fellow conspirators at once into stone.

—Apollodorus, *The Library,* bk. 1, 153, 155, 157, 159, 161

Thro' devious Wilds, and trackless Woods he past,
And at the *Gorgon*-Seats arriv'd at last:
But as he journey'd, pensive he survey'd,
What wasteful Havock dire *Medusa* made.
Here, stood still breathing Statues, men before;
There, rampant Lions seem'd in Stone to roar.
Nor did he, yet affrighted, quit the Field,
But in the Mirror of his polish'd Shield
Reflected saw *Medusa* Slumbers take,
And not one Serpent by good chance awake.
Then backward an unerring Blow he sped,
And from her Body lop'd at once her Head.
The Gore prolifick prov'd; with sudden Force
Sprung *Pegasus,* and wing'd his airy Course.
. . . .
Medusa once had Charms; to gain her Love
A rival Crowd of envious Lovers strove.
They, who have seen her, own, they ne'er did trace
More moving Features in a sweeter Face.
Yet above all, her Length of Hair, they own,
In golden Ringlets wav'd, and graceful shone.
Her *Neptune* saw, and with such Beauties fir'd,
Resolv'd to compass, what his Soul desir'd.
In chaste *Minerva's* Fane, he, lustful, stay'd,
And seiz'd, and rifled the young, blushing Maid.
The bashful Goddess turn'd her Eyes away,
Nor durst such bold Impurity survey;
But on the ravish'd Virgin Vengeance takes,
Her shining Hair is chang'd to hissing Snakes.
These in her *Aegis, Pallas* joys to bear,
The hissing Snakes her Foes more sure ensnare,
Than they did Lovers once, when shining Hair.
. . . .
His Feet again the valiant *Perseus* plumes,
And his keen Sabre in his Hand resumes:
Then nobly spurns the Ground, and upwards springs,
And cuts the liquid Air with sounding Wings.
O'er various Seas, and various Lands he past,
'Till *Aethiopia's* Shore appear'd at last.
Andromeda was there, doom'd to attone
By her own Ruin, Follies not her own:
And if Injustice in a God can be,

Such was the *Libyan* God's unjust Decree.
Chain'd to a Rock she stood; young *Perseus* stay'd
His rapid Flight, to view the beauteous Maid.
So sweet her Frame, so exquisitely fine,
She seem'd a Statue by a Hand Divine,
Had not the Wind her waving Tresses show'd,
And down her Cheeks the melting Sorrows flow'd.
Her faultless Form the Hero's Bosom fires;
The more he looks, the more he still admires.
. . . .
Too long you vent your Sorrows, *Perseus* said,
Short is the Hour, and swift the time of Aid,
In me the Son of Thund'ring *Jove* behold,
Got in a kindly Show'r of fruitful Gold.
Medusa's Snaky Head is now my Prey,
And thro' the Clouds I boldly wing my Way.
—Ovid, *Metamorphoses,* bk. 4, 144, 145, 141–42

CHAPTER 1
"TWO BY TWO"

THIRTY-SIX
POEMS

Warren's first volume of poetry, the *Thirty-Six Poems* of 1935, has been practically unknown to a generation of readers, or at least it had been until the *Collected Poems* appeared in 1998. Three of the thirty-six were never published again; fifteen more never reappeared after *Selected Poems 1923–1943*—in other words, half the collection vanished for more than fifty years. Only sixteen were included in the *Selected Poems* of 1966, fourteen in 1975, ten in 1985. Even the title disappeared, as those three editions listed the poems as coming from *Selected Poems 1923–1943*, not *Thirty-Six Poems*. It is not surprising, therefore, that the volume has received little attention. To be sure, some of Warren's most important poems, such as "The Return: An Elegy," "Kentucky Mountain Farm," and "Pondy Woods," come from that sequence, and those poems have enjoyed canonical status. But the sequence as a whole has not, though I hope that with its reemergence in the *Collected Poems* it will. It certainly has never been read as a sequence.

A few months before the volume assumed its final form, Warren was not entirely sure which poems he would include and how he would arrange them. In a letter to Allen Tate on February 4, 1935, he wrote: "I am still debating with myself over *To One Awake,* probably because forty makes such a good round number for the poems of a book. Your suggestion for making a new arrangement for the poems se[e]ms to be a good one. I was trying for something more complicated, but it now appears quite empty to me; and I can scarcely remember what principle I was working on. I am enclosing a new table of contents. How does it look to you?"[1] It is not clear whether Tate was suggesting a particular new arrangement or just that Warren rearrange the poems in some way. But it is intriguing to learn that there had once been an organizing principle that Warren claimed (whether sincerely or not is a question) no longer to remember, and that it was rather complicated. That he sent Tate a new table of contents suggests that he had abandoned the first arrangement. The question remains, Was the new arrangement based on a new, if less "empty" and perhaps less "complicated" principle? He did in the end include "To One Awake," the third poem from the last.

Three months later, he was hesitating between including thirty-six or forty poems, but that hinged (and back in February it may have only hinged) on just one decision, whether to keep the four-sonnet sequence "Images on the Tomb." On May 10, he wrote to accept Ronald Lane Latimer's offer to publish the volume for the Alcestis Press:

> I am sending forty poems, which I believe are the best and which, at least, are more consistent in tone. I have discarded other pieces, because they were really incidental and had no definite relation to the rest of my work. As the matter stands now it might be better to print the work up in two sections, the second beginning with *Pacific Gazer*. This second group is essentially more miscellaneous than the rest and it might be best to make an arbitrary separation. There is another matter in connection with the manuscript: I have included four sonnets at the very end, not mentioned in the table of contents, *Images on the Tomb*, which are very early work. I'm not certain that I want them in the volume at all; I am sending them merely because they have received a modest amount of mention. What do you think about them? I have no title for the collection. In the last few weeks I have been flirting with *Kentucky Mountain Farm* or *Cold Colloquy*, but something seems wrong with both. The first is pretty well occupied now by my friend Jesse Stuart, and the second seems a bit fancy. I have about decided to use *Thirty-Six Poems* (or Forty, as the case may be). What do you think? Although the poems are not arranged in chronological order, I believe that the dates on the poems might be of some interest. (*Selected Letters* 2: 39)

"Pacific Gazer," the tenth poem from the end, does transport the reader to California, a place he has not been in any of the previous poems, but as I will argue later, it is as connected to its immediate predecessor, "The Last Metaphor," as any poem in the sequence is to an immediate neighbor. Warren does makes two statements that are consistent with the theory that the *Thirty-Six Poems* constitute an organized collection: (1) he discarded poems that did not fit (having "no definite relation" with the rest), and (2) the poems are not arranged in the order in which he wrote them. Including their dates, which the publisher did not do, would have had the effect of alerting the reader to the possibility that there *was* an order to their arrangement.

Whether or not Warren consciously arranged his poems to be read this way (though I believe the preponderance of the evidence indicates that he did), looking at the poems "two by two" (40)—the way the golden and hieratic eyes of buzzards burn through the night in "Pondy Woods"—is at least a useful way of focusing one's attention. In "Ransom" (49), Warren alludes to the Roman augurs' divination from the flight of birds: "Doom has, we know, no shape but the shape of air. / That much for us the red-armed augurs spelled, / Or flights of fowl lost early in the long air." Taking the *auspicium* involved drawing a *templum,* an imaginary rectangle on the sky, and observing the birds that flew through that space. To read the poems two by two is to make of each pair a *templum* in which the passage of certain words and images from one poem to the other will be worth our observation.[2] By "passage," I mean that the same words and images appear in both poems and thus seem to pass from one poem to the next, from one part of the *templum* to the other. The "flights of fowl" in "Ransom" are an example of this, for in the immediately preceding "Late Subterfuge" (48), the flights of birds are also noted: "The grackles, yellow-beaked, beak-southward, fly / To the ruined ricelands south, leaving empty our sky." In fact, "Ransom" is at the center of five poems about birds: kildees fly south in "Letter from a Coward to a Hero" (46), the poem before "Late Subterfuge"; the catbird returns in time for an ironic spring in "Aged Man Surveys the Past Time" (49), the poem following "Ransom"; and the "seaswoop fisher" (50) is described as an "abler Ptolemy" (the avian astronomer navigates by the stars) in "Toward Rationality."

But to return to the beginning of the volume, in "The Return: An Elegy" (33), the poet imagines himself returning from the East Coast for his mother's funeral.[3] "Kentucky Mountain Farm" (35), a mini-sequence of seven numbered poems that counts as seven among the thirty-six of the volume's title but that I will consider as a single poem in its relations to the poem before and after it, is a reflection on the "little stubborn people of the hill" of eastern Kentucky, a region that Warren had not yet visited at the time he wrote the poem. These two contexts are connected in that the train carrying the poet home in "The Return" crosses the eastern continental divide in the Appalachians, where the hill people in the other poem reside. Warren uses the same language and imagery in both poems to mark this division between water that flows to the Atlantic and water that flows to the Mississippi:

> Locked in the roaring cubicle
> Over the mountains through darkness hurled
> I race the daylight's westward cycle
> Across the groaning rooftree of the world.
> The mist is furled.

> a hundred years they took this road
> the lank hunters then men hard-eyed with hope:
> ox breath whitened the chill air: the goad
> fell: here on the western slope

> the hungry people the lost ones took their abode
> here they took their stand. ("The Return: An Elegy" 34)

> From this high place all things flow.
> Land of divided streams, of water spilled
> Eastward, westward, without memento . . . [ellipses in poem]
> Land where the morning mist is furled
> Like smoke above the ridgepole of the world.

> The sunset hawk now rides
> The tall light up the climbing deep of air.
> Beneath him swings the rooftree that divides
> The east and west. ("Kentucky Mountain Farm" 38)

In both poems, "mist is furled" about a "rooftree," a divide that paradoxically unites them. In "The Return: An Elegy," the continental divide parallels the divide separating mother and son. To say they had not been on good terms would be an understatement. When the speaker thinks of gazing into her eyes, maternal affection is not what he expects to find: "O eyes locked blind in death's immaculate design / Shall fix their last distrust in mine" (33). In the rolling train, he catches himself saying "the old bitch is dead" and then asks, "what have I said!"

The divide also separates the present from the past. The Pullman takes him back in time, or at least gives that illusion:

> O wheels
> Pursue down backward time the ghostly parallels
> Pursue past culvert cut embankment semaphore
> Pursue down gleaming hours that are no more.
> . . . .
> turn backward turn backward o time in your flight
> and make me a child again just for tonight
> good lord he's wet the bed come bring a light. (34)

The third and second lines from the end, as John Burt notes, are adapted from "Rock Me to Sleep," by Elizabeth Akers Allen (1832–1911) (809n).[4] They may themselves be pursued backward in time, for Allen was probably remembering one of the most famous lines in French literature: "Ô temps, suspends ton vol! et vous, heures propices, / Suspendez votre cours! / Laissez-nous savourer les rapides délices / Des plus beaux de nos jours!" (O time, suspend thy flight! And you, happy hours, / Suspend your course! / Let us savor the fleeting delights / Of our most beautiful of days!), from "Le Lac," by Alphonse de Lamartine (1790–1869). In the poem, the speaker recalls that a woman he loved but who has since died once spoke those words, which now take on an additional layer of meaning as he repeats them in grief for her passing, and in the place where she said them.

Lamartine was actually quoting a poem from the century before his, the "Ode sur le Temps," by Antoine-Léonard Thomas (1732–1785), in which—ironically, considering the context the words will acquire in Warren's poem—the poet asks that Time spare his life so that he may have the opportunity of expressing his love to his mother: "Ô Temps, suspends ton vol, respecte ma jeunesse; / Que ma mère, longtemps témoin de ma tendresse, / Reçoive mes tributs de respect et d'amour" (O Time, suspend thy flight; respect my youth; / May my mother, who has long been witness to my affection, / Receive my tributes of respect and love).[5]

Warren's decision to interrupt those lines with a recollection of having wet the bed has been interpreted in various ways. Victor Strandberg sees it as "Warren's sarcasm towards the concept of time in a famous sentimental poem. . . . [S]uch an escapist view of time, Warren implies, is the intellectual equivalent to wetting the bed" (*A Colder Fire* 11). James Justus calls it a "brilliant passage" that "is an affective conjunction of sentimental song and childhood trauma in a mature mind resisting both sentimentality and dependency, but . . . is also contextually obtrusive in its strengths and aggressively flashy in its effects" (52). John Burt, in a meditation on Warren's elegies, a category in which the poem's subtitle would appear to place it, says at this juncture, "the imagined recovery of the past for which elegy strives seems to blow up in the speaker's face. . . . But the joke here seems to be as much at the narrator's expense as it is at the expense of the sentimentalist he was never in much danger of becoming, for even as it removes the speaker from silly displays of feeling it marks him as someone who must bear the responsibility for his incapacity to mourn. The discontinuities of tone here do not purify but rather abolish elegy" (*Robert Penn Warren and American Idealism* 77). I think, however, that the bed-wetting is more than sarcasm, an obtrusive interruption, or a joke. Urination is serious business in Warren. It kills Old Grammy in "Minnesota Recollection" (534) in *Altitudes and Extensions,* when he freezes to death for having stepped outside in a snowstorm in response "to the call of nature."[6] It kills Jed Tewksbury's father in the opening pages of *A Place to Come To,* when he falls off his mule-drawn wagon and is crushed under the wheels as he was performing an act that was variously interpreted as urination and masturbation. The golden shower by which Zeus impregnated Danae—to which Warren alludes in "No Bird Does Call" (416) in *Being Here:* "The hollow is Danae's lap lavished with gold by the god"—lends itself to being read as a similar combination, urine with seminal power (in paintings the golden shower is sometimes represented as liquid, sometimes as dust, sometimes as gold coins). From that union came Perseus, who confronted and killed the Medusa.

The myth containing those two events is pervasive in Warren, as I have argued for the novels in *The Taciturn Text* and the last four volumes of poetry in *The Braided Dream.* For example, on the way to visit the site where the events recounted in *Brother to Dragons* (Jefferson's nephews' murder of a slave) had taken place, Warren and his father pull off the road to answer the call of nature: "we . . . stopped just once to void the bladder. . . . / The sunlight screamed, while urine spattered the parched soil" (15). Here father and son are united as they both create a golden stream in the sunlight. That sunlight is the first thing Warren thinks of when he thinks of his father a little later in *Brother to Dragons:*

> in a café once, when an old friend said,
> "Tell me about your father," my heart suddenly
> Choked on my words, and in the remarkable quiet
> Of my own inwardness and coil, light fell
> Like one great ray that gilds the deepest glade,
> And thus I saw his life a story told,
> Its glory and reproach domesticated,
> And for one moment felt that I had come
> To that most happy and difficult conclusion:
> To be reconciled to the father's own reconciliation. (27–28)

Warren offers us a concrete image of that reconciliation when father and son stand by the side of the road, performing together an act that would be trivial did it not so deeply draw upon his personal poetic myth. A third passage from *Brother to Dragons* comes closer to paralleling the bed-wetting of "The Return": "that is why you wake sweating toward dawn / And finger the cold spot in your side with no fantasy now for the matutinal erection" (29). Matutinal erections do not need sexual fantasies since they have a nonsexual cause, a buildup of urine in the bladder—though they can contribute, as a somatic cause, to sexual dreams.

The need to urinate can give rise to nonsexual dreams, too. In "Literal Dream" (542), Warren dreams of a stain of liquid on the ceiling "gathered to a / Point. / Which hung forever. / Dropped" and then "I woke at the call of nature" (543). The story the dream tells was provided by Thomas Hardy's *Tess,* but the physical stimulus was the need to void his bladder. In the succession of poems constituted by "Literal Dream" and the two poems that follow it in *Altitudes and Extensions,* the liquid on the ceiling that turns out to be blood returns in the form of "the last red / Liquid" (544) in a wineglass in "After the Dinner Party" and as "The pink / Of sunset [that] tints the ceiling" (545) at which both Warren and his dying mother stare in "Doubleness in Time" (544). In "Literal Dream," Warren dreams himself to be in the downstairs room in *Tess,* looking up at the ceiling as the old lady in her rocking chair does the same. The strong parallels between this dreamed scene and the remembered scene of his mother's death in the hospital recounted in "Doubleness in Time" (where Warren and his mother both gaze at a pink tinge on the ceiling) suggest a hidden connection, already evident in "The Return: An

Elegy," between his mother's death and lying in bed with the need to urinate, a need eventuating in a dream in "Literal Dream" (as Freud explains in *The Interpretation of Dreams,* such dreams allow the sleeper to continue to sleep)[7] but into wetting the bed in the earlier poem.

"Doubleness in Time" is the poem that "The Return: An Elegy" could not be, a genuine grieving for his mother. Its first words—"Doubleness coils in Time like / The bull-snake in fall's yet-leafed growth" (544)—are a reminiscence of the older poem: "honor thy father and mother in the days of thy youth / for time uncoils like the cottonmouth" (35). Its last words are a commentary on his long-standing inability, which he had made thematic in "The Return: An Elegy," to adequately grieve: "I do not know . . . / Why my grief has not been understood, nor why / It has not understood its own being. // It takes a long time for it to learn / Its many names: like / *Selfishness* and *Precious Guilt.*"[8] That selfishness and precious guilt was certainly evident in the earlier poem.

The return to the mother was presented there as a hopeless pursuit "down backward time" (34). In the final section of "Kentucky Mountain Farm," appropriately titled "The Return," a similar backward return is desired but likewise impossible:

> Again the timeless gold
> Broad leaf released the tendoned bough, and slow,
> Uncertain as a casual memory,
> Wavered aslant the ripe unmoving air.
> Up from the whiter bough, the bluer sky,
> That glimmered in the water's depth below,
> A richer leaf rose to the other there.
> They touched; with the gentle clarity of dream,
> Bosom to bosom, burned on the quiet stream.
>
> So, backward heart, you have no voice to call
> Your image back, the vagrant image again.
> . . . And he, who had loved as well as most,
> Might have foretold it thus, for long he knew
> How glimmering a buried world is lost
> In the water's riffle, the wind's flaw;
> How his own image, perfect and deep
> And small within loved eyes, had been forgot,
> Her face being turned, or when those eyes were shut
> Past light in that fond accident of sleep. (38–39)

As Strandberg points out, the two characters here are "apparently mother and son." The "lack of recognition on the part of the mother shows that the son has changed since his departure, as any intelligent boy will in later adolescence and early manhood. The old image of his identity—'perfect and deep / And small within loved eyes'—has lost its accuracy with the youth's internal changes, and in any case has been forgotten in his long absence ('her face being turned')" (*A Colder Fire* 22). Thus "The Return" restates the problem set out in "The Return: An Elegy," but with the difference that while in the latter the son's selfishness and anger prevent a reconciliation, in the former the anger and selfishness are gone but the passage of time gets in the way. The image of the leaf touching its reflected version "Bosom to bosom" recalls the proximity of the mother's breast to the son in the final lines of "The Return: An Elegy": "If I could pluck . . . / To lay upon the breast that gave me suck / Out of the dark the dark and swollen orchid of this sorrow" (35).

"Kentucky Mountain Farm" is followed by "Pondy Woods" (39), in which a golden-eyed buzzard chides Big Jim Todd, pursued for some misdeed at the Blue Goose saloon, for being "more passionate / than strong" (40). The rocks that speak in "Kentucky Mountain Farm" employ the same terms in rebuking Appalachian farmers for not being more like themselves, for not "Renouncing passion by the strength that locks / The eternal agony of fire in stone" (35). The rocks exhort the hill people to "breed no tender thing," to "quit yourselves as stone and cease / To break the weary stubble-field for seed" and "Let not the naked cattle bear increase." The rocks, in other words, urge them to renounce life itself, to give up reproducing (for which some measure of passion is required), a renunciation they apparently were not persuaded to make.

Despite the racial divide separating the white mountaineers from Jim Todd, who is lumped with his fellow blacks in the buzzard's rebuke, "'Nigger, your breed ain't metaphysical'" (39), they are alike in preferring what their rebukers call passion to what they call strength. Even the infamous line I have just quoted[9] is part of the play of allusions linking black and white, for that Todd's "breed" should lack metaphysicality, though an objectionably racist assertion in itself, is actually an echo of "But breed no tender thing among the rocks" (35) in the rebuke addressed to the mountaineers. Both breeds breed.

The buzzard's sermon differs from that of the rocks in that he preaches not renunciation but patience. We "'swing against the sky and wait,'" he tells Todd. "'You seize the hour, more passionate than strong.'" Scavengers, buzzards, and their ilk wait until their food is safely dead before attacking it:

> "The Jew-boy died. The Syrian vulture swung
> Remotely above the cross whereon he hung
> From dinner-time to supper-time, and all
> The people gathered there watched him until

The lean brown chest no longer stirred,
Then idly watched the slow majestic bird
That in the last sun above the twilit hill
Gleamed for a moment at the height and slid
Down the hot wind and in the darkness hid." (40)

This bird seems a parody of the "sunset hawk" in "Kentucky Mountain Farm" that "rides / The tall light up the climbing deep of air. / Beneath him swings the rooftree that divides / The east and west" (38). Both catch the last light of the setting sun; the swinging motion that the talking buzzard attributes to his kind ("'We swing against the sky'") and to his cousin at Golgotha parallels that of the earth beneath the hawk; the eyes of both are gold. The hawk's "gold eyes scan" the swinging world below, while at the close of "Pondy Woods" the buzzards are "Drifting high in the pure sunshine / Till the sun in gold decline; / Then golden and hieratic through / The night their eyes burn two by two." The buzzard's Syrian kin kept watch above the expiring Jesus, waiting until his "lean brown chest no longer stirred." The sunset hawk likewise looks down on the "lean men" (35) who live in the hills and who at this evening hour "take their rest" (38). Attention is paid here as well, as it was in the case of the lean-chested Jesus, to whether they stir: "Forever, should they stir, their thought would keep / This place."

The buzzards who resemble the rocks as rebukers of the passionate and the sunset hawk in their golden-eyed gaze at the lean men below bear as well an intriguing resemblance to the rocks' antagonist, "the obscene moon whose pull / Disturbs the sod" (35), for they too are obscene, "Black figments that the woods release, / Obscenity in form and grace" (39). It is easier to see why buzzards should be so characterized than the moon. Buzzards are ugly, grotesque, and feed off the dead. The moon's obscenity is apparent only to the rocks, who are the speaker at this point in the poem. The moon, in their estimation, "dictates," as Strandberg explains, "an endless cycle of reproduction and death" (*A Colder Fire* 13), while the rocks prefer "the sweet sterility of stone" and stasis. The moon's "pull / Disturbs the sod," thereby disturbing the rocks, ultimately breaking them, indeed, destroying them in the poem's second section, "At the Hour of the Breaking of the Rocks" (36). The moon's effects in the first section were felt at the time of "the hungry equinox" (35), pulling the world into spring. The rocks in the second section, as spring advances, are "tortured" and "stricken" (36), eventually disintegrated by spring floods. Their "fractured atoms now are borne / Down shifting waters to . . . the profound deeps." As Strandberg puts it, in this second section "the rocks receive their own final rebuke. Here even the seemingly ageless, changeless rocks are subject to the immutable laws of change and destruction" (*A Colder Fire* 14).[10]

The Kentucky mountain farmers pay no heed to the rocks' injunction but till the soil and plant their seeds, with the result that in the poem's third section, "History Among the Rocks," we can see "ripe wheat" (36) appear. That ripe wheat returns in "Pondy Woods," where its creation comes at the expense of the rocks that in "Kentucky Mountain Farm" had prided themselves on "Renouncing passion by the strength that locks / The eternal agony of fire in stone" (35). We can see it when Todd emerges from his night in the woods: "At dawn unto the Sabbath wheat he came, / That gave to the dew its faithless yellow flame / From kindly loam in recollection of / The fires that in the brutal rock once strove. / To the *ripe wheat* fields he came at dawn" (40).

Strandberg notes the persistence of a theme from one poem to the next: "Towards the conclusion of 'Pondy Woods,' Warren reiterates his vision of total mutability, much as we had seen it at the beginning of 'Kentucky Mountain Farm.' Here, too, the rocks have disintegrated—this time into loam—and the fires that once burned within stone are transmuted into the 'yellow flame' of a wheat field" (*A Colder Fire* 25). The "recollection" in which the wheat is engaged as it gives the dew its flame almost hints at another possibility of recollection, as the "ripe wheat" and the fire in the stone recall the same elements in "Kentucky Mountain Farm." There is a bit more to that recollection, for death lurks for a man in both ripe wheat fields. In "Kentucky Mountain Farm," we see it when "Under the shadow of ripe wheat, / By flat limestone, will coil the copperhead, / Fanged as the sunlight, hearing the reaper's feet" (37). In "Pondy Woods," the buzzard seems to predict that Big Jim Todd will die in the wheat field: "you'll sweat cold sweat . . . / When down your track the steeljacket goes / Mean and whimpering over the wheat" (39). The narrator appears to confirm this by leaving him there at the end of the poem, allowing him (and us) to be lulled into a false sense of security, when the morning's silence is suddenly broken by the baying, from the woods, of "the musical white-throated hound" (40). Exposed as he is in the open field, I would not give much for his chances.

The death that comes to all, from the reaper the copperhead awaits to the fugitive in the wheat, is part of the cycle in which scavengers like buzzards and vultures play a part, as Warren would later note in "Dead Horse in Field" (471), in *Rumor Verified,* where he notes that one day after its death, a horse's "eyes / Were already gone—that / The beneficent work of crows. . . . / At evening I watch the buzzards, the crows, / Arise. They swing black in nature's flow and perfection." He would return to the theme in "Immanence" (472), the next poem in *Rumor Verified,* labeling this Lucretian recycling "Nature's Repackaging System." Buzzards and the moon, then, are alike—and to some, obscene—because of their participation in what Strandberg calls the "endless cycle of reproduction and death."

The hounds that bayed at the end of "Pondy Woods" are still at it in "Eidolon" (41), whose narrator is a boy kept awake by the sounds of a distant hunt. Warren recycles the "throat" and "belled" of that passage from "Pondy Woods"—"there belled / The musical white-throated hound"—in "Eidolon": "the throaty, infatuate timbre. . . . The rangers / Of dark remotelier belled." Such reappearing words resemble the "fractured atoms" of rock that "are borne / Down shifting waters" in "Kentucky Mountain Farm," carried from one poem to the next.

But in such recycling, nothing is ever quite the same. It was the hunted prey who spent the night "Laying low" in the dark of Pondy Woods, but in "Eidolon" it is the boy, not the hunted, who "all night, lay in the black room," listening to the hunt. Todd and the boy were probably equally uncomfortable, the former lying "in the mud and muck," the latter with "Tick-straw, all night, harsh to the bare side." The pursued in "Pondy Woods" was black; in "Eidolon," it is white: "Who saw, in darkness, how fled / The white eidolon from the fangèd commotion rude?"

The theme of pursuit, begun in "Pondy Woods" and continued in "Eidolon," persists in "Letter of a Mother" (41). There, the narrator is again portrayed as a son, as he was in "Eidolon." In that poem, he shared the house with his father ("the man, clod-heavy, hard hand uncurled") and grandfather ("The old man, eyes wide, spittle on his beard"), inhabiting an upper room: "under the rooftree / The boy." In "Letter of a Mother," he again inhabits an upper room: "Shuffle of feet ascends the darkened stair. // The son . . . / Inherits now his cubicled domain." The son, who in "Eidolon" heard the "far clamor" of pursuing hounds, now becomes the object of pursuit: "the flesh cries out unto the black / Void, across the plains insistently . . . / The mother flesh that cannot summon back // The tired child it would again possess." The insistence of her distant cries matches the "unappeasable" quality of the dogs' "far clamor." Death awaits the hunted "at dawn" in the wheat field in "Pondy Woods" (40) and "Eidolon" (41): "blood black on / May-apple at dawn." It comes for the son in "Letter of a Mother" not from the mother herself but as what she prefigures: "a womb more tender than her own / That builds not tissue or the little bone, / But dissolves them to itself in weariness." The son, though acknowledging the inevitability of this tenderer womb, resists his mother's attempt at repossession: "'By now this woman's milk is out of me. / I have a debt of flesh, assuredly, / Which score the mintage of the breath might pay . . .'" (ellipsis in the poem). I interpret this to mean that living in the world, simply breathing, might be, he hopes, sufficient repayment of the debt he owes her for the "gift of her mortality." Living itself is the "sweet process" that "may bloom in gratitude" for that gift. It is important to note that Warren here speaks of the gift not of life but of mortality, thereby including death in the gift in addition to life. And it is intriguing that he should have written not "her gift of mortality" but "the . . . gift of *her* mortality"—as if to include in the gift the fact of her death. She is not, it would appear, dead in this poem, having presumably penned the letter only recently, but she was already so in "The Return: An Elegy."

The theme of animosity toward one's parents continues in "Genealogy" (42), which concludes with "a curse of hell-black hate" for the speaker's father. The poem begins with the recreation of an ancestral past: "Grandfather Gabriel rode up to town," where "he rallied and whored and ginned with the best— / O an elegant son-of-a-bitch, I guess." Unlike in his later poems, where he uses his actual personal past as raw material, here much is fictional. Warren did have a grandfather named Gabriel, but that was his mother's father, not, as here, his father's. The Gabriel in "Genealogy" "rode from town / With Grandmother Martha in a white wedding gown" (the real Gabriel's wife was named Mary).[11] A son is born. Martha dies in childbirth, and the speaker then reflects on himself as the descendant of these forebears: "Your grandson keeps a broken house. / . . . / There's a mole in the garden, fennel by the gate, / In the heart a curse of hell-black hate / For that other young guy who croaked too late." The other young guy could only be the "fine little bastard," as Grandfather Gabriel calls him, to whom Martha gave birth—that is, the speaker's father. Warren's own father would not die until two decades after he wrote this poem, so he could not be referring to him (who in any event was not Gabriel's son). The speaker seems to regret that he had ever been born, an event that could not have transpired had his father died soon enough.

Before the poem arrives at this sad conclusion, the speaker conjures up an image of his grandparents in their graves in ways reminiscent of the previous poem. The phrase "In . . . dissolute bone adrowse" in "Genealogy" is a variation on what he said in "Letter of a Mother" about the womb more tender than his mother's that "builds not tissue or the little bone, / But dissolves them." In writing about nature's process of recycling, he imitates it by recycling fragments of his text. In "Letter of a Mother," the force that holds a living body together is described as "hunger . . . bred in the bitter bone / To cleave about this precious skeleton." In "Genealogy," the body's disintegration after death is described as a hunger for those bones: the "elegant" grandfather's "bones have fed the elegant grass" (the grandfather's elegance is appropriated by the grass in the recycling).

"History" (43) is another exercise in recreating an ancestral past, going back before the grandfather's generation to that of the pioneers who crossed the Appalachians, descended into the fertile lands to the west, and exterminated the native inhabitants. This new Canaan was "a land of corn . . . / And wine," as it still would be when Grandfather Gabriel rode from town with his new bride: "Wine-yellow was sunshine then on the corn." His triumph is predicted, retrospectively, by the pioneers in "History," for whom the "bride's surrender will be sweet."

Both poems detail the degeneracy of subsequent generations. The speaker in "Genealogy" reports to his deceased grandfather, "Your grandson keeps a broken house" with maggots in the meal and a mole in the garden. The pioneers in "History" can somehow foretell that "Our sons will cultivate / Peculiar crimes" (one thinks of the grisly murder Jefferson's nephews would commit in *Brother to Dragons*).[12] That degeneracy takes different forms, for though Gabriel's grandson is full of hate, the pioneers' criminal descendants have "not love, nor hate." Some, though, will resemble the grandson in their distaste for life: "defective of desire," they "Shall grope toward time's cold womb." The grandson seems to wish for death, in regretting that he was ever born. This characterization of the tomb as womb recalls, of course, the same image in "Letter of a Mother" ("a womb more tender than her own"). Those in "History" who grope toward that womb "In dim pools peer / To see, of some grandsire, / The long and toothèd jawbone greening there," as the grandson in "Genealogy" sees, though in his mind's eye, the bones of his buried grandfather, whose "bones have fed the elegant grass" and whom he imagines keeping company with Martha "In fragrant hair and dissolute bone adrowse."

In "Resolution" (45), one of those descendants speaks, and some, at least, of what was predicted in "History"—the sons' "Having not love, nor hate, / Nor memory"—has come to pass. For the speaker in "Resolution," reflecting on what the passage of time has wrought, finds it difficult to call up the face of one he once loved: "I tried to frame your face / In the mind's eye; / And could, a little space." Hate, too, disappears: "Hates cold, once hot; / Ambitions thewless grown; / Old slights forgot." That thewlessness is a pointed recollection of the last lines of "History": "Let us go down," Canaan's invaders tell themselves as they pause before descending to pillage and take possession, "before / Our thews are latched in the myth's languor, / Our hearts with fable grey." Myth and fable accrue through time, which can thus bring about thewlessness in both poems. The speaker in "Resolution" makes it quite clear that "Time, / . . . / Keen heart-divider / Who deepest vows unspeaks," is responsible for loss of love, hate, and even memory. Time in "Resolution" is "fangèd" ("O fangèd paradox!"), not unlike what the pioneers' sons will seek in "time's cold womb," some grandsire's "toothèd jawbone." In both poems, Time is apostrophized: "O Time," the poet in "History" exclaims, "for them the aimless bitch" quarters the ground where "The blank and fanged / Rough certainty lies hid." "Resolution" begins with a similar address: "Grape-treader Time . . . / O fangèd paradox!" The two poems had originally appeared together—in reverse order, "Resolution" preceding "History"—as sections 1 and 2 of "Two Poems on Time" in the *Virginia Quarterly Review* of July 1935 (as Burt notes in *Collected Poems* 650n).

Warren changed their order for *Thirty-Six Poems,* evidently so that connections could emerge between "History" and "Genealogy" and between "Resolution" and "Letter from a Coward to a Hero" (46). In both of the latter, the poet addresses an absent acquaintance—in "Resolution" a former lover, in "Letter" a childhood friend who has died in combat. In both he finds it difficult to call up images from the past: "I tried to frame your face / In the mind's eye; / And could, a little space" ("Resolution"); "The scenes of childhood . . . The thicket where I saw the fox, / And where I swam, the river. / These things are hard / To reconstruct" ("Letter from a Coward to a Hero"). The hero was brave ("I have not seen your courage to pawn"), naturally, but so too was the lover, in that she denied the existence of Time ("You said: / *There is no Time*"), an assertion that the poet, who disagrees, describes as "most brave." In "Resolution," the speaker takes note of Time's power to destroy both love and hate (it is the "Keen heart-divider / Who deepest vows unspeaks," leaving "Hates cold, once hot"); by contrast, the hero has "been strong in love and hate."

"Letter from a Coward to a Hero" closes with the image of the brave friend "Clutching"—apparently in death—"between the forefinger and thumb / Honor, for death shy valentine." "Late Subterfuge" (48) begins by linking honor and a lost friend in a different way: As the year moves toward its end, "We have kept honor yet, or lost a friend." In "Letter," the poet had said to the hero, "Though late at night we have talked, / I cannot see what ways your feet in childhood walked," going on to say that he does not know how his friend acquired his notable courage. In other words, in childhood they talked but did not walk together. But in "Late Subterfuge," he does walk with another friend: "Our feet in the sopping woods will make no sound." Those wet woods recall a similar landscape encountered in "Letter," the "sodden ground" from which "wind rouses / The kildees," sending them south in migration, "At the blind hour of unaimed grief." It is a time for grief in "Late Subterfuge" as well, where the poet speaks of a "grief" that "can be endured." In both poems, grief is felt in the wet season of the year's approaching close, the time when birds head for warmer latitudes. In "Late Subterfuge," the "year dulls toward its eaves-dripping end. / . . . The grackles . . . fly / . . . south, leaving empty our sky."

The theme of birds that fly away continues in "Ransom" (49): "Doom has, we know, not shape but the shape of air. / That much for us the red-armed augurs spelled, / Or flights of fowl lost early in the long air." Though in a new context, for these birds are not migrating, as in the preceding two poems, but taken as auguries.

In "Late Subterfuge," Warren writes of "being inured / To wrath, to the act unjust, if need, to blood." In "Ransom" (the title alludes to the ransom paid by

Christ's Atonement), he again speaks of a bloody act: "The mentioned act: barbarous, bloody, extreme, / And fraught with bane. The actors: nameless and / With faces turned (I cannot make them out). / Christ bled, indeed, but after fasting and / Bad diet of the poor; wherefore thin blood came out." As John Burt notes, the "mentioned act" is "lust in action, according to Shakespeare" (809n), in Sonnet 129: "The expense of spirit in a waste of shame / Is lust in action; and till action, lust / Is perjured, murderous, bloody." Yet while reiterating Shakespeare's language, Warren seems to put it in the context of the Crucifixion. Who are these nameless actors whose faces are turned? Lovers engaged in lust? Perhaps. But in light of the allusion to the Crucifixion in the immediately following line ("Christ bled . . ."), could they not also be the crucifiers?

In any event, Warren returns to the Crucifixion in "Aged Man Surveys the Past Time" (49): "Once softlier far did Pontius ponder on / His jest before our Lord the steel partook." "Ransom" began with a reflection on "Old bottles but new wine, and newly spilled," while "Aged Man" begins with another liquid being spilled from eyes that, like the bottles, are old: "Adept, too late, at art of tears he stands / . . . / And aged eyes, like twilit rain, their effort / Spill." The "Aged Man" is preceded in "Ransom" by another "old man": "At night the old man coughs: thus history / Strikes sum." The combination of time ("history") and mathematics ("sum") will return, though in a negative formulation, in "Aged Man": "Time has no mathematic."

Strandberg finds that "Aged Man Surveys the Past Time" and "Toward Rationality" (50) "both deal with the same subject, confronting the fact of self-annihilation" (*A Colder Fire* 41). Indeed, the two poems were originally linked in their earlier publication in the *American Review* in 1934 as section 1 and 2, respectively, of "Two Poems on Truth" (650n). The "Aged Man" is contemplating his approaching death; in "Toward Rationality" Warren asserts that death comes to all, including himself: "Brothers, stones on this moraine of time, / And I, a stone: for you were Xerxes' guests / In littoral picnic by the unfettered brine." Warren here alludes to Xerxes' attempt to cross the Hellespont, which was initially frustrated when a storm destroyed the bridges he had made. In his anger he ordered that the sea be given three hundred lashes, as Herodotus writes, "and that a pair of fetters be cast into it."[13] Herodotus also records that later, when his army successfully crossed over, as the Persian monarch "saw the whole Hellespont covered with the vessels of his fleet, and all the shore and every plain about Abydos as full as possible of men, Xerxes congratulated himself on his good fortune; but after a little while he wept." When asked why, "'There came upon me,' replied he, 'a sudden pity, when I thought of the shortness of man's life, and considered that of all this host, so numerous as it is, not one will be alive when a hundred years are gone by'" (224). Thus the allusion to Xerxes and his locus classicus on the inevitability of death resonates well in Warren's poem. Continuing to address Xerxes' men, whom he characterizes as "perpetual, blithe, armed cap-a-pie," the speaker asserts, "Too happy, happy gentlemen, you freeze / Downward." I take the freezing as a way of speaking of their turning to stone, with the coldness attributable to their becoming amassed in time's moraine, a moraine being composed of earth and stones deposited by a glacier.[14] The downward direction corresponds to the Orphic image introduced into "Aged Man Surveys the Past Time": "Could Orpheus map / The rocky and bituminous descent?" The answer to this question is no, for as Strandberg observes, the aged man has no faith in the Christian hope "and the victory of Orpheus"—in returning back to the surface after his descent into the underworld—"holds no promise for him" (*A Colder Fire* 40).

Pontius Pilate, who allowed Jesus' execution to take place, is appropriately followed in "Toward Rationality" by another executioner, when Warren remarks of Xerxes' "too happy" soldiers that their "kind faces all reflect / The rude Abhorson's spittlebearded grin." Abhorson is the comic headsman in Shakespeare's *Measure for Measure* (as Burt notes, 809n).[15] Abhorson's grin parallels what Warren, alluding to Pilate's question—What is truth?—calls his "jest." As he likens Xerxes' soldiers to Abhorson, he also sets up a parallel in "Aged Man Surveys the Past Time" between the aged man and Pilate:

> And aged eyes, like twilit rain, their effort
> Spill gentlier than herb-issue on a hill.
>
> Grief's smarting condiment may satisfy
> His heart to lard the wry and blasphemous theme.
> (Once softlier far did Pontius ponder on
> His jest before our Lord the steel partook.)
>
> Truth, not truth. (49)

Actually, there are two parallels: (1) "softlier" is compared to "gentlier" and (2) the aged man's wryness matches Pontius's jest-making. Indeed, the parentheses setting off the sentence about Pontius make it appear that the aged man actually makes the same jest as he did, "the wry and blasphemous theme" of "Truth, not truth."

Strandberg says of the fourth stanza of "Aged Man"—"By fruitful grove, unfruited now by winter, / The well-adapted and secular catbird / Whimpers its enmity and invitation. / Light fails beyond the barn and blasted oak."—that the old man saddened by thoughts of his impending death "is mocked in his unbearable anxiety by a 'secular' and 'well-adapted' catbird, who represents the fallacies of modern positivism" (*A Colder Fire* 40). Remarkably well adapted, too—that is, to its place in the natural world—is the bird in "Toward Rationality: "Red kine err not, nor under Capricorn / The seaswoop fisher, abler Ptolemy." The king-fisher (known to the ancients as the halcyon), that is, has a deeper knowledge of the stars than the ancient Egyptian astronomer, navigating by them flawlessly when it flies south for the winter. The catbird, likewise a migratory bird, has made it back to a spring-awakened landscape that the aged man, whose days are short, will soon depart. Both the kingfisher and the catbird can be said to know more than we do. I am not sure I agree with Strandberg about the catbird being a sym-bol of modern positivism, for when considered with the kingfisher he seems more appropriately to represent nature's realm, not a human construct.

The question of what a bird can tell us about our mortality is asked as well in "To a Friend Parting" (50): "We saw above the lake / Tower the hawk, his wings the light take. / What answer to our dread?" We are put in mind of the buzzard "Drifting high in the pure sunshine" in "Pondy Woods," who had an answer to the dread Jim Todd was feeling: "*Non omnis moriar,* the poet saith." The speaker in "To a Friend Parting" and his parting friend, whom he addresses as "old sol-dier," saw the hawk from the "shore" of a lake, a circumstance that parallels what happens in "Toward Rationality," when the speaker addresses Xerxes' soldiers on another shore: "In littoral picnic by the unfettered brine." The wrath of Xerxes, to which the adjective "unfettered" alludes, is paralleled by that of the "old soldier" who was the speaker's companion by the shore: "Much you have done in honor, though wrathfully. / That, we supposed, was your doom." Xerxes' soldiers "freeze / Downward," a reworking of Orpheus's "rocky and bituminous descent" in "Aged Man Surveys the Past Time." That downward movement returns in "To a Friend Parting" in an allusion to the journey on which the friend is embarking: "Follow the defiles down" into a "Rough country of no birds." There may be no birds because the journey could be an Orphic one, into the depths of the earth. In any case, the birds that have been accompanying our journey through this part of the book's sequence (grackles, flights of fowl as augury, a catbird, a kingfisher, and a hawk) will desert us for the next four poems.

Yet the theme of the creature that knows its own business, whether bird or mammal or insect, persists. It was apparent in "Toward Rationality" not only in the "seaswoop fisher" that outdoes Ptolemy in its knowledge of the stars but also in "Red kine" that "err not." The hawk in "To a Friend Parting" may or may not have an answer to our dread. In "Letter to a Friend," what we might learn from such creatures as these is not a message, not a reply to our questioning, but through their example they can teach us that a certain knowledge is possible: "The caterpillar knows its leaf, the mole / Its hummock, who has known his heart, or knows / The trigger of this action, set and sprung?"

It is immediately after asking what answer the hawk might have "to our dread" that the speaker in "To a Friend Parting" gives some practical advice that is probably the best answer available, since none could be had from the hawk:

> Follow the defiles down. Forget not,
> When journey-bated the nag, rusty the steel,
> The horny clasp of hands your hands now seal;
> And prayers of friends, ere this, kept powder dry.
> Rough country of no birds, the tracks sly:
> Thus faith has lived, we feel.

In the same way that the hawk gave no reply to "our dread," a painted image of the world ("Here the narrator and his friend have witnessed eternity, evidently through the medium of art" [Strandberg, *The Poetic Vision* 61]) in "Letter to a Friend" is incommensurate with "our terror": "Our eyes have viewed the burnished vineyards where / No leaf falls, and the grape, unripening, ripes. / It was a dream without fruition as / Without our terror." In parallel terms, "We saw" the hawk (in "To a Friend Parting"), "We have seen" the painting of the vineyard (in "Letter to a Friend"), as well as one of an "Unmoving" ship on a "moveless" sea (doubtless an allusion to the lines "As idle as a painted ship / Upon a painted ocean" in Coleridge's "Rime of the Ancient Mariner"), a "voyage, then each to each we said," that "rendered // Courage superfluous, hope a burden. / But living still, we live by them." It is in the living that one realizes that hope and courage are required for the voyage—just as, in the other journey (in "To a Friend Parting"), it is because faith "has lived" thus that one realizes the importance of not forgetting the clasped hands of a friend and the efficacy of friends' prayers.

By contrast to the painted grape that "unripening, ripes," a very real "wild plum" (the tree) in "To a Friend Parting," "Rock-rent ax-bit, has known with the year bloom." It has known it with the year because unlike the grape it has dwelled in Time. It has also had to contend with rocks (and an ax). Like the grape, and unlike the plum, the addressee of "Letter to a Friend" has not (yet) had to contend with Time: "I write to you, to you unfrighted." The grape in the picture from which Time is absent was similarly incommensurate with both fruition and our terror. Xerxes' soldiers and the speaker as well, evidently by virtue of the mere fact of being mortal, *were* commensurate with stone, because they dwelled in Time: "Brothers, stones on this moraine of time, / And I, a stone" ("Toward Rationality"). In "Kentucky Mountain Farm," the "lean men" were, unlike the friend not yet frighted by Time, commensurate with stone, for they "of all things alone / Were

. . . / Figured in kinship to the savage stone" (36). For like the stone, they dwelled in Time. Unlike "water or the febrile grass," men and stones not only live in Time but also struggle with it, are "frighted" by it. Like the "little stubborn people of the hill," the "tortured and reluctant" stone resists time's disintegration.

The "dream without fruition" in "Letter to a Friend" that was a metaphor for reality as viewed through the medium of art is followed by some real dreaming in "Aubade for Hope" (51). In this poem, morning sounds and the light of dawn awaken "them that wallowed in / The unaimed faceless appetite of dream." Strandberg makes the observation that the dreamers would "prefer to remain in a world where hope . . . is irrelevant by reason of the withdrawal of the consciousness from contact with reality. . . . Dawn intrudes upon the dulled consciousness, alerting it heartlessly, as always, to time and pain and the nagging necessity of hope" (*A Colder Fire* 45). For hope is here associated with the morning events that impinge on one's dreams:

> Light; the groaning stair. . . .
> . . . .
>   —I name some things that shall,
>
> As voices speaking from a farther room,
> Muffled, bespeak us yet for time and hope:
> For Hope that like a blockhead grandam ever
> Above the ash and spittle croaks and leans.

The "dream without fruition" in "Letter to a Friend," it had seemed to the speaker and his friend, "rendered // Courage superfluous, hope a burden." In both poems, hope is at first rejected by the dreamer but then accepted. Immediately after calling hope a burden, the speaker reverses himself: "But living still, we live by them"—that is, by courage and hope—"and only / Thus, or thus, stuttering, eke them out, / Our huddled alms to crammed Necessity" (that huddled posture anticipating that of the grandam leaning over the ash in "Aubade for Hope"). In both poems, the speaker realizes that he must live in Time, and in both, Time is associated with stone: In "Letter to a Friend," as long as the friend is "unfrighted yet" by Time, his "triumph is not commensurate with stone"; in "Aubade for Hope," the morning sounds that tear us from our dreams and "bespeak us yet for time and hope" include a "Thump of wood on the unswept hearth-stone." The hardness of the stone contributes to the racket that wakes the sleeper; the hearth is part of "crammed Necessity" because the fire must be lit for breakfast and to warm the house (we know it is winter, for "All night, the ice sought out the rotten bough"). But to the dreamer reluctant to awaken, that thump "is / Comment on the margin of consciousness, / A dirty thumb-smear by the printed page." The poem returns to that hearth-stone, without naming it explicitly as such, in the final lines, when hope "Above the ash and spittle croaks and leans."

Strandberg expresses surprise that in the second of these poems the speaker does not appear to have retained the lesson he learned in the first: "Since 'Letter to a Friend' warns against calling 'courage superfluous, hope a burden,' we might expect the next poem, 'Aubade for Hope,' to be reasonably affirmative in tone and content. But it is clear that Warren's morning song for hope is not meant to inspire exhilaration. As a matter of fact, its main function is to express the speaker's dismay and resentment at being recalled from the land of 'unaimed faceless appetite of dream' into a world less congenial to the heart's desire" (*A Colder Fire* 44–45). I have a two-part reply: First, While it is true that "Aubade for Hope" concludes with the rather off-putting image of Hope as a "blockhead grandam" who "ever / Above the ash and spittle croaks and leans," in the line just before, the speaker says of the noise she and others make that draws the dreamers from their dreams (the speaker, incidentally, is not the only one awakened: "wakes *them* that wallowed in / . . . dream") that they "bespeak us yet for time and hope." That "yet" plays the same reversing role in this poem as the "But" in "But living still, we live by [courage and hope]" in the other poem. Both mark the moment the speaker changes his mind, however reluctantly, rejecting life as a dream for life as lived in time and hope. Second, Strandberg reads the *Thirty-Six Poems* as a continuous sequence, and so do I, but with the difference that I also read them as continuously doubling themselves. Thus "Aubade for Hope" repeats "Letter to a Friend" even to the extent of repeating the initial error of preferring dream to reality and refusing to shoulder the burden of hope.

"Man Coming of Age" (52), like "Aubade for Hope," depicts a wintry dawn: "What rime, what tinsel pure and chill, / At dawn defines the new-spied hill? // This brilliance in the night was wrought." The ice was produced in the night, as it was in "Aubade," where "All night, the ice sought out the rotten bough." That it was the rotten bough the ice sought out is paralleled in "Man Coming of Age" by what the glitter of ice on the hill is compared to: "So settles on a dying face, / After the retch and spasm, grace." Rotten, the bough was dying. The ice-struck bough is replaced in "Man Coming of Age" by a "snowy bough." The hill covered with rime and tinsel creates a "light that glitters"; in "Aubade," a hill shines too: the "gleam of landscape sun / Has struck . . . the hill."

"Aubade" begins with a disturbing tread, the "foot on the cold stair treading" that is the first to be listed of the morning noises that awaken the speaker. "Man Coming of Age" ends with a disturbing tread, that is, with the injunction to avoid making one: "go! lest he, before you tread / That ground once sweetly tenanted, /

Like mist, down the glassy gloom be fled." The "he" whom a tread would cause to flee is the "*alter ego*" of the potential treader, the person he had been when he had "roamed" that landscape "In season greener." The disturbing tread that persists from one poem to the next links having an alter ego with dreaming, which is appropriate since it is the sleeper's other self, the unconscious, that dreams.

"Man Coming of Age" concludes with the speaker ordering the protagonist to leave: "Walker in woods that bear no leaf, / Climber of rocks, assume your grief // And go! lest he, before you tread / That ground once sweetly tenanted, / Like mist, down the glassy gloom be fled." So too does "Croesus in Autumn" (53): "So haul your careful carcass home, old fellow . . . / Now green is blown and every gold gone sallow." In both poems the present colder season is contrasted with a past warmer one: "Man Coming of Age" is set in winter, but a "season greener" is there recalled; in "Croesus," set in autumn, summer's "green is blown" and the title character "might consider a little piteous / The green and fatal tribe's decline." The colder and leafless season is reason for regret in both poems: "Walker of woods that bear no leaf, / . . . assume your grief" ("Man Coming of Age"); "If the distrait verdure cleave not to the branch . . . / Should then gruff Croesus on the village bench / Lament the absolute gold of summer gone?" ("Croesus in Autumn").[16] That is, the speaker deems it cause for lament, but it appears that his protagonist does not share his concern about the leaves not cleaving "to the branch / More powerfully than flesh to the fervent bone." Autumn may presage death for the speaker, but not for Croesus—nor, in fact, for the trees themselves: "He might consider a little piteous / The green and fatal tribe's decline. // But in Kentucky against a dwindling sun / The riven red-oak and the thick sweet-gum / Yet hold the northward hills whose final stone / In dark ogive supports the fractured loam." Though their leaves, their "flesh," may disappear, the trees' trunks, branches, and roots, their "fervent bone," holds fast.

The same thing happens in the next two poems, "So Frost Astounds" (53) and "The Last Metaphor" (54). In the former, the speaker recalls observing a woman,[17] whom he addresses in the second person, sitting by a window in "the season when blackbirds go":[18]

I observed your hands which lay, on the lap, supine.

So frost astounds the summer calyxes

And so was locked their frail articulation
by will beneath the pensive skin:
as though composed by the will of an artist on dull blue cloth,
forever beyond the accident of flesh and bone

or principle of thief and rat and moth,
or beyond the stately perturbation of the mind.

As the trees' skeletal structures in "Croesus in Autumn" hold firm ("Yet hold the
. . . hills"), here the bones of the hands are locked by strength of will. Similarly, in
"The Last Metaphor," bare autumnal trees, "Purged of the green that kept so fatal
tenure / . . . are made strong; no leaf clings mortally." Freed from the mortal
leaves, the trees seem freed from mortality, as the articulated bones in the hands
in "So Frost Astounds" seem to the speaker "forever beyond the accident of flesh
and bone . . . rat and moth." Of course, it is only "as though" they were beyond
it, since they are mortal after all, "frail" ("their frail articulation") like the "frail ver-
dure" of the leaves ("Now flat and black the trees stand on the sky / Unreminiscent
of the year's frail verdure"). But as it turns out, the trees show evidence of some-
thing approaching frailty, too, in the speaker's "final metaphor," which in the
poem's conclusion he substitutes for the one according to which the leaves' disap-
pearance "made strong" the trees. In this last metaphor, "when the leaves no more
abide / The stiff trees rear not up in strength and pride, / But lift unto the grad-
ual dark in prayer." Which is to say that their branches now look like praying
arms, and hands—reminiscent of the supine ones in "So Frost Astounds."

We might note, in passing, a few more reminiscences among these three
poems. The birds are flying south in "So Frost Astounds"—"it was the season
when blackbirds go"—while in "The Last Metaphor," "no tardy bird may sing."
The speaker suggests that what happens to flowers struck by sudden cold happens
to the woman: "*So frost astounds the summer calyxes*"; the speaker in the other
poem says that what happens to the tree at the approach of winter happens to
him: "'I am as the tree and with it have like season.'" The "frail verdure" in "The
Last Metaphor" recalls both the "frail articulation" of "So Frost Astounds" and the
"distrait verdure" of "Croesus in Autumn." The "green that kept so fatal tenure"
in "The Last Metaphor" restates "The green and fatal tribe's decline" in "Croesus
in Autumn." "The Last Metaphor" closes with "a final metaphor" (that of the
praying trees), and so does "Croesus in Autumn": "I bring you but this broken
metaphor." The "stately perturbation of the mind" that the hands' locked articu-
lation gave the impression of being forever beyond in "So Frost Astounds" recalls
the way that in "Croesus in Autumn" the "seasons down our country . . . stir the
bald and metaphysic skull, / Fuddling the stout cortex."

Paralleling the protagonist in "The Last Metaphor," who "came out with his
mortal miseries" to a lonely windswept landscape (a "rocky crest" where "Only the
wind sang"), is a "gazer of saddest intent" in "Pacific Gazer" (55), who walks "On
scarp rim that winds gnaw" and likewise finds that nature echoes his deepest sen-
timents. The landscapes are different, one inland and the other coastal, yet they

share the elements of wind, water, cold, and setting sun. The man in "The Last Metaphor" found "a water, profound and cold, / whereon remotely gleamed the violent west"; in "Pacific Gazer," in the west, over the sea's "cold horizon," "Day's nimb recedes." In both poems, the protagonist's heart bears witness to the desolate land- or seascape and blowing wind: "he took counsel of the heart alone / To be instructed of this desolation" ("The Last Metaphor"); "Can the griding ocean's unease / Or leaning furious blast / Hurt heart appease?" ("Pacific Gazer"). Both see themselves in what they see: "'I am as the tree and with it have like season'" ("The Last Metaphor"); "What wrath he owes / Abides in the water's might: / Only the blind blast echoes / His wrath" ("Pacific Gazer").

"Pacific Gazer" and "Calendar" (56) share the same poetic form (as did "Aged Man Surveys the Past Time" and "Toward Rationality"): seven five-line stanzas with the same meter (2 + 3 + 3 + 3 + 2) and rhyme scheme (ABABA). "Calendar" echoes what was said in "Pacific Gazer" about day's dying in the west, but with the difference that day is now disappearing toward the south. In "Pacific Gazer," "Day's nimb recedes" and "Day's lamp is sped," while in "Calendar," "The days draw in: / Southward, the red suns trim / Daily." The westward sun dips increasingly southward every evening as "the grinding orbit veer[s] / Coldward." In "Pacific Gazer," the light dying over the ocean is likened to a thread of steel that "Marks taut the cold horizon," while in "Calendar" the wind will play a "cold-taut harp." Both poems speak of anger that is matched by the anger of someone or something else, as the Pacific gazer finds that his "wrath . . . / Abides in the water's might" and that its "blind blast echoes / His wrath" while the speaker in "Calendar" wonders if his rage is in fact inherited from past generations: "is their wrong / Our wrong . . . / And all our young rage strong / Tinct of an elder cark?"

In "Problem of Knowledge" (57), "we . . . under the solstice turn" and "sow where once our mattock cracked the clod." The seasons pass in "Calendar," too, as the speaker considers "summer's heart . . . locked in the burr from frost." But the principal common ground between the two poems lies elsewhere: "Loving, with Orphic smile, we yearn / Down the deep backward our feet, we think, have trod" ("Problem of Knowledge"). Such a backward pace, if traced in the sequence itself of these poems, would soon encounter, in "Calendar," its double: "Do memories [the dead] keep / Backpace our calendar / To an age that knew no hap / Of coil, nor jar?" There are three parts to the echo: "backward"/"backpace," "pace"/ "feet," and "our"/"our." In both poems, the speaker seeks to know the past. In "Calendar," he wonders what the dead remember; in "Problem of Knowledge," he asks, "Was it a sandal smote the troughèd stone?" That is, is the depression in the stone the trace left by a footstep? Actually it was created by repeated footsteps over many years, which do in the end leave traces, for example, on the stairs to an ancient temple. What of the past can be recaptured in the present? That question also arises in "Calendar," but from the perspective of a present that will one day be the past: "Long past our hence-going / Will our hurt in the wind's voice / Speak so to men unknowing / Of our hugged joys . . . ?"

The past is difficult to "snare": "What years, what hours, has spider contemplation spun / Her film to snare the muscled fact?" "Cold Colloquy" (57), like the two poems that precede it, is also about excavating the past. In "Problem of Knowledge," the past is recalcitrant; in "Cold Colloquy," however, the recalcitrance lies not in the past but in the one who is invited to step back into it: "She loitered to heed his heart's pouring-out, / Her heart sick within her, she sickening with doubt / That again it might stir, as it once had stirred, / At another's pain snared in gesture or throaty word." (The sort of backward reading these poems encourage would snare these "snares.") She is afraid of her own past, of her history of being stirred at the recital of another's pain. In "Problem of Knowledge," the question was raised of whether it had been a sandal that "smote the troughèd stone." It is appropriate that when "stone" reappears in "Cold Colloquy," it should apply to the one who is recalcitrant there: "She hearkened, eyeless and sunk like the uncarved stone." What is past bears a mark, even if it be impossible to determine what made it; she refuses the past so bears none.

There is a turning point in both poems:

> Loving, with Orphic smile, we yearn
> Down the deep backward our feet, we think, have trod:
> Or sombrely, under the solstice turn,
> We sow where once our mattock cracked the clod. ("Problem of
>   Knowledge")

> She turned, a puzzlement on fair features wrought
> That of words so freighted with woe so little she caught.
> She turned; with fair face troubled thus would go,
> In season of sun when all the green things grow
> Or of dry aster and the prattling leaves,
> To stand apart, pondering, as one who grieves
> Or seeks a thing long lost among the fallen leaves. ("Cold Colloquy")

The "solstice turn" would be the turning of the year, yet there is also a hint of the disastrous turn that Orpheus made, by which he lost Eurydice. That mythic turn is repeated here, the woman playing Orpheus's role to the man's Eurydice. For despite her recalcitrance, she did listen to him, "She hearkened, . . . / Till the light in his face, an empty candle, was blown"—his fading to darkness evoking Eurydice's as she redescended into hell's shadows. "She hearkened, and all was something once read about, / Or a tale worn glossless in time and bandied about." In these lines, Warren seems to allude to the story itself, "read about," for example, in Ovid. The last lines of the poem, quoted above, make her into another Orpheus, searching for his lost beloved "as one who grieves / Or seeks a thing long lost."

The words "once read about" may be read again in "For a Self-Possessed Friend" (57): "But you, my friend . . . you do not praise at all, / Or praising, stop and seem to cast your eye / Toward some commensurate cold finality / That once you guessed, or dreamed, or read about" (ellipsis in the poem). Allusions to the Orpheus myth continue here, too: "spectres spring / Irresolutely to the mind and fade," as did Eurydice, together with the man in "Cold Colloquy" to whom the woman "hearkened . . . / Till the light in his face, an empty candle, was blown." That extinguished candle also returns, in the form of a "candle gone black out." This candle appears to allude to the eventual demise of the self-possessed friend, whom the speaker predicts will thereafter show up in that place to which Eurydice was obliged to return: "when, self-possessed, you stand / . . . where await, / . . . the bored and bland / Incurious angels of the nether gate." The stone that was "troughèd" in "Problem of Knowledge" and "uncarved" in "Cold Colloquy" returns, but carved: "The impeccable unspeaking line of art / In brute stone cut."

"For a Self-Possessed Friend" and "For a Friend Who Thinks Himself Urbane" (58) are connected in an obvious way by their titles (as were "To a Friend Parting" and "Letter to a Friend"). The self-possessed friend does not praise enough: "you do not praise at all, / Or praising, stop and seem to cast your eye / Toward some commensurate cold finality." The urbane friend praises too much, having tried to "make the worse appear the better reason."[19] The self-possessed friend will, the speaker predicts, go after death to where the "bland . . . angels of the nether gate" await; the urbane friend resembles those angels, being of "bland brow."

The friend's urbanity is described as ineffectual sunshine: "you have tried to . . . follow / The sunshine of consent's good season; / But cannot." "The Garden" (59), set on "a fine day in early autumn," receives the doubtful blessing of a similarly feeble sun: "now the leaves will bloom / Their time, and take from milder sun / An unreviving benison." The first lines of "The Garden"—"How kind, how secret, now the sun / will bless this garden frost has won"—share a "secret" connection with the last lines of the immediately preceding poem: "But we, among all men, / Share this in secrecy: a little while / And you . . . will try again" ("For a Friend Who Thinks Himself Urbane"). Though it also shares a connection with the last lines of "For a Self-Possessed Friend," which spoke of the "bland" angels of the nether gate awaiting "In darkling kindliness," for the sun is not only "secret" but also "kind."

Indeed, the three poems work together in an allusive network, for the frosty yet sunny garden is a place of binary contradiction the two poles of which evoke the preceding two contrasting friends. The garden is "poised between the two alarms / Of summer's lusts and winter's harms," as if between the "sunshine of consent's good season" that the urbane friend tried to follow and the "cold finality" on which the self-possessed one cast his eye.

In "To One Awake" (59), darkness, like "dim autumnal rain," bestows "Its weary kiss," recalling "the kiss" of lovers recalled "in early autumn" in "The Garden." "To One Awake" is a poem about dreaming: "in the unclean flesh of sleep are caught / The sightless creatures that uncoil in dream." But it is also, like "The Garden," a poem about walking in a landscape: "this hollow hinterland you walk / Is of a swarthy liege your fief, / Whose bitter milk / Is wrung from out a barren stalk." An echo, though faint, links "this hollow hinterland" with "these precincts" from "The Garden." Whiteness from a stalk recalls whiteness from a shaft: "No marbles whitely gaze . . . / But . . . far more bold and pure / Than marble, gleams the sycamore, / Of argent torse and cunning shaft / Propped nobler than the sculptor's craft." The "bitter milk / . . . wrung from out a barren stalk, / Whose honey is the sap of grief / And its dark leaf" can be identified if we reread the stanza before: "If in the unclean flesh of sleep are caught / The sightless creatures that uncoil in dream, / Mortal, you ought / Not dread fat larvae of the thought / That in the ogival bone preform / The fabulous worm." The fabulous worm is likely an engorged penis, and the dream a wet one ("fat larvae of the thought"), hence "unclean" and the object of apprehension. The milk from a bitter stalk is semen wrung out in masturbation; the grief of the sapped member is the accompanying sadness of guilt. In "The Garden," the "cunning shaft / Propped" assumes phallic proportions, its "torse" not just "torse" but "torse" in the word's other sense: twisted, wrung. No wonder that "The Garden" is the site where "summer's lusts" are alarming. In "Letter of a Mother," the "illegal prodigality of dream" was the product of "cunning flesh . . . a subtile engine, propped / In the sutured head beneath the coronal seam," which is to say the brain. The brain, cunning and propped, is described in the same terms as the phallic sycamore. This makes perfect sense, for the brain is a sexual organ, particularly in "To One Awake," where "fat larvae of thought / . . . preform / The fabulous worm" that "uncoil[s] in dream."

At the same time, the third of three landscape poems and the second of two dream ones, "Garden Waters" (60), synthesizes elements of the two poems that precede it: "If in his garden all night fell the stream, / Noisy and silver"—recalling the sycamore's "argent torse" in "The Garden"—"over the moon-dark stone, / It was not so with the voiceless waters of dream, / Monstrously tumbled, falling with no tone." The monstrousness of the water's tumbling recalls that of the monsters caught in the unclean flesh of sleep in "To One Awake," in particular the "sightless creatures that uncoil in dream," here evoked in the "voiceless waters of dream." A "hollow-bosomed flood" answers to "hollow hinterland," thanks to a change Warren made in "To One Awake," which in its original publication had "this sable hinterland" (52n). "To One Awake" ends with a "dark leaf," while "Garden Waters" concludes with the revelation of something (including the same thing) hidden that comes from the season—and the poem—just past: "Within them [the garden waters] still sometimes, I think, is hid / The obscure image of the season's wreck, / The dead leaf and the summer's chrysalid."

"To a Face in the Crowd" (61), like "To One Awake" and "Garden Waters," is about what is perceived in dreams. "In dream, perhaps, I have seen your face before," the speaker tells the "Face" of the title, whom he also addresses as "Brother." And like "Garden Waters," the poem is about the noise water makes. In it, "taciturn tall stone" on a shore "Repeats the waves' implacable monotone." The speaker knows "how black and turbulent the blood / Will beat through iron chambers of the brain" were the brother to stand between the stone and the sea and hear it repeat the sound the latter makes. The effect on the blood of the noise water can make is likewise detailed in "Garden Waters": "men by crags have stopped against the loud // Torn cataract or hollow-bosomed flood / In solace of that full nocturnal tongue / Calling in kinship to the buried blood." Those in "To a Face in the Crowd" who can hear the taciturn tall stone echo the waves—the speaker, who seems to have done this already, and his "brother," whom he invites to do so—are linked by kinship: "We are the children of an ancient band / Broken between the mountains and the sea, / A cromlech marks for you the utmost strand // And you must find the dolorous place they stood." As the cataract or flood calls in kinship to the buried blood of the men who stop to hear it, the fathers call to their blood descendants, through their cromlech that echoes the sound of the waves. Water itself calls in one instance, while in the other fathers do, but through the intermediary of the sound water makes (and of the stone that reflects the sound).

This difference corresponds to a difference made within "Garden Waters" between real waters that make noise at night and dream waters that do not: "If in his garden all night fell the stream, / Noisy and silver over the moon-dark stone, / It was not so with the voiceless waters of dream, / Monstrously tumbled, falling with no tone." Real waters may call in kinship to the buried blood, but "More terrible breaks the torrent with no song." The waves that make their monotone in "To a Face in the Crowd" correspond to the real waters here, while the fathers' tall stone in its taciturnity corresponds to the waters of dream in their voicelessness. All the more so for the fact that the "monotone" the stone repeats itself repeats the "no tone" of the waters of dream.[20] In a way perhaps emblematic of their own sequential construction and that of so many of Warren's volumes to come, the *Thirty-Six Poems* thus conclude with the creation of a tone out of silence, an echoing monotone out of none at all. Something out of nothingness: meaning through an insistent echoing, a copy of no original.

CHAPTER 2
"IN MIRRORED-MIRRORED-MIRROR-WISE"

ELEVEN POEMS
ON THE SAME THEME

What is the "Same Theme" on which the *Eleven Poems* are based? Leonard Casper maintained that each is "an exploration of that original sin which every man commits" (*The Dark and Bloody Ground* 64). For Victor Strandberg, the "master metaphor" of the poems is the "undiscovered self" (*A Colder Fire* 75). James A. Grimshaw Jr. writes that what unites the poems is "the theme of love," not just romantic, but also fraternal, maternal, and divine (*Understanding Robert Penn Warren* 117). William Bedford Clark sees them as chronicling "the efforts of their unnamed, and therefore representative, protagonist to deny his personal past and abandon as well the accompanying burdens of history" (*The American Vision* 61). John Burt finds that the "theme mentioned in the title is that of human fallenness—not just the fallenness of original sin, but the fallenness of finding one's self thrown into a world in which one feels the demand of having a metaphysical purpose but can't find any that are not already somehow shot through with fakery."[1]

Though Warren never claimed to know much about music,[2] his title does suggest the traditional musical form of theme and variations, except that the *Eleven Poems* may not resemble, say, Bach's *Goldberg Variations,* which like nearly all other examples of the form begin with a statement of the theme, so much as Elgar's *Enigma Variations,* in which no such statement appears, with the result that one is left forever guessing what in fact it is.

Invoking another kind of musical structure, however, Casper calls Warren's volume "contrapuntal," having "the range of a prolonged fugue" in that "each part" is "an exploration" of the given theme (*The Dark and Bloody Ground* 64). I propose that we take the fugal model seriously as a way of reading the *Eleven Poems,* realizing how much it differs from the theme-and-variations one. To the extent that one sees the poems as exploring a theme rather than imitating one another, however, one is still in the realm of theme and variations. What the poems actually do is more complicated than that. Like sequentially entering voices in a fugue, each imitates its predecessor yet also embodies the enigmatic theme of the collection. There is, in other words, repetition on two levels, through development of the theme and imitation of the previous poem. The elements of one poem that are imitated in the next may be less universally significant than the "Same Theme," whether we read that as original sin, the undiscovered self, varieties of love, the burden of history, or something else. Indeed, they may often be devoid of any meaning outside their immediate context (which is always at least two contexts, given that each appears in more than one poem). Yet they are part of the substance of which these poems, collectively considered, are made.

The *Eleven Poems* begin with an echo: "Among the pines we ran and called / In joy and innocence, and still / Our voices doubled in the high / Green groining our simplicity" ("Monologue at Midnight" 65)—quite literally begin, as these are the first words of the first poem. They echo the echo that linked the last two poems of Warren's immediately preceding sequence, *Thirty-Six Poems*, and thus create a continuity from one sequence to the next. The waves' implacable "monotone" in "To a Face in the Crowd" (61) was repeated (within that poem) by the "taciturn tall stone" but itself echoed (within the sequence) the "no tone" in "Garden Waters" (60), transforming by the echoing process *none* (the "no tone") to *one* (the "monotone"). The "simplicity" of "Our voices"—their singleness, their monotone—is here "doubled" by the acoustical properties of the overarching trees, an echo transforming one ("simplicity") to two (now "doubled"). This effect is explicitly named later in "Monologue at Midnight" as an "echo": "The hound, *the echo*, flame, or shadow . . . / And which am I and which are you?" (ellipsis in the poem). Among the echoes linking this poem with "Bearded Oaks" (65), which follows it in the sequence, is this "echo": "Our feet once wrought the hollow street / With *echo*" ("Bearded Oaks"). In both instances it is "we"—the lovers who are the protagonists of the first three poems of the sequence (of which the third is "Picnic Remembered" 66)—who make the sound that finds an echo. My candidate, therefore, for the secret theme of the sequence is echo itself.

There are other instances of doubling in "Monologue at Midnight": "The match flame sudden in the gloom / Is lensed within each watching eye / Less intricate, less small, than in / One heart the other's image is." One match flame image within one eye is visually echoed in another eye, as the images of the lovers are echoed in each other's hearts.[3] Yet another analogue for echo is offered by the shadows that consistently follow, and imitate, the lovers: "And always at the side, like guilt, / Our shadows over the grasses moved." That combination of grass and shadowing (in the sense of imitation) will recur, in a different formulation, in "Bearded Oaks": "So, waiting, we in the grass now lie / Beneath the languorous tread of light: / The grasses, kelp-like, satisfy / The nameless motions of the air." The grasses, that is, shadow the motions of the air, moving when they do.

"Bearded Oaks" imitates "Monologue at Midnight" in other ways, too. In the latter, "How soundlessly / The maple shed its pollen in the sun"; in "Bearded Oaks," gold again descends from a sunlit sky:

> The storm of noon above us rolled,
> Of light the fury, furious gold,
>
> . . . .
>
> Passion and slaughter, ruth, decay
> Descend, minutely whispering down,
> Silted down swaying streams, to lay
> Foundation for our voicelessness.

The pollen fell "soundlessly" in "Monologue at Midnight"; what descends in "Bearded Oaks" does so almost as silently, since it whispers and makes "voicelessness" possible.[4] What descends from the "furious gold" of the "storm of noon" is of a different nature. The two lines preceding the passage from "Bearded Oaks" just quoted make the same statement: "violence, forgot now, lent / The present stillness all its power." Clark explains that this violence is "worldly" (*The American Vision* 61), that it is related to world events at the time the poem was written (it was first published in 1937), especially the rise of fascism in Europe. The lovers lie down beneath the bearded oaks to escape those storms, abandoning what Clark calls "the burdens of history." The stillness beneath the bearded oaks is made powerful by its contrast to the violence raging above and beyond. In the next stanza (immediately following the line "Foundation for our voicelessness"), explicit reference is made to history: "All our debate is voiceless here, / As all our rage, the rage of stone; / If hope is hopeless, then fearless fear, / And history is thus undone." The burden of history can be shaken off, and history itself "undone," by escaping the world in the peace beneath the oaks. But that peace is a kind of death, as the poem's final stanza makes clear: "we may spare this hour's term / To practice for eternity." Lying together in the grass, "as light withdraws, / Twin atolls on a shelf of shade," the lovers are playing at being dead. They are turning into stone, as Warren returns to the metaphor he explored in *Thirty-Six Poems* of stone as the opposite of life and time. He had already returned to it in "Monologue at Midnight": "are we Time who flee so fast, / Or stone who stand, and thus endure?"

That theme undergoes further development in "Picnic Remembered" (66): "Our hearts, like hollow stones, have trapped / A corner of that brackish tide." The brackish water is associated with the increasing darkness of the end of day: "darkness on the landscape grew / As in our bosoms darkness, too." It is the darkness of death, as the lovers seemed to have but partly realized: "we did not know / How darkness darker staired below; / Or knowing, but half understood." In "Bearded Oaks," they also saw the darkness come: "I do not love you less that . . . all that light once gave / The graduate dark should now revoke."

In both poems the lovers imagine themselves floating in an ocean. In "Bearded Oaks," they saw the grass in which they lay as "kelp-like. . . . / Upon the floor of light, and time, / Unmurmuring, of polyp made, / We rest; we are . . . / Twin atolls." In "Picnic Remembered," they "moved, as swimmers," like the light that "swims" above the bearded oaks.

As fear became "fearless" in "Bearded Oaks," fear is negated as well in "Picnic Remembered": "all the wild / Grief canceled; so with what we feared." The golden pollen that sifted down in "Monologue at Midnight," replaced by the fragments of the "furious gold" of noon that descended through the trees in "Bearded Oaks," is now an "amber light" that "laved" the trees above "and us." "Twin atolls" in "Bearded Oaks," the lovers in "Picnic Remembered" become "Twin flies . . . as in amber tamed."

The first three poems seem to form a cluster, as the next three form another. The speaker in the first three addresses "us"; in the second three, he addresses "you." The "we" are lovers taking refuge under trees (pines, bearded oaks, and unspecified "painted trees") from fear, time, and history. The "you" in "Crime" (68), "Original Sin: A Short Story" (69), and "End of Season" (70) is seeking refuge too, from an insistent past.

"Envy the mad killer who lies in the ditch and grieves," the speaker in "Crime" tells "you," "for what he buried is buried" even if "he cannot seem / To remember what it was he buried." The killer at least "grieves" (evidently because he cannot remember), whereas the "we" in "Picnic Remembered" did not, for "all we had endured / Seemed quaint disaster of a child, / Now cupboarded, and all the wild / Grief canceled." The two poems interflow, for in "Crime" a "disaster of a child" is suggested when the narrator wonders if the murderer's victim had been a child: "was it . . . the child who crossed the park every day with the lunch-basket?" Though the victim could also have been "An old woman" or a "stranger," the child image persists, as the killer himself is likened to "a child asleep with a bauble" as he hugs his "treasure," the memory of his victim's "lyric scream." And the darkness that "darker staired below" in "Picnic Remembered" becomes in "Crime" memory dripping like "a pipe in the cellar-dark." The stairs in one poem, in other words, seem to lead down to the cellar in the other.

The child image continues into "Original Sin: A Short Story" (69), in which a mysterious entity from the past who haunts the "you" whom the speaker addresses "comes, its hand childish. . . / Clutching the bribe of chocolate or a toy you used to treasure." It keeps showing up, fumbling at the door, snuffling like an old hound, trying the lock. "You thought you had lost it when you left Omaha, . . . / But you met it in Harvard Yard." Strandberg calls it "the shadow-self within, the dark, hidden self" we (or "you") "have slain and buried" (*A Colder Fire* 82). It already made an appearance in "Crime" in the form of "the letter" in the attic that "Names over your name, and mourns under the dry rafter." In "Original Sin," pains are taken to avoid receiving such a letter: "You have moved often and rarely left an address."

The hidden self that keeps showing up in "Original Sin" comes more and more to resemble the mad killer in "Crime." As indeed it should, if we agree with Strandberg that what is slain and buried is the slayer's hidden self. We have seen this already in the child image, which in "Crime" applies to the mad killer and in "Original Sin" to that hidden self. The child in both instances is holding something he treasures: "His treasure . . . / Hugged under his coat . . . like a child asleep with a bauble" ("Crime"); "Clutching . . . a toy you used to treasure" ("Original Sin"). Both are "nodding": the mad killer is depicted as trying, "nodding and serious," to remember who it was he killed, while the secret self is presented in the first words of "Original Sin" as "Nodding . . . its great head."

The second stanza of "Original Sin" presents a portrait of "your" grandfather, to which the speaker says the secret self is connected: "You thought you had lost it when you left Omaha, / For it seemed connected then with your grandpa, who / Had a wen on his forehead and sat on the veranda / To finger the precious protuberance, as was his habit to do, / Which glinted in sun like rough garnet or the rich old brain bulging through." The glinting garnet on the brow echoes the image of a glittering jewel in another brow in "Crime": "when the earth gets warmer, // The cold heart heaves like a toad, and lifts its brow / With that bright jewel you have no use for now."[5] "Your grandpa" returns in "End of Season" (70), in which the connection with the hidden self, asserted yet still obscure in "Original Sin," is made explicit: "The Springs where your grandpa went in Arkansas / To purge the rheumatic guilt of beef and bourbon, / And slept like a child, nor called out with the accustomed nightmare, / But lolled his old hams, stained hands, in that Lethe, as others, others, before. // For waters wash our guilt." It is that the grandfather did what "you" have tried to do: to forget the past. The Arkansas waters, Lethe-like, washed away his guilt, while in "Original Sin" "you" have sought a "sense of cleansing." The grandfather "slept like a child," as the hidden self in "Original Sin" clutched its treasure with "childish" hand and the mad killer in "Crime" hugged his treasure "like a child asleep with a bauble." Having successfully forgotten his guilt, the grandfather no longer dreamed "the accustomed nightmare," which Warren's sequencing leads us to connect with the "nightmare" in "Original Sin" that is the secret self: "The nightmare stumbles past, and you have heard / It fumble your door before it whimpers and is gone."

In another instance of cleansing in "End of Season," the speaker recalls how Virgil, "With rushes, sea-wet, wiped from that sad brow the infernal grime," where Dante's brow recalls both the grandfather's wen-bedecked "forehead" in "Original Sin" and the toad's "brow" in "Crime." If these sea-wet rushes recall the "locks like seaweed" on the "great head" of the hidden and rejected self as it makes its first appearance in "Original Sin," then it may be that only by confrontation with that self can true cleansing be achieved.

The "letter" that has been hidden in the attic in "Crime," and that "you" tried to evade in "Original Sin" by having "rarely left an address," turns up again in "End of Season": "But the mail lurks in the box at the house where you live." It will be waiting when "you" return from the beach vacation where you have gone, as your grandfather had gone to an Arkansan spa, for a plunge into oblivion, "Down the glaucous glimmer where no voice can visit."

"Revelation" (71) is the only poem of the eleven in which the protagonist is neither "you" nor "we" but "he":

> Because he had spoken harshly to his mother,
> The day became astonishingly bright,
> The enormity of distance crept to him like a dog now,
> And earth's own luminescence seemed to repel the night.
>
> Roof was rent like the loud paper tearing to admit
> Sun-sulphurous splendor where had been before
> But the submarine glimmer by kindly countenances it,
> As slow, phosphorescent dignities light the ocean floor.

Despite the change of person, certain continuities with the preceding poems are evident (as if such a change were a futile effort to shake off a persistently return-ing past). The "submarine glimmer" here is of a piece with the "glaucous glimmer" into which "you" dived in "End of Season" and recalls as well the underwater region where the lovers took refuge in "Bearded Oaks" and "Picnic Remembered." It ceases to be a refuge for the boy when the world's light invades it as a consequence of his having spoken harshly to his mother. The outside world makes its presence known, creeping up to him "like a dog," as in "Original Sin" the nightmare vision of the old self is likened to "the old hound that used to snuffle your door and moan." In "End of Season," the grandfather "slept like a child," having purged his past; but the child in "Revelation," troubled by the outrage he committed in the very recent past, did not: "tears, that night, wet the pillow where the boy's head was laid."

In "Pursuit" (72), we return to "you," whom we find consulting a doctor. The physician, "Listening . . . bends at your heart; / But cannot make out just what it tries to impart." This scene echoes, with a reversal of roles, a scene in "Revelation" in which the boy, made suddenly aware of the world because of what he said to his mother, perceives that chrysanthemum and aster "lean, confer, / And his ears, and heart, should burn at insidious whisper / Which concerns him so, he knows; but he cannot make out the words." The doctor bends; the flowers lean. The doctor "cannot make out just what" the protagonist's heart is saying; the protagonist "cannot make out" what the flowers are saying. The theme of the difficulty of understanding what is spoken actually began in "End of Season," where "You will have to learn a new language to say what is to say" when obliged to converse with one whose face "wears / The . . . smudge of history." The underwater diver had sought out a place where he could be uncommunicative, that glaucous region "where no voice can visit." Similarly, in "Bearded Oaks," the lovers found their underwater retreat to be "Foundation for our voicelessness." To engage in history, to shoulder its burden, is to be obliged to speak a language, and perhaps to learn a new one. To retreat from it, on the other hand, is to dwell in silence. "Solution, perhaps, is public, despair personal" ("Pursuit"): in other words, one can choose to remain in personal solipsistic despair ("you sit alone—which is the beginning of error" ["Pursuit"]) or to work toward a solution by going public, joining the conversation.

"Question and Answer" (73) continues the theme of the difficulty of communicating, but a new problem arises: "never demand . . . answer," we (addressed as "you") are told, of the sand, the gull, the sky, nor even "of your true love." Why? Because "all— / Each frescoed figure leaning from the world's wall . . . — / Demand / In truth the true / Answer of you; / And each, / Locked lonely in its valveless speech, / Speaks, / And without resting, seeks / Answer and seeks to speak: / That conversation is not loud." Those quietly conversing "leaning" figures evoke the flowers in "Revelation" that "lean" and "confer" in a "whisper" (together with the doctor who "bends" to make out what the heart is saying in "Pursuit"); in fact, a little later in the poem the leaning frescoed figures are said to "flower from the stalk, and bend," which underscores their connection with the flowers. These figures are difficult to communicate with because "all / Rehearse their own simplicity"; this is likely the same simplicity as that seen in the solipsistic lovers in "Monologue at Midnight," whose "voices doubled in the high / Green groining our simplicity." Like the figures leaning from the world's wall, they spoke, but only to each other.

The speaker in "Question and Answer" complains that the figures from the world's wall "all repeat / In mirrored-mirrored-mirror-wise / Unto our eyes / But question, not replies." That mirroring mirrors a mirror in "Pursuit":

> But history held to your breath clouds like a mirror.
> There are many states, and towns in them, and faces,
> But meanwhile, the little old lady in black, by the wall,
> Who admires all the dancers, and tells you how just last fall
> Her husband died in Ohio, and damp mists her glasses;
> She blinks and croaks, like a toad or a Norn, in the horrible light,
> And rattles her crutch, which may put forth a small bloom, perhaps white. (73)

It is not clear how we should take this woman. Is she held up as a figure of scorn? Or is she worth paying attention to, both on "your" account and ours? A small but persistent detail links her both to the leaning flowers in "Revelation" and to the leaning frescoed figures in "Question and Answer": the flowers were encountered "by walls" (though also "by walks"), the frescoed figures lean "from the world's wall," while the old lady is "by the wall." Another detail links her in another way to the frescoed figures: they "flower from the stalk," while the old lady's crutch may miraculously "put forth a small bloom." Yet another detail connects her to the hidden self that, like the burden of history, "you" are learning it is best not to ignore. Strandberg notes that "the little old lady in black, who blinks and croaks like a toad, may remind us (uncomfortably) of that shadow-self back in 'Crime,' whose 'cold heart heaves like a toad' in the cellar-dark" (*A Colder Fire* 92). Finally, the way her glasses mist up parallels the way that history "clouds like a mirror," which aligns her with the burden of history that it is becoming increasingly evident one should not shirk. In other words, she represents both history and the hidden self and is scorned at our ("your") peril.

All this prepares us to appreciate what is at stake in the question the next poem, "Love's Parable" (75), will ask: "Are we but mirror to the world?" The statement made in "Question and Answer" to the effect that "all repeat / In mirrored-mirrored-mirror-wise" the question "you" would ask them now takes on additional meaning, for there are mirrors on either side of the poem, the one in "Pursuit" that is history clouding up to "your breath" and the one in "Love's Parable" that "we" present to the world. The mirrors on either side of "Love's Parable" are mirrored by each other, for in the developing argument of the *Eleven Poems* "history" and "the world" become the same thing. The poem to follow, "Terror" (77), will remind us that at the time *Eleven Poems* were being written, history was being made "In the Piazza or the Wilhelmplatz," as Mussolini and Hitler were being encouraged by onanistic crowds each "to follow his terrible / Star." This was the world, the burden of that time.

The "we" who may mirror it are two lovers, each likened in "Love's Parable" to a kingdom long troubled by civil war that welcomes the arrival on their shores of an alien prince who can bring peace, one "whose tongue, not understood, / Yet frames a new felicity, / And alien, seals domestic good: / Once, each to each, such aliens, we." Thus the theme of the difficulty of communicating continues. It began in "End of Season" with a suggestion that now proves prophetic: "You will have to learn a new language to say what is to say." Each of the two lovers in "Love's Parable" will have to learn a new tongue in order to communicate with the other. The theme continues in "Revelation" with the whispered words of chrysanthemum and aster that the boy feels "concerns him so, he knows; but he cannot make out the words." It developed in "Pursuit" into the doctor who "cannot make out just what" the protagonist's heart is trying to impart. Then in "Question and Answer," we see it again in the frescoed figures leaning from the world's wall of whom "each" is "Locked lonely in its valveless speech" in a "conversation" that "is not loud."

Peace then came, as each lover became "the other's sun" and every day a "miracle." They discovered "love's mystery," which is "That substance long in grossness bound / Might bud into love's accident." This budding picks up the theme begun in the old lady's crutch "which may put forth a small bloom" in "Pursuit" and continued in the flowering ("All flower from the stalk") in "Question and Answer." But since that time "we have seen the fungus eyes / Of misery . . . / And marked how ripe injustice flows, . . . / How proud flesh on the sounder grows / Till rot engross the estate of men." The lovers have also discovered "within, the inward sore / Of self" and "Contempt of very love we bore / And hatred of the good." It is after reaching this state that they ask, "Are we but mirror to the world? / Or does the world our ruin reflect, / Or is our gazing beauty spoiled / But by the glass' flawed defect?" Such despair was likewise reached in "Question and Answer," when "you" found that the figures on the world's wall had no answer to his question but instead would ask the same question of him. In response, he exclaims, "Then let the heart be stone," as if he had returned to that sad state the lovers in

"Picnic Remembered" had reached when they found that "Our hearts, like hollow stones, have trapped / A corner of that brackish tide" and in "Bearded Oaks" that "all our rage [is] the rage of stone" and "hope is hopeless."

Yet at this point the speaker makes a virtue of necessity, finding something good in stoniness by evoking the rock Moses struck and consequently "Like a pealing bell ring / And in the general sight / Gave forth to tongue and gut the living stream's delight." But is he confident of repeating Moses' success? Evidently not, for he continues: "But if not that, then know / At least the heart a bow / Bent" from which one might let "the arrow fly / At God's black, orbèd, target eye." Strandberg sees in these lines "intimations of divine love" (*A Colder Fire* 94), though it seems to me as likely to be an expression of God-hatred. In "The Mango on the Mango Tree" (98) from "Mexico is a Foreign Country: Five Studies in Naturalism," published the following year in *Selected Poems 1923–1943*, God's eye is hardly an object of devotion: "The mango is a great gold eye, / Like God's, set in the leafy sky / To harry heart, block blood, freeze feet, if I would fly. // For God has set it there to spy / And make report." (In both, Warren rhymes God's "eye" with "fly.") But however we interpret the attention paid to God at the end of "Question and Answer," at the end of "Love's Parable" the speaker turns heavenward as well, expressing "hope" that the "falling-off" between the lovers may be overcome by the power of prayer: "for there are testaments / That men, by prayer, have mastered grace."

In "Terror," we return from "we" to "you," and from lovers' concerns to the world's, but the connections between this poem and "Love's Parable" are such that we can see why the question was raised in that poem of whether the lovers "Are . . . but mirror to the world." For the world as depicted in "Terror" mirrors the lovers in "Love's Parable." In the early stages of their relationship, "joy sought joy then when we loved, / As iron to the magnet yearns." In "Terror," the speaker criticizes those who fought alongside the Communists in the Spanish Civil War and then against them in Finland for being motivated not by a cause, but by their own "emptiness" and "Lust" for combat: they "seek" to "polarize their iron of despair." Joy seeking joy in one poem has yielded to despair seeking despair in the other; both the joy and the despair are likened, through simile or metaphor, to "iron" under the influence of a magnetic—that is, polarized—field. The speaker in "Terror" elaborates: "They fight old friends, for their obsession knows / Only the immaculate itch, not human friends or foes." Itching was a problem in "Love's Parable," too, when rot set in: "we at length, / Itching and slumwise, each other infect." It is in the very next line that the question arises, "Are we but mirror to the world?" The propinquity of the itch to the mirror in these two lines suggests not only, given that itching will recur in "Terror," that the two poems—the one about lovers, the other about the world—mirror each other, but also that they infect each other through a contagious itch. Indeed, the speaker in "Terror" warns of the danger of contamination that may come from getting too close: "contagion may nook in the comforting fur you love to caress."

The *Eleven Poems* are so interconnected that their common mysterious theme seems to be what so many of their contiguous echoes self-referentially express: the doubling of echoing, mirroring, and infection.

CHAPTER 3
"THIS COLLOCATION/ OF MEMORIES"

PROMISES:
POEMS 1954–1956

After a decade of silence, Warren returned to poetry in 1953 with the book-length *Brother to Dragons* and to the lyric poetic sequence with *Promises: Poems 1954–1956*. He emerged from that chrysalis transformed. Joy had entered the picture, no doubt for reasons of personal happiness; archaic language, ruined gardens, and intimations of terror were gone. His Kentucky boyhood, his happy second marriage, his children, and European travels provided new material appropriate to this major transformation. All these changes were immediately apparent to his readers, but beneath it all, the fundamental desire to write poems that mirrored and reinterpreted one another remained.

The five poems of "To a Little Girl, One Year Old, in a Ruined Fortress," the first of the two sequences that make up *Promises*, "exhibit," as Victor Strandberg has convincingly shown, an "interlocking continuity" (*A Colder Fire* 207). That continuity is sometimes maintained through sameness, as in the anguish of the "anguished" Philip of Spain in "Sirocco" (103), who built the fortress before which the poems unfold, and that of the "irrelevant anguish of air" in the windless landscape of "Gull's Cry" (103), which follows it (*A Colder Fire* 181). Sometimes it is maintained through an opposition grounded in an underlying sameness, as in the reason itself the air is anguished, which is that it is stifled by windlessness—in contrast to the force of the wind that dominates the first poem and gives it its title: "the sirocco, the dust swirl is swirled / Over the bay face, mounts air like gold gauze whirled; it traverses the blaze-blue of water," carrying desert sand from North Africa across the Mediterranean to the Italian coast. In "Gull's Cry," as Strandberg points out, "[i]nstead of the 'air like gold gauze whirled,' we have . . . a heavy, stagnant atmosphere of total stasis: 'I do not think that anything in the world will move, not goat, not gander . . . ; the sun beats'" (*A Colder Fire* 179). He reveals a third linkage as well: "the same focus of vision which picked out the garbage of the moat in 'Sirocco'"—the garbage beneath which Philip's great stone scutcheon languishes—"is similarly at work noting the refuse of the animal kingdom in 'Gull's Cry': 'Goat droppings are fresh in the hot dust'" (*A Colder Fire* 179).

Strandberg has so thoroughly analyzed these five poems that at first it may seem difficult to find a part of that "interlocking continuity" that he has not already brought to light, but I propose that we take a closer look at the stone of the ruined *rocca* in "Sirocco"—"To a place of ruined stone we brought you . . . / We have brought you where geometry of a military rigor survives its own ruined world"—in connection with its reappearance in "Gull's Cry": "let the molecular dance of the stone-dark glimmer like joy in the stone's dream." Commenting on this line, Strandberg writes, "The choice of the stone to represent a fallen but redeemable nature is particularly effective here . . . because it ties in with the 'ruined stone' that composes the 'ruined fortress' of the world in 'Sirocco'" (*A Colder Fire* 183). What catches my eye here is the parallel between the survival of the geometry in the stone and the life still present in the dance of the stone's molecules, which is geometrical too, though in a different way: an inner molecular geometry as opposed to an outer one imposed by the fortress's architect "with most fastidious mathematic and skill" ("Sirocco"). In Warren's poetic practice, the mathematic and skill imposed from without corresponds to his own imposition of form on his material, in both the structure of individual poems and their arrangement in the volume, while the inner dance of molecules corresponds to what words do on their own, beyond the conscious oversight of a poet who, like Mallarmé, "lets the words take the initiative" with the result that, "set in motion by the collision of their difference, they illuminate each other by reciprocal reflections" ("L'oeuvre pure implique la disparition élocutoire du poëte, qui cède l'initiative aux mots, par le heurt de leur inégalité mobilisés; ils s'allument de reflets réciproques" ["Crise de vers"]). Mallarmé probably did not have sequentially occurring reflections in mind, but it is a fair way of describing what happens in Warren's sequences: a word in one poem illuminates the same word or a similar one appearing in a neighboring poem.

The poems in *Promises*' first sequence, unlike those in the second, are already connected by virtue of telling a continuous story in the same setting. Thus we read of a "defective child" in "Gull's Cry" and read of it again in "The Child Next Door" (104). With regard to the defective child (since it is the same child), we have none of the "collision of . . . difference," as Mallarmé put it, that we find in abundance elsewhere in Warren's sequences. Yet we can find it in this sequence, too, not only in the recurring anguish of Philip and the wind and in the life hidden in stone but also in the collision between the defective child and the poet's perfect daughter—each, by Strandberg's reckoning, the twin half of the other: "The child is an infant whose 'defective' body bears tragic testimony of original sin and whose proximity ('next door') to Rosanna—indeed they become almost twin halves of the same total human Self—brings her perfection under such a pall as nearly to annihilate the narrator's tentative 'redeem, redeem!' of the previous poem" (*A Colder Fire* 175). Between one child and the other, there is both collision and reciprocal reflection.

In the last line of "Gull's Cry," Warren writes (alluding to another defective individual, a hunchback who also lives in the neighborhood): "And in that moment of possibility, let *gobbo, gobbo's* wife, and us, and all, take hands and sing: redeem, redeem!" Yet expressing a redeeming hope through hands is precisely what he will find fault with when someone else tries it in "The Child Next Door":

> The sister is twelve. Is beautiful like a saint.
> Sits with the monster all day, with pure love, calm eyes.
> Has taught it a trick, to make *ciao*, Italian-wise.
> It crooks hand in that greeting. She smiles her smile without taint.
>
> I come, and her triptych beauty and joy stir hate
> —Is it hate?—in my heart. Fool, doesn't she know that the process
> Is not that joyous or simple, to bless, or unbless,
> The malfeasance of nature or the filth of fate?

Here is another collision with reciprocal illumination. On the surface, we can see the conflict between the poet's expression of the hope of redemption in the second poem and his dashing of that hope in the third, between his approval of expressing the hope himself and disapproval of someone's acting on that hope. But beneath the surface, the collision: for it is a hand-held hope in both instances, hands that clasp and hands that greet—and a hand that imitates another, as the defective child slowly learns, through his instructor's patient repetition, the communicating gesture. At the close of "The Child Next Door," the poet also has finally learned: "I smile stiff, saying *ciao*, saying *ciao*, and think: this is the world."

The poems imitate each other, too, as "The Flower" (104) presents another repetitive gesture involving a hand. The poet and his wife escort their one-year-old daughter up the hill from the beach, and when they arrive at the place on the path where earlier in the summer the parents had plucked her a flower, she reaches out and demands another:

So here you always demand
Your flower to hold in your hand,
And the flower must be white,
For you have your own ways to compel
Observance of this ritual.
You hold it and sing with delight.

In a reversal of the relationship between child and teacher in "The Child Next Door," where the older sister taught the child, here it is the child who teaches the ritual to her parents. Because the season has advanced, the parents can find "No bloom worthily white." Those available are "disintegrated" or turned brown by the salt air and the passage of time (the flowers were fresher in June): "We give the best one to you. / It is ruined, but will have to do." Yet the child is just as happy with the imperfect flower: "you sing as though human need / Were not for perfection." In this she resembles the older sister in the poem before, as Strandberg explains: "The girl's response to the ruined flower is such indiscriminate joy . . . as to suggest a comparison between Rosanna and the saintly sister. . . . Both of these girls . . . seem to transcend the ruins . . . through an attitude of total acceptance of things as they are. . . . [T]hese girls cheerfully work with whatever is available, content with whatever the ruins offer, however imperfect a defective brother or a ruined flower might be" (*A Colder Fire* 193). The connection between the defective child and time's ruining power (and consequently between the defective child and the defective white flowers) is underscored by the expression "defection of season" (in the sense of time running out) in "Colder Fire" (107), the fifth and final poem in the sequence.

In "Colder Fire," the time-ruined and disintegrating white flowers are replaced by "time-tattered and disarrayed" white butterflies, and the "ritual" involving the flowers is replaced by the "ritual" (in the word's only other appearance in *Promises*)[1] the butterflies enact: "the late / White butterflies over gold thistle conduct their ritual carouse. // . . . Pale ghosts of pale passions of air, the white wings weave. / In tingle and tangle of arabesque, they mount light, pair by pair, / As though that tall light were eternal indeed, not merely the summer's reprieve." Like the butterflies themselves, the poems in this sequence dance in pairs, but with the difference that each poem after the first is part of two pairs, uniting with its predecessor and its successor. Warren seems to comment on this state of affairs at the close of "Colder Fire": "I cannot interpret for you this collocation / Of memories. You will live your own life, and contrive / The language of your own heart, but let that conversation, / In the last analysis, be always of whatever truth you would live." There are two messages here, and two audiences. The first and more obvious is the lesson for living he addresses to his daughter. But he is speaking to the reader as well, leaving it to the reader to *interpret* this *collocation* of memories. A curious but well-chosen word, a collocation is a co-location, for to collocate is to "place side by side, or in some relation to each other; to arrange" (*OED*), from "com" (together) and "locare" (to place). The memories are collocated, but so are the poems, the time-damaged and dying white butterflies collocated with the time-damaged and dying white flowers, the butterflies' ritual with the flower ritual, the learned behavior of the hand reaching out for a flower with the learned behavior of the hand saying *ciao*.

The first two lines of the final stanza of the poem are likewise open to more than one interpretation: "For fire flames but in the heart of a colder fire. / All voice is but echo caught from a soundless voice." Strandberg writes:

> The "fire" and the "voice," it seems to me, refer to the poet's motive and to what that motive produces—what through his art he says. The "colder fire" and the "soundless voice" tie in with the exhortation to recognize honestly "whatever truth you would live" in the previous stanza. . . . [T]hat private truth . . . is . . . not so private after all. The vision of truth which each heart claims as distinctly its own partakes in fact of a larger vision, a generalized truth, embracing in composite all the lesser ones: "For fire flames but in the heart of a colder fire." Consequently, the body of art (the "voice") whereby the individual seer renders his particular vision of truth may appear distinct from all others, but actually every artist is only adding his strength to a composite voice—the voice, which is ultimately inarticulate, of all men seeking truth. (*A Colder Fire* 202–3)

Another interpretation, however, might emerge from our listening closely to (1) the "conversation" carried on in the "language of [his] own heart" (to borrow some terms from the preceding stanza)—by this I mean what such words and concepts as "voice," "echo," "colder fire," and the echo of a silence appear to signify in Warren's private language, as we see them in other poems (and novels); and (2) the collocation of soundless voices and cool-burning fires available for our perusal at this particular moment in *Promises,* as we see what Warren will make of the pairing of "Colder Fire" with the next poem, "What Was the Promise that Smiled from the Maples at Evening?" (109)

Taking the first approach, we might remember that *Thirty-Six Poems* ended with the "monotone" of "the waves' implacable monotone" ("To a Face in the Crowd" 61), echoing yet adding a syllable to the "no tone" of "the voiceless waters of dream, / . . . falling with no tone" ("Garden Waters" 60). As I suggested, this anticipates the supposed text from the father that sons in Warren's novels will feel obliged to interpret even though its existence as a text is doubtful. The line "All voice is but echo caught from a soundless voice" replicates this situation: the voice could be the son's, echoing the father's soundless voice. The father's voice might be soundless because, like the wink that Willie Stark might not have meant to convey anything by, it was not meant to say anything. The defective child's gesture is a variation on this theme, for it might be so mentally deficient that its crooked hand does not really mean *ciao* or anything else. It is a copy without an original, an echo of no voice—or at least of a voice no one (except perhaps the one echoing it—the son, in the novels—can hear.

Likewise through that first method of approach, we might find a clue to what Warren means by "a colder fire" in the later poem "Fox-fire: 1956" (157), where he speaks of the old Greek grammar his father left behind when he died: "that poor book burns / Like fox-fire in the black swamp of the world's error." Fox-fire (phosphorescent decaying wood) is an instance of cold fire, and here it is a father's text.

Taking the second approach (yet also the first, as it turns out), we can almost immediately see another "colder fire," after the one four lines from the end of the poem of that title, in the sixth line of the next poem: "Beneath pale hydrangeas first firefly utters cold burning" ("What Was the Promise that Smiled from the Maples at Evening?"), as the second sequence of *Promises* begins, which is itself titled "Promises" (and is dedicated to Gabriel, Warren's son). And still another colder fire makes its appearance a little later in the poem, when he stands at his parents' graves: "Then sudden, the ground at my feet was like glass, and I say / What I saw, saw deep down, and the fleshly habiliments rent— / But agleam in a phosphorus of glory, bones bathed, there they lay, / Side by side, Ruth and Robert: the illumination then spent." This phosphorescence was announced by the firefly earlier in the poem, yet also by the "colder fire" in the poem just before. That colder fire was there paired with a "soundless voice" ("All voice is but echo caught from a soundless voice"), and that pairing is repeated here, for the long-dead parents speak, "in silence": "Then her voice, long forgotten, calm in silence, said: 'Child.' / Then his with the calm of a night field, or far star: / 'We died only that every promise might be fulfilled.'" Now we can understand why the white butterflies in "Colder Fire" are "Pale ghosts": they anticipate the ghosts of the parents, glowing in their graves (their pairing replicated by that of the poems themselves). Like Ruth and Robert, they are perceived in pairs ("pair by pair, / As though that tall light were eternal"); and like them, they are "time-tattered and disarrayed," disarrayed as in "no longer arrayed": "of fleshly habiliments rent." The connection between cold burning and ghosts had already been made in "What Was the Promise" in the "spectral" setting in which the firefly appeared: "In first darkness hydrangeas float in their spectral precinct. / Beneath pale hydrangeas first firefly utters cold burning. / The sun is well down now, first star has now winked." The pale hydrangeas float like pale butterflies, suspended in their spectral precinct like ghosts. The butterflies that took the place of flowers (in "The Flower") are now flowers again.

In "Court-martial" (110), the poet remembers sitting as a young boy at the feet of his grandfather, a Confederate veteran, in the shade of a cedar tree. He would "say to me / Some scrap of old poetry— / Byron or Burns—and idly / The words glimmer and fade / Like sparks in the dark of his head"—another fire in the dark that is a father's text, like the fox-fire of the father's Greek grammar.

"Court-martial" reworks several moments from "What Was the Promise." The poet recalls, "In the dust by his chair / I undertook to repair / The mistakes of his old war. / Hunched on that toy terrain, / Campaign by campaign, / I sought, somehow, to untie / The knot of History." That "toy terrain" is a pun on the toy trains featured in "What Was the Promise": "Children gravely, down walks, in spring dark, under maples, drew / Trains of shoe boxes, empty, with windows, with candles inside, / Going *chuck-chuck,* and blowing for crossings, lonely, *oo-oo.*" Both are improvised toys on the ground (in "Court-martial" the ground itself is a toy).

After his grandfather recounted how he meted out summary justice to bush-whackers, "I snatched my gaze away. / . . . The far woods swam in my sight," and "the fields fell away" as he began to meditate on what he had heard. Similarly, when he was standing at his parents' graves, "the farms and far woods fled away." In *Promises,* the expression "far woods" appears only in these two passages. This is also true of the words "my gaze," which appear in the passage from "Court-martial" just quoted and in "What Was the Promise," after he had seen his parents' bones bathed in phosphorescence but before he heard their voices: "in earth-dark no glow now, therefore I lifted / My gaze to . . . / Swell of woods and far field-sweep." In this passage, the "woods and far field-sweep" repeat the "farms and far woods" of which he spoke just before he had the vision of his parents glowing in their graves; at this point in "What Was the Promise" he is about to be granted his second hallucination, the one in which he hears their voices. Thus the combination "woods" + "far" + "farms" / "fields" twice marks in "What Was the Promise" the moment just before he experiences an hallucinatory dream of his parents. Similarly, in "Court-martial" the same combination, in the form "far woods . . . fields" (with "fled away" echoing the "fell away" preceding the first of the two visions in "What Was the Promise"), immediately precedes another vision of another progenitor, his grandfather:

> Calmly then, out of the sky,
> Blotting the sun's blazing eye,
> He rode. He was large in the sky.
>
> . . . .
>
> To the great saddle's sway, he swung,
> Not old now, not old now, but young,
> Great cavalry boots to the thigh. . . .

Behind him is something like a cloud, a shadowy mass that gradually comes into focus: the bushwhackers his grandfather had, in his swift roadside justice, hanged: "Ornaments of the old rope, / Each face outraged, agape, / . . . out-staring eye, / And the spittle not yet dry / That was uttered with the last cry." These, too, find their counterpart in "What Was the Promise," where other creatures were murdered and the poet was afterward impressed by their open eyes and wetness: "The guns of the big boys on the common go *boom,* past regret. / Boys shout when hit bullbat spins down in that gold light. / 'Too little to shoot'—but next year you'll be a big boy. / So shout now and pick up the bird—Why, that's blood, it is wet. / Its eyes are still open." The boys who shot the birds were "past regret"; the grandfather who hanged the guerillas may have been past all regret as well, but that did not prevent him from reacting somewhat defensively to his grandson's gaze: "'By God, they deserved it,' he said. / 'Don't look at me that way.'"

In this "shadowy autobiography," a term Warren applies to *Being Here* (in "Afterthought" 441) but which is also descriptive of *Promises,* the boy the poet was is growing up, will by "next year . . . be a big boy," will some day accept the necessity of the kind of action his grandfather took. In "Gold Glade" (113), the next poem in the sequence, hidden connections to "Court-martial" show that he is now following his grandfather's path. He is "Wandering . . . the woods of boyhood" with a "Heart aimless as rifle, boy-blankness of mood." The rifle and the blankness hearken back to the two preceding poems, the rifle to the "guns of the big boys" they trained on the bullbats, the blankness to the last glimpse he had of his grandfather at the conclusion of "Court-martial": "The horseman does not look back. / Blank-eyed, he continues his track, / Riding toward me there, / Through the darkening air. // The world is real. It is there." The boy in "Gold Glade" is beginning to resemble both the gun-toting big boys and the grandfather who hanged bushwhackers, seen in these final lines of "Court-martial" in a vision of his youthful glory.

Aimless though his heart may be, the boy follows, in a sense, in his grandfather's footsteps: "I came where ridge broke, and the great ledge, / Limestone, set the toe high as treetop by dark edge / Of a gorge, and water hid, grudging and grumbling, / And I saw, in mind's eye, foam white on / Wet stone." Hidden water was a feature of the ideal spot to hang bushwhackers, according to the former Confederate captain: "Find a spring with some cress fresh beside it, / Growing rank enough to nigh hide it." As the grandfather made his way to such a place, so too the boy in "Gold Glade" descends to where "water hid," and continued

> through the beech wood:
> There, in gold light, where the glade gave, it stood.
>
> The glade was geometric, circular, gold
> No brush or weed breaking that bright gold of leaf-fall.
> In the center it stood, absolute and bold
> Beyond any heart-hurt, or eye's grief-fall.
> Gold-massy in air, it stood in gold light-fall,
>
> No breathing of air, no leaf now gold-falling,
> . . . .
> Silence: gray-shagged, the great shagbark
> Gave forth gold light. There could be no dark.

Beyond a grove of beeches, a shagbark hickory; beyond the father's trees, the grandfather's.

Here are my reasons. In "No Bird Does Call" (416), in the later sequence *Being Here,* Warren will crawl back into his mother's lap, a cave-like hollow surrounded by beeches that lavish that lap with their golden leaves in a reenactment of Zeus's impregnation of Danae through a shower of gold:

> Bowl-hollow of woodland, beech-bounded, beech-shrouded,
> With roots of great gray boles crook'd airward, then down
> To grapple again, like claws, in the breathless perimeter
> Of moss, as in cave-shadow darker and deeper than velvet.
>
> And even at noon just a flicker of light,
> In summer green glint on darkness of green,
> In autumn gold glint on a carpet of gold, for then
> The hollow is Danae's lap lavished with gold by the god.

Similarly, the entrance to the cave in Warren's novel *The Cave* (1959) is located under the roots of "the biggest beech of all" (16), the mother (as cave) and the father (as beech) conjoined. Jeremiah Beaumont in *World Enough and Time* once plucked an icicle from a big beech tree and put it in his mouth. "At that instant he . . . seemed to become the tree" (29)—as if becoming his father (that icicle may prefigure the dagger with which he would slay Colonel Fort, who had been a father to him).

As for the shagbark, it is gray ("gray-shagged") like the grandfather, an "old man, now shrunken, gray"—who had fought for the Gray. And the massyness of the "Gold-massy" shagbark was also seen in the hallucinatory vision of the grandfather as a young Confederate officer: "Behind, shadow massed, slow, and grew / Like cloud on the sky's summer blue. / Out of that shade-mass he drew." The mass out of which he drew was part and parcel of his identity, the cluster of hanged heads for which he was responsible.

Warren says of the shagbark that it is "Perhaps just an image that keeps haunting me," which is an apt description of the vision of the grandfather riding toward him out of the sky. But then he recants his doubt and claims the tree was real: "No, no! in no mansion under earth, / Nor imagination's domain of bright air, / But solid in soil that gave it its birth, / It stands, wherever it is, but some- where. / I shall set my foot, and go there." This is how "Gold Glade" ends, and "Court-martial" concludes similarly, with an affirmation, as if there were any doubt, that something—in this case, the world itself—exists and that there is a place where it may be found: "The world is real. It is there."

Although Strandberg finds that "the nineteen poems . . . of the Gabriel sequence do not exhibit the interlocking continuity of the shorter Rosanna sequence" (an opinion I do not share), "Gold Glade" and "Dark Woods" (114) are connected more than most by "their use of a common image—the moment of vision in the forest—to show the bright and the dark of mystic perception" (*A Colder Fire* 207). "Dark Woods" is divided into three parts, each with its own title: "1. Tonight the Woods Are Darkened," "2. The Dogwood" (115), and "3. The Hazel Leaf" (115). It is evidently a single poem, however, for the first words of its second part, "*All right:* and with that wry acceptance you follow the cow-track," pick up the thread of the last lines of the first part: "Beyond the old field and pale cow-track, / The woods wait. They wait. *All right.*" (*All right* is italicized in both.) The second part continues the story of his venturing into the woods, and the first lines of the first and third part are identical: "Tonight the woods are darkened." In both "Gold Glade" and "Dark Woods," the poet makes a solitary trek into the forest, where he confronts a tree. Yet each poem is in several respects the opposite of the other:

1. "Gold Glade" takes place in autumn, "Dark Woods" (except for part of "The Hazel Leaf") in spring. Strandberg writes of this polarity that it is "an inver- sion of the usual seasonal setting" (*The Poetic Vision* 67), because the fall becomes

"the setting for a prelapsarian epiphany" while spring is the backdrop for an encounter with death (the skull of a cow).

2. "Gold Glade" is set in broad daylight, "Dark Woods" on a dark night lit only by stars.

3. The shagbark in "Gold Glade" is an object of reverence, but the dogwood in "Dark Woods" incites rage: "you felt a strange wrath burn / To strike it, and strike, had a stick been handy."

In both poems, the boy has a moment of fear. Coming to the stream in "Gold Glade," he "went down, and with some fright on / Slick boulders, crossed over"; recalling his nocturnal journey in "Dark Woods," he asks "Did nerve fail?" Hearing whispers, he asks if there were ghosts "In the field-dark to spy on and count you," who "leer in their spooky connivance . . . ?" His foot is seduced in one poem, trapped in the other: "declivity wooed / My foot . . . and so I / Went on" ("Gold Glade"); "the pale dust, / How soundless, accepted the foot! // Foot trapped in that silken compulsion" ("Dark Woods"). Geometry is evoked in both poems to describe what he finds: "The glade was geometric, circular" ("Gold Glade"); the path forms "the ectoplasmic bisection / Of the dark field-heave" ("Dark Woods"). The shagbark in "Gold Glade" "stood, absolute . . . / Gold-massy"; he finds mass and the absolute in "Dark Woods," too: "where woods massed their darkness / A darkness more absolute." Both trees emit light, in quietness: "Silence: gray-shagged, the great shagbark / Gave forth gold light"; "White-floating in darkness, the dogwood . . . glimmered in darkness, and uttered no word."

The shagbark was "bold / Beyond any heart-hurt, or eye's grief-fall." Though he had said his heart was "aimless," one wonders if the boy did not carry some heart-hurt with him that he found the hickory to be beyond (beyond deigning to care about? or showing a boldness that made heart-hurts unimportant?) The combination in that line of heart-hurt with the grief an eye might suffer is curious, especially when we reflect that (1) Warren suffered a near-blinding injury to his left eye in the spring of 1921 at age sixteen (it was removed thirteen years later [Blotner 30, 136]), and (2) in "Dark Woods," "one eye grieves in the socket." It grieves in the poem because "A bough finds your face" and hits the eye. But aware of the injury and of how autobiographical his poetry can be, we are justified in seeing the eye injury as a likely candidate for the "pain" that sent him into the woods in the first place, that "Had once drawn you forth: / To remember it might yet be some pain. / But to forget may, too, be pain" ("Dark Woods"). In "Nocturne," an early version of this poem (published in *The Fugitive* in 1924), no mention of the eye is made, but the hurt that sends him forth into the woods is, as it is in "Gold Glade," a pain of the heart: "Tonight the woods are darkened. /

We have forgot our pain, / The pain of hearts that hearkened / To an old abysmal strain" (10). "Nocturne" and "Dark Woods" (and within it, "The Hazel Leaf") all begin with the same first line, possibly suggesting that the earlier poem should be read in conjunction with the later one.

The dogwood, like the shagbark hickory, was a surprise—he did not expect to see it there, "sudden at path-turn." But he did expect to find, and did, the cow skull, remembering what it looked like in daylight:

> Here the dead cow was dumped, and by buzzards duly divested.
> All taint of mortality's long since wiped clean as a whistle.
> Now love vine threads eyehole, God's peace is by violet attested.
>
> The bones are long lost. In green grass the skull waits, has waited:
> A cathedral for ants, and at noon, under white dome, great transept,
> They pass in green gloom, under sunlight by leaf mitigated.
> For leaf of the love vine shuts eyehole, as though the eye slept.
>
> But now it's not noon, it is night, and ant-dark in that cow skull.

The fact that he went looking for the cow skull lends support to the theory that the pain that sent him there was what "Gold Glade" calls "eye's grief-fall"—a strange, compacted, expression that seems to allude to the way his eye was injured: by an object *falling* into it, a chunk of coal his brother had aimlessly tossed into the air from the other side of a hedge. For his attention is focused on the skull's blocked eyehole. In other words, his grief over the injury to his eye drew him into the woods, for it was the "pain [that] / Had once drawn you forth" (in the retrospective look that the third part of "Dark Woods," "The Hazel Leaf," casts on the events recounted in the first two parts), but the cow's skull that he remembered from an earlier journey there in daylight drew him there as well, and with good reason, for its blocked eyehole matched his own. The reenactment of that injury by the bough hitting his eye is connected to the realization that he was near the cow skull and its blocked eyehole by an intervening event that resembles both. For the next thing that happens after the bough hits his eye is that he notices that "something blots star." It turns out to be a passing owl. This blotting out of the only available light announces what immediately follows, the realization that he is near the cow skull, with its vine-blocked eye.

What the owl does is what the grandfather did in "Court-martial": "out of the sky, / Blotting the sun's blazing eye, / He rode." This reminiscence might serve to remind us that in each of these three poems we are in some sense in the same place, for like the other two, "Dark Woods" concludes by emphasizing what is "there":

Do not forget you were once there. ("Dark Woods")

I shall set my foot, and go there. ("Gold Glade")

The world is real. It is there. ("Court-martial")

As we have already seen, the "there" that concludes "Court-martial" and "Gold Glade" is in both instances part of an affirmation that something (the world, the mysterious glade) does indeed exist. What the two "theres" at the end of "Gold Glade" and "Dark Woods" have in common is that they designate the mysterious place in the woods where the boy encountered a tree that would forever haunt him.

"Country Burying (1919)" (116) concludes with the same word, though not the same note: "*Why doesn't that fly stop buzzing—stop buzzing up there!*" Yet the "there" in this poem, a "little white church . . . / Bone-white," is strangely like the cow skull that drew the boy into the woods, as if it were somehow the same place. The country church is "Bone-white"; the skull is a "white dome" made of bone. In the church, a fly buzzes; the skull is a "cathedral for ants." The ants "pass in green gloom, under sunlight by leaf mitigated" (because the leaf is blocking the eyehole through which sunlight enters). The church is suffused by a "Light [made] religiously dim by painted paper on window glass," that paper being to the window glass what the leaf is to the eyehole. The green leaves frame another aspect of the church: "through dust-pale green / Of oak leaf, the steeple pokes up in the bright air." The poet, still a boy as in the preceding several poems, had been brought to the church by his mother, who wanted to attend the funeral of someone she barely knew; he waits outside by the parked cars, unhappy at having lost an afternoon. In one more reminiscence of the closed-up hole, the funeral over, "we, too, now go, down the road, where it goes, / My mother and I, the hole now filled." The way this hole is filled sheds a new light on the shut eyehole in "Dark Woods": it is not only an emblem of the boy's life-altering injury, but a memento mori.[2]

Death reigns as well in "School Lesson Based on Word of Tragic Death of Entire Gillum Family" (117). Warren recalls being a boy in school and getting the news that five of his classmates would not be coming back because their father had stabbed them to death. The buzzing fly becomes a more irritating insect as one poem fades into the next: "An ice pick is a subtle thing. / The puncture . . . hurts no more than a bad bee sting." The church's windows were blocked by painted paper; in the schoolroom "the window panes steam" as the pupils reflect on the news. The afternoon drags on in both: for the boy outside the church, "the afternoon glares," as he complains to himself that he has "lost a boy's afternoon, /

When summer's so short." In the schoolroom, "In the afternoon silence the chalk would scrape. / We sat and watched the windowpanes steam." What shoe was Brother putting on when his father approached him? "That was something, it seemed, you just had to know. / But nobody knew, all afternoon, / Though we studied and studied, as hard as we could, to know . . . / We studied all afternoon, till getting on to sun."

Both the woman whose funeral it was and the Gillum family are of a certain "kind." "That kind came to town," the boy in "Country Burying" said, "Some butter to swap, clutch of eggs in a basket." The Gillum children's "toes were the kind that hook round the legs of chairs." And their mother was the "clabber kind that can catch just by honing after a man." The same colors predominate in the description of Mr. Gillum in "School Lesson"—"from yellow toenail to old black felt hat, / Gillum was scarcely the type to set a lady dreaming"—and the deceased in "Country Burying": "Gnarled hands in black mittens, old face yellow as a gourd."

Strandberg says of "Country Burying," "School Lesson," and the next poem in the sequence, "Summer Storm (Circa 1916) and God's Grace" (119), that they form "a subgrouping set off in contrast to the mystical 'Dark Woods' and 'Gold Glade'" and share "a common mood, realism; a common theme, the awakening of young Robert Penn Warren to tragedy . . . ; and a common subject, the actual experiences of Warren's adolescence" (*A Colder Fire* 207). The characteristic soil of his native region is evident in all three:

> Red clay, the road winds, goes on where it goes. ("Country Burying")

> That morning blew up cold and wet,
> > All the red-clay road was curdled as curd. ("School Lesson")

> Redder than ever, red clay was red. ("Summer Storm")

Yet these three instances of red clay betray a subtler arrangement in accord with the poems' persistent pairing, the first and second having in common that the red clay is what the roads are made of, the second and third that the red clay, which is not a road in the third poem, is depicted under the effect of a change in the weather. In "Summer Storm," the red clay was redder than ever because as the storm approached, "the sun flamed suddenly red," intensifying the soil's natural color.

The concluding lines of "School Lesson"—

> Studying the arithmetic of losses,
> > To be prepared when the next one,

By fire, flood, foe, cancer, thrombosis,
             Or Time's slow malediction, came to be undone.

We studied all afternoon, till getting on to sun.
There was another lesson, but we were too young to take up that one.

—are particularly connected to "Summer Storm" in two ways. First, they announce that other grave events, including "flood," are still to come, and the summer storm does in fact bring a flood: "the bridge had washed out. / A drowned cow bobbled down the creek." "Summer Storm," as the sequence in *Promises* doubles reality, seems indeed to be that "next one" for which one should be prepared. Second, "School Lesson" ends as it was "getting on to sun," meaning sundown, while "Summer Storm" begins at that same moment in time, picking up where "School Lesson" leaves off. Its first words are "Toward sun," indicating the hour the first sign of the storm appeared, the sun suddenly turning red.

The father's murder of his children seems inexplicable, given what he had said about his devotion to their welfare:

". . . a man's got his chaps to love and to cherish,
        And raise up and larn 'em so they kin git they chance."

So mud to the hub, or dust to the hock,
             God his helper, wet or dry,
Old Gillum swore by God and by cock,
             He'd git 'em larned before his own turn came to die.

That morning blew up cold and wet,
             All the red-clay road was curdled as curd,
And no Gillums there for the first time yet.

I have extended the quotation a little past Gillum's expression of fatherly concern in order to show Warren's irony in following it immediately with the first inkling of the terrible news and that he provides a premonition of that news with a turn for the worse in the weather. God, who sent the storm, is as insane as Gillum: "The pitchfork lightning tossed the trees, / And God got down on hands and knees / To peer and cackle and commend / His own sadistic idiocies." In addition to saying he was dedicated to his children's getting an education, Gillum had expressed contempt for the human race: "Human-man ain't much more'n a big blood blister, / All red and proud-swole, but one good squeeze and he's gone." Perhaps the ice pick was his way of popping the blister. He seems to have gone about it with a sadistic coolness: "Dollie-May was combing Susie-May's head. /

Sam was feeding, Forrest milking, got nigh through. / Little Brother just sat on the edge of his bed. / Somebody must have said: 'Pappy, what now you aimin' to do?'"

Warren's sympathies in "Summer Storm" lie with the farmers who have to cope with God's caprices. In "Founding Fathers, Nineteenth-Century Style, Southeast U.S.A" (120), they lie with his ancestors and those of his neighbors in southwest Kentucky, the farmers of the preceding poem. Those forebears, staring out from daguerreotypes and oil paintings, "beg us only one word to justify their own old life-cost. // So let us bend ear to them in this hour of lateness, / And what they are trying to say, try to understand." But it is not easy to lend a sympathetic ear, for as much as the farmers in "Sudden Storm" are victims, their progenitors were victimizers. God, in whom the farmers of "Sudden Storm" in their weakness know better than to trust, seems by contrast to have been a source of reassurance to their forefathers, for even the nameless ones lost to history always kept, along with the Decherd rifle, "the mold-yellow Bible, God's Word, in which, in their strength, they had also trusted." They knew how to stand for their portrait in the "pose of the patriot, left hand in crook of the spine or / With finger to table, while right invokes the Lord's just rage." With God on their side, "Some prospered, had black men and lands." They scattered their children "like millet seed flung in a wind-flare. / Wives died, were dropped like old shirts in some corner of country. / Said, "Mister," in bed, the child-bride; hadn't known what to find there; / Wept all the next morning for shame." These last four lines contain three subtle echoes of "Summer Storm" through which the ancestors are likened to the God of the storm and their victims to his. First, the "wind-flare" recalls the sun-flare ("the sun flared suddenly red") that announced the destructive wind. Second, the ancestors dropped wives like old shirts; the plowhands fleeing the storm lost their hats as they came pelting back astride a mule at breakneck pace: "the hat that jounced off stayed off, like as not." Warren's irony places the act of leaving behind an article of clothing into contrasting contexts. The ancestors abandoned their deceased spouses, worn out from childbearing and the rigors of the frontier, as if they were worn-out shirts; the plowhands could not stop to retrieve their hats because their own lives were in danger. And third, the wives wept in the morning; so did the farmers, after the flood that wiped out their crops: "Next morning . . . / Raw-eyed, men watched" as a drowned cow floated by. The God of the storm knows how to make even the animals grieve: "The mole, in his sod, can no more hide, / And weeps beneath the naked sky."

The plowhands fleeing the storm—"Astride and no saddle, and they didn't care / If a razor-back mule at a break-tooth trot / Was not the best comfort a man ever got"—form a particularly telling contrast to one of the poet's own ancestors: "One of mine was a land shark, or so the book with scant praise / Denominates him, 'a man large and shapeless, / Like a sack of potatoes set on a saddle.'" The plowhands can ride without a saddle, if they have to, while the ancestor looks as if he is plopped on a saddle when he is not even on a horse.

"Foreign Shore, Old Woman, Slaughter of Octopus" (122) at first seems oddly placed. Preceded and followed by poems set in Kentucky—or the "Southeast U.S.A.," in the case of its immediate predecessor—its setting as the title indicates is a foreign clime, most likely (in light of the other poems in *Promises* that have that setting) Italy.[3] Yet the way that title announces its geographical setting actually links it to "Founding Fathers, Nineteenth-Century Style, Southeast U.S.A.," for these are the only two poems in *Promises* to do so. And the order of the three elements in the two titles is such that the first's indication of place is backed up right against the second's, as if it were Warren's intention to make the contrast as clashing as possible.

At sunset, an old woman, barefoot and dressed in "peasant black," walks the beach among volcanic boulders: "What can the sea tell her, / That she does not now know, and know how to bear? / She knows, as the sea, that what came will recur, / And detached in that wisdom, is aware / How grain by grain, last sun heat from sand is expended on night air." Warren finds her unforgettable, saying at the conclusion of the poem that he will quit this foreign shore soon, leaving behind "much, but not . . . her image." It will return to him in "day traffic" or "night dark," assuaging the "mind's pain of logic somewhat, or the heart's rage."

A tower of wisdom and strength, this woman forms a marked contrast to the brides who wept for shame in "Founding Fathers." Her detachment ("detached in that wisdom") is of a different sort than that suffered by the wives who, having "died, were dropped like old shirts." Unlike them, she is a survivor. But Warren points us toward another comparison by the detail of her clothing: "She wears peasant black," like the founding fathers who "wore long black coat" in their daguerreotype portraits. These two instances of wearing black are the only ones in *Promises* apart from the deceased woman's "black mittens" in "Country Burying" and the "old black felt hat" that belonged to Gillum in "School Lesson" and to the unnamed tramp in "Dark Night of" (123). They are the only instances at all in which the verb "to wear" has black clothing for its object, and the only ones in which a person's costume (as opposed to just a hat or mittens) is predominantly of that color. The founding fathers' long black coats, with their accompanying "gold watch chain," were signs of wealth and authority, while the "peasant black" of the old woman denotes the opposite end of the social scale. Yet what the peasant woman wore also enhances her contrast to the frontier brides, who despite their shame "took pleasure in silk; wore the keys to the pantry." What they wore defined them, too.

The founding fathers, however, find an additional counterpart in "Foreign Shore"—in the octopus that comes "up from some cold coign and dark lair of water, / Ectoplasmic, snot-gray, the obscene of the life-wish, / Sad tentacles weaving like prayer, eyes wide to glare-horror of day-wash." Despite its prayer to be spared, the beast is slain, while "Boys yelled at the knife flash." Afterward, "Pearl slime of the slaughter, on black stone, glints in last light." Though it is "with severe reprehension" that the "merciless" eyes of the founding fathers "stare" from their portraits in the poems' opening lines (eyes that in their self-assurance convey something quite different from the doomed octopus's "wide to glare-horror"), in its closing ones we hear those ancestors adopt a different tone, a pleading more like the sea-creature's prayer. They "beg us" some "word to justify their own old life-cost." That "life-cost" anticipates the "life-wish" that motivates the octopus's prayer; indeed, no other hyphenated "life-" appears in *Promises*.

"Dark Night of" brings us right back to Kentucky, though with haunting recollections of "Foreign Shore." The narrator, a twelve-year-old boy, encounters a vagabond hiding on his family's land and reluctantly performs the duty of chasing him off. The events of both poems take place as afternoon slowly fades to night. In Italy, "Saffron-saddening the mountain, the sun / Sinks, and from sea, black boulder by boulder, / Night creeps." In Kentucky, "afternoon, strand by gold strand, / Raveled out." The saffron is answered by the gold; "boulder by boulder" by "strand by . . . strand." Like the old woman who "follows her slow track," the old man ("He was old . . . / Old and spent") follows his, "a track no man would have planned." Both cross the poet's field of vision, and their image will stay with him. The woman possesses a wisdom he admires, while he attributes glory and an enviable joy to the man: "His head, unbared, moves with the unremitting glory of stars high in the night heaven there. / He moves in joy past contumely of stars or insolent indifference of the dark air. / May we all at last enter into that awfulness of joy."

But the man also oddly resembles the slaughtered octopus. The boy catches sight of him hiding in the underbrush: "Beneath elder bloom, the eyes glare," echoing the octopus's "eyes wide to glare-horror." Like a creature from watery depths ("up from some cold coign and dark lair of water"), the vagrant, "In a voice like a croak from an old well," begs the boy to leave him alone. "'Caint you git on away?' / . . . 'Caint you let a man lay!'"—a pleading paralleling that of the "Sad tentacles weaving like prayer." The boy recalls, "I stared down the dank depth and heard / That croak from cold slime," compelling us to recall the "Pearl-slime of the slaughter" that was all that was left of the octopus. Both the octopus and the hobo emerge from concealment to their detriment, the former gazing in horror at "day-wash" and about to be sacrificed under the knife, the latter coming out of the "black safety of shade" to "the world's bright vacancy" and "light's malevolent stare" as if "to see if he'd proved / That a man could survive half a minute / Outside the woods and not in it." The concealing woods are his natural element; once out of them, he is a fish out of water.

The fact that the wanderer should combine in his person aspects of both the old woman and the tentacled creature raises the possibility that even within "Foreign Shore," both of the latter may be part of the same reality. Indeed, they are, for together the woman and the "Ectoplasmic, snot-gray . . . obscene . . . nightmare" are a figure for Warren's Medusa, in a recurring myth in which a "knife flash" (Perseus's dissevering act) and a saffron light (in the golden shower that made him) likewise find their place. The weaving tentacles are the Gorgon's serpentine locks, returning in the honeysuckle's "white strands" that "wreathed" the head of the vagrant when the boy first saw him. Medusa's gaze turned men to stone; her reincarnation in the glaring eyes of the tramp had a similarly paralyzing effect on the beholder: "My heart clenched hand-hard as I stood."

The phenomenon reappears in "Infant Boy at Midcentury" (125): "the heart will compress / Like stone"—but with what a difference in context! The heart is now a parent's, and Medusa has nothing to do with its compression to hardness, though the old man in "Dark Night of" does. Parents' hearts do that when they see their child take that first step, the step that will eventually take him out of their sight, out of their lives: "when we see that rosy heel learn, / With its first step, the apocalyptic power to spurn / Us, and our works and days, and onward, prevailing, pass." In a beautiful symmetry, the boy who sees the stranger pass out of his field of vision is balanced by the father who foresees his son continuing past his. The old man is insistently said to "move" past the boy: "At last he would . . . / Move in the dark air. / . . . / His head, unbared, moves with the unremitting glory of stars. . . . / He moves in joy" ("Dark Night of"). As the other boy "moves" past the old man the poet will have become: "And think, as you move past our age that grudges and grieves, / How eyes, purged of envy, will follow your sunlit chance. / Eyes will brighten to follow your brightness and dwindle of distance. / From privacy of fate, eyes will follow, as though from the shadow of leaves" ("Infant Boy at Midcentury"). The poet, in the shadow of leaves, has even taken the place occupied in the preceding poem by the old man, "Couched under elder bloom," hiding in the honeysuckle, in the "black safety of shade." That old man from "Dark Night of" is evoked in these lines from "Infant Boy" immediately preceding the quatrain quoted above: "And remember that many among us wish you well; / And once, on a strange shore, an old man, toothless and through, / Groped hand from the lattice of personal disaster to touch you. / He sat on the sand for an hour; said *ciao, bello,* as evening fell." Like the homeless wanderer, a product of "pellagra and spite," the man on the beach is fenced in by "personal disaster"; like the hobo, "Old and spent," he is "old . . . and through." He both recalls his counterpart from the poem before, of whom he is a happier avatar, and prefigures the poet as an old man in the stanza to follow.

"Lullaby: Smile in Sleep" (127) is, like "Infant Boy at Midcentury," addressed directly to Gabriel, Warren's son (born in 1955). Yet the poems differ from each other in that "Infant Boy" is an almost unremitting jeremiad, but "Lullaby: Smile in Sleep" a hopeful paean to new possibility. The "Midcentury" of the first poem's title is a bad time to be born: "You have entered our world at scarcely its finest hour, / And smile now life's gold Apollonian smile at a sick dialectic. // You enter at the hour when the dog returns to his vomit, / And fear's moonflower spreads." But that smile, however sad its object, is transformed in "Lullaby: Smile in Sleep" into a joyful command:

> Sleep, my son, and smile in sleep.
> You will dream the world anew.
> Watching you now sleep,
> I feel the world's depleted force renew,
> . . . .
> Feel wink of warmth and stir of spirit,
> As though season woke in the heart's cold underwood.
> The vernal work is now begun.

In "Infant Boy," spring was apprehensive: "petal fears the late, as fruit the early frost-fall." The "wink of warmth" apparent in "Lullaby: Smile in Sleep" was prefigured in "Infant Boy" by an eye movement that had a quite opposite meaning: "Some will glorify friendship, but watch for the slightest motion / Of eyelid . . . and the longed-for betrayal it indicates."

Yet in both poems Warren foresees the possibility that his son might "command" a better world, whether consciously—"To pause, in high pride of undisillusioned manhood, / At the gap that gives on the new century, and land, /And with calm heart and level eye command / That dawning perspective and possibility of human good" ("Infant Boy at Midcentury")—or unconsciously: "For you now dream Reality. / Matter groans to touch your hand. / Matter now lifts like the sea / Toward that cold moon that is your dream's command. / Dream the power coming on" ("Lullaby: Smile in Sleep"). Among the poems in *Promises,* "command" appears only in these two.

"Man in Moonlight" is composed of three sections, "1. Moonlight Observed from Ruined Fortress" (129), "2. Walk by Moonlight in Small Town" (130), and "3. Lullaby: Moonlight Lingers" (131). In the first, Warren continues to focus his attention on the moon, which at the conclusion of "Lullaby: Smile in Sleep," quoted above, is the "dream's command" of the sleeping Gabriel. Warren addresses his son as "you" in "Lullaby: Smile in Sleep"; he addresses the moon as "you" in "Moonlight Observed." He praises it for the universality of its splendor, visible not just on the Mediterranean but also on the Gulf Coast or from Cumberland's bluffs: "Décor must be right, of course, for your massive effect, / But a Tennessee stock-pond is not beneath your contempt, / Though its littoral merely a barnyard with cow-pats unkempt. / No, even a puddle is not too small for respect." In "Walk by Moonlight in Small Town," he rises from bed in the middle of the night to wander the streets of what is probably his native Guthrie, Kentucky, viewing moonlight's effect on lawns, windowpanes, department store dummies, and freight cars on a siding. Childhood memories are awakened, culminating in the hallucination he could see children "playing, with no sound. / They ceased their play, then quiet as moonlight, drew, slow, around." He tried, as he gazed at each, to recollect the names of these friends of his youth. "Each small, upgazing face would lie / Sweet as a puddle, and silver-calm, to the night sky." The puddle each face formed in the moonlight is itself an eerie recollection of the "puddle [that] is not too small" for the moon to respect it in "Moonlight Observed from Ruined Fortress" (the only puddles to appear in *Promises*).[4] Both sorts of puddles receive moonlight and are located in Warren's native region.

"Lullaby: Moonlight Lingers," the third section of "Man in Moonlight," braids together elements from the first two as well as from the poem that immediately precedes "Man in Moonlight" in *Promises'* sequence, "Lullaby: Smile in Sleep." Like the latter, it is a lullaby addressing Gabriel as "you": "Sleep, my son . . . / You will dream" ("Lullaby: Smile in Sleep"), "Sleep deep, son, and dream" ("Lullaby: Moonlight Lingers"). As in "Walk by Moonlight in Small Town," here too Warren is provoked by the moonlight to recall moments from his childhood, the way it shone on a certain oak near his house, how it "glimmered down a summer lane." He even hears his own father's voice telling him what he is now telling his son: "*Sleep, son. Good night.*" The first section of "Man in Moonlight" focused on how the moon's splendor can be beheld anywhere in the world; the second section found it shining on children's faces from a distant past ("puddles" in both instances). The third section recapitulates these two phenomena in a single statement: "Moonlight . . . fell in far times and other places."

"Mad Young Aristocrat on Beach" (132) has an Italian setting and features a protagonist as alien to Warren's experience as the old woman in "Foreign Shore, Old Woman, Slaughter of Octopus." The poet appears to be observing a young man on the beach and inventing an entire life story for him, surmising that he is lamenting the fate of being the younger son who will not inherit the family title.

What he imagines for him is the opposite of what he imagined for himself in "Man in Moonlight." Walking the moonlit streets of Guthrie in the second section of that poem, he was surrounded by silent children ("children were playing, with no sound"); the mad young aristocrat is confronted by children, too, but they are not silent: "He sits in blue trunks on the sand, and children sing. / Their voices are crystal and sad, and tinkle in sunlight." Their "tinkling . . . crawls on his quivering heart in its midnight. / . . . / Oh, Lord, let us pray that the children stop singing before he begins to weep." The children make him sad; the children in the other poem are strangely affecting, too: "something grew in their pale stare: / Not reprobation or surprise, / Not even forgiveness in their eyes, / But a humble question . . . like beseechment."

The poet was delighted by the moon's splendor as it played on the sea in "silver scintillance" in the first section of "Man in Moonlight"; the young aristocrat is dismayed by the "freaking and fracture and dazzle of light" as the sun shines on the sea off the same Italian coast where the poet had stood and enjoyed the lunar light show: "You strike our cliff, and then lean on to Carthage. / We stand on the crumbling stone and ruins of rage, / To watch your Tyrrhenian silver prank the sea." Unlike the poet, who leaves his bed to savor the moonlight's transformation of the town, the aristocrat "is tired, and wants only sleep"; he "longs for bed."

The young man thus seems a double for the poet, yet he also seems a double for his son, who smiled in sleep: "He ponders how charming it is to smile, and magnanimous. / And his smile, indeed, is both sweet and beguiling, / And joy floods his heart now like hope. . . . / He is . . . smiling now on us, / And smiles at the sea." Warren is gently telling his son to sleep in the three immediately preceding poems; the young aristocrat seems sleep-deprived ("he is tired, and wants only sleep"; he "closes his eyes, . . . longs for bed"). Warren tells his son to smile in "Lullaby: Smile in Sleep," and in "Infant Boy at Midcentury," Gabriel does "smile . . . life's gold Apollonian smile"; the young aristocrat smiles at the sea and is "smiling now on us" and recalls that "his mother once said that his smile was sweet." But in the immediately following lines, he turns on her and rejects the smile: "Curse the bitch, it is power man wants, and like a black cloud now he mounts to his feet. / . . . / He will swim in the sea, the water will break to his will." A young man's desire for power coupled with turning his back on parents was presented in more positive terms in "Infant Boy at Midcentury," when Warren foresaw his son developing "the apocalyptic power to spurn / Us." And in "Lullaby: Smile in Sleep," the sea, on which the young aristocrat will exert his power, making it "break to his will," will succumb to a power Gabriel unconsciously exerts in a gentler way: "Matter now lifts like the sea / Toward that cold moon that is your dream's command. / Dream the power coming on. / Dream, strong son."[5]

The poet finds that the moon's splendor is as dazzling in America as it is on the Tyrrhenian sea: "once on Cumberland's bluffs . . . my eyes / were trapped in gleam-glory." Even a Tennessee pond by "a barnyard with cow-pats" is not too small to receive the moon's attention. Excrement and America combine in a different way in the thoughts he attributes to the young aristocrat. Musing that he might make up for being denied the title by marrying a rich American, "sudden as death, a thought stops him chillingly short: / *Mais l'Amérique, merde!* why it's full of Americans there."

Shit persists into the next poem, "Dragon Country: To Jacob Boehme" (133), where a dragon's "great turd steams." The beast has been wreaking havoc in Todd County, Kentucky, killing the occasional mule driver and traveling salesman and defying all attempts at capture. This has created a financial hardship for the Todd Countians: "Land values are falling . . . certain fields go untended, the local birth rate goes low"—all because of the dubious honor of having been chosen by God, or fate, for this visitation. The mad young aristocrat faces financial difficulties for not having been chosen for God, or fate, to be the first born and "never come to the title" and estate. Though at a certain moment he begins (as the poet, watching his expression, imagines) to smile and see himself receiving applause and "joy floods his heart now like hope," the joy is fleeting, and he returns to his essential sadness. In contrast to the aristocrat, the inhabitants of Dragon Country in the end embrace their condition, finding in it "the fearful glimmer of joy, like a spoor"—yet another excremental image, echoing the "merde" and "cow-pats" of the two preceding poems. It frees them from concern with the ordinary problems and hopes of their neighbors:

Yes, other sections have problems somewhat different from ours.
Their crops may fail, bank rates rise, on rumor of war loans be called,
But we feel removed from maneuvers of Russia, or other great powers,
And from much ordinary hope are now disenthralled.

The Baptists may pray that the affliction be lifted,

But if the Beast were withdrawn now, life might dwindle again
To the ennui, the pleasure, and night sweat, known in the time before
Necessity of truth had trodden the land, and heart, to pain,
And left, in darkness, the fearful glimmer of joy, like a spoor.

The same decision to accept whatever necessity deals out for the sake of avoiding ennui is made in *Promises*' other supernatural poem, "Ballad of a Sweet Dream of Peace" (135). There, the role the dragon plays is fulfilled by hogs, with the difference that the hogs consume the same victims night after night. The narrator's guide to the infernal woods where these strange events take place suggests that "when you are ready, our clients usually say / That to shut the eyes tight and get down on the knees is the quickest and easiest way." But there are those "who, when ennui gets great, / Will struggle, or ingeniously irritate / The helpers to acts I won't state: / For Reality's all, and to seek it, some welcome, at whatever cost, any change." The only "ennui" in *Promises* is that found, and eluded, in these two neighboring poems. Those who eschew it seek, in both instances, "reality." The hogs' more jaded victims find it to be "all, and to seek it," and, as the wiser denizens of Dragon Country (wiser, that is, than the Baptists who pray that the evil be removed) put it, "We are human, and the human heart / Demands language for reality that has not slightest dependence / On desire, or need." In other words, they seek a name for that reality that derives not from the needs provoked by crop failures, rising rates, or called-in loans, or from the desires of "ordinary hope." Yet while both the Todd Countians and the more adventurous of the hogs' clients wish to avoid ennui and seek a more than ordinary reality, they are opposites in that the latter "welcome . . . change" while the former, having lived with the dragon for many years—the narrator "was only a boy" when the first depredation was reported and appears to have reached adulthood now—want things to remain the same.

The desire for change evident in the more jaded of the hog's victims in "Ballad of a Sweet Dream of Peace" is evident as well in the boy Warren remembers himself to have been in "Boy's Will, Joyful Labor without Pay, and Harvest Home" (1918)" (138): "Blood can't abide the status quo," the boy seems to say to himself (or the poet observes in recalling the event) as he bolts down his oatmeal and hurries outside to take part in the harvest, his blood unable to stand the status quo and eager for the change in routine this day will bring. Warren at thirteen (if we can judge by the date in the title) gets to drive the tractor that pulls the thresher. "You stoke the tractor. You *gee* and *haw*. / You feed the thresher's gap-toothed maw. / Then on a load-top, high, you stand / And see your shadow, black as law, // Stretch far now on the gold stubble." The boy rejoices in his power, as the young aristocrat did in his: "He will swim in the sea, the water will break to his will. / Now emerging on shore, he is lethal, he shows it."[6] The boy on the tractor is lethal too, or, rather, the chain of events he sets in motion proves lethal to one of God's creatures, one whose blackness matches that of the shadow he sees himself cast on the field. As he drives the tractor and thresher through the wheat, "a black snake rears big in his ruined room. // Defiant, tall in that blast of day, / Now eye for eye, he swaps his stare. / His outrage glitters on the air." One is reminded of the "big black son-of-a-bitch" that "Reared from the stones" in *Brother to Dragons* (35). The snake in the field is soon surrounded, and killed.

> Men shout, ring around. He can't get away.
> Yes, they are men, and a stone is there.
>
> Against the wounded evening matched,
> Snagged high on a pitchfork tine, he will make
> Slow arabesque till the bullbats wake.
> An old man, standing stooped, detached,
> Spits once, says, "Hell, just another snake."

Actually, it is more than just another snake. As Strandberg suggests, the snake may be raised on the pitchfork "as though in a religious parody" (*A Colder Fire* 209), reenacting what was itself a reenactment: "as Moses lifted up the serpent in the wilderness, even so must the Son of man be lifted up" (John 3:14). The Israelites in the desert suffered a plague of fiery serpents; to counteract their poison, "the Lord said unto Moses, Make thee a fiery serpent, and set it upon a pole: and it shall come to pass, that every one that is bitten, when he looketh upon it, shall live" (Num. 21:8). Moses successfully fulfilled the command with a serpent made of brass. Christ as the raised serpent thus counteracts the serpent in Eden—Satan himself—as Moses' serpent on a pole counteracted the fiery serpents that wounded the Israelites, redeeming the human race from the Fall.

That evening, after the laborers have left the field, "the propped pitchfork lifts / Its burden, hung black, to the white star." And the "little blood that smeared the stone / Dropped in the stubble, has long since dried." Warren, though avowedly not a believer,[7] alludes to Christ in the conclusion to "Ballad of a Sweet Dream of Peace" in such a way as to make it connect to the Christ imagery behind the raised-up serpent in "Boy's Will":

> there's a rumor astir
> That the woods are sold, and the purchaser
> Soon comes, and if credulity's not now abused,
> Will, on this property, set
> . . . heel that, smiting the stone, is not what is bruised.
> And subdues to sweetness the pathside garbage, or thing body had refused.

Strandberg sees this "redemptive supernatural" as "counteracting the ravaging Beast of 'Dragon Country'" (*A Colder Fire* 220), thus further connecting those neighboring poems. The connection to "Boy's Will" is that in "Ballad," Christ (or perhaps a parody of him) can bruise the stone that in "Boy's Will" kills the serpent, which in fact does not represent Christ on the cross but parodies him, turning him back into a serpent.

For instead of embracing the Christian hope, Warren insists on the necessity of a boy's shedding blood. We saw this in "What Was the Promise that Smiled from the Maples at Evening?" when the boy is assured that "next year you'll be a big boy" and can shoot bullbats himself—the same birds that come into view when the snake's writhing ceases ("Slow arabesques till the bullbats wake"). As it is, he is not too young to pick up the dead ones, wet with blood, and find that the "heart in the throat swells like joy." The original sin that cannot be avoided is, for Warren, not to be seduced by the serpent but to kill it. In the characteristic reversal through which poems in Warren's sequences tend to reenact their immediate predecessor, the boy in "Boy's Will," proud of the black shadow he casts atop the thresher, assumes something of an executioner, the role played in "Ballad of a Sweet Dream of Peace" by the hogs. Two textual clues confirm this. First, the line "In the field the old red thresher clatters." The thresher becomes the extension of the boy's will to power and sets in motion the chain of events the leads to the death of the snake. The only other things that clatter in *Promises* are Granny's bones when the hogs attack her in "Ballad of a Sweet Dream of Peace": "they will sit in a ring, / Till she finishes work, the poor old thing: / Then old bones get knocked down with a clatter to wake the dead." The ring the hogs form before they attack the old woman is reenacted by the men who "ring around" the snake the boy unearthed with the thresher, the only other instance in *Promises* of that kind of ring.[8]

Another clue connecting "Boy's Will" with "Ballad of a Sweet Dream of Peace" can be found in the blood-stained stone that killed the snake: "The little blood that smeared the stone / . . . has long since dried." Seeing Granny's night dress, the interlocutor asks, "*what is that stain?* / It's only dried blood," his guide replies. These are the only two instances of dried blood in *Promises* (or indeed of "dried" anything). The blood on her clothes comes from the fact that every night she goes to the woods "to embrace a thorn tree, to try to understand pain" and then exclaims, "Oh, we need not despair, / For I bleed, oh, I bleed, and God lives!" As the poet in "Boy's Will" recalls the events of that day, his memories stab his heart, as thorns pierced the grandmother:

> In the star-pale field, the propped pitchfork lifts
> Its burden, hung black, to the white star.
>
> And the years go by like a breath, or eye-blink,
> And all history lives in the head again,
> And I shut my eyes and I see that scene,

And name each item, but cannot think
What, in their urgency, they must mean,

But know, even now, on this foreign shore,
In blaze of sun and the sea's stare,
A heart-stab blessed past joy or despair,
As I see, in the mind's dark, once more,
That field, pale, under starlit air.

The blood from Granny's thorn-stab was proof that "we need not despair"; the poet's heart-stab, similarly, is "blessed past . . . despair."

"Lullaby: A Motion like Sleep" (141) concludes, as does "Boy's Will" in the lines just quoted, by combining "blaze," "joy," and self-inflicted wounding:

So, son, now sleep

Till clang of cock-crow, and dawn's rays,
Summon your heart and hand to deploy
Their energies and know, in excitement of day-blaze,
How like a wound, and deep,
Is Time's irremediable joy.

In "Ballad of a Sweet Dream of Peace," the wound is an antidote to despair; in "Boy's Will," it is past both joy and despair; in "Lullaby: A Motion Like Sleep," it is what joy is said to be like. The apparent discrepancy may be explained by the fact that the heart-stab in one poem is not the same as the wound in the other. The blessèd heart-stab is the pain of Warren's bittersweet recollection of that day four decades before; the wound that he invites his son to "know"—as he says that the heart-stab he feels on the foreign shore is something he knows ("But know . . . / A heart-stab")—is the wound of joy itself (what happened on harvest day, the subject of his recollection). When he urges his son to summon his heart and hand "to deploy / Their energies" in the "excitement of day-blaze," he is inviting him to live the kind of energetic moment he thrilled to that dawn in 1918: "The world is panting, the world won't wait. / All energy's unregenerate. / Blood can't abide the status quo."

"Lullaby: A Motion like Sleep" is so tightly interwoven with "Boy's Will" that not only do its concluding lines echo those of its neighbor, but the latter's last words—"under starlit air"—are restated, almost verbatim, in the other's first line:

Under the star and beech-shade braiding,
Past the willow's dim solicitude,

Past hush of oak-dark and stone's star-glinted upbraiding,
Water moves, in a motion like sleep,
Along the dark edge of the woods,
So, son, now sleep.

Like the water in its sleeplike motion, Warren's poems in sequence braid. They do so with such constancy that one could go to sleep to its interflow, its hidden circulation, and perceive it unconsciously, in what Warren in a later poem will call "the braiding texture of dream" ("Dream of a Dream," in *Now and Then* 354).

The co-presence of pleasure and pain in the concept of joy that is like a wound may offer a way to interpret the puzzling conclusion to the sequence, "The Necessity for Belief" (142), remarkable for its brevity and doubling structure, a strange combination of concision and repetitiveness:

> The sun is red, and the sky does not scream.
> The sun is red, and the sky does not scream.
>
> There is much that is scarcely to be believed.
>
> The moon is in the sky, and there is no weeping.
> The moon is in the sky, and there is no weeping.
>
> Much is told that is scarcely to be believed.

Not only does line 2 repeat line 1, but line 6 comes close to doing the same to line 3, and the structure of lines 1–2 is largely, though not entirely, repeated in lines 4–5. Why does the sky not scream? Why would the sun's redness be a reason for the sky to scream, if that is the implication? Are we supposed to think that the moon's presence in the sky would normally be a reason for weeping? Who is not weeping—the sky, because it is what does not scream in the first two lines?

Strandberg sees a progression in the poem: "Replacing the vanished light of the day is another, more enchanting light, whose radiance transfigures all it illuminates. And so the faith which the sky showed at the setting of the sun ('and the sky does not scream') is here rewarded: 'And there is no weeping'" (*A Colder Fire* 242). The sky has a "secret knowledge" not available to humanity but in which we might do well to trust.

The sky's secret knowledge may be akin to what the poet had learned by the end of the preceding poem, that joy bears a significant measure of pain, being very much like a wound. Thus the sun's blood-red death is not a reason to despair. Indeed, as the grandmother asserts in "Ballad of a Sweet Dream of Peace," bleed-

ing is a sign that God lives. While the unbelieving Warren may not share her the-
ology, he does believe there is power in the blood, particularly when it flows: "for
sleep and stream and blood-course / Are a motion with one name, / And all that
flows finds end but in its own source, / And a circuit of motion like sleep, / And
will go as once it came" ("Lullaby: A Motion like Sleep"). This comes close to
describing what happens in a sequence of poems like *Promises,* so interconnected
as to resemble living tissue, with words circulating from poem to poem like red
corpuscles, enriching and enlivening the whole.

CHAPTER 4

"THE LOGIC OF DREAM"

YOU, EMPERORS, AND OTHERS:

POEMS 1957–1960

Warren's most successful volume—for *Promises* won both a National Book Award and a Pulitzer Prize—was followed by what many readers consider his least. Including Warren: "I've made some very bad slips, such as in the volume of poems called *You, Emperors, and Others*. When I came to do my *Selected Poems* a few years later, I discarded many of those poems entirely. I was on the wrong track; I was writing poems that were not on my line, my basic impulse. I got stuck with a lot of sidetrack poems."[1] He was alluding to the 1966 *Selected Poems*, from which he excised "Lullaby: Exercise in Human Charity," "The Self that Stares," "Fatal Interview," "He Has Fled," "Nocturne," "So You Agree with What I Say? Well, What Did I Say?" "Prognosis," "The Bramble Bush," and numbers 2–7 of "Short Thoughts for Long Nights." Even so, the poems, whether or not they were off the basic impulse, do work as a sequence. All the poems in the volume, whether failures or such magnificent successes as the "Mortmain" series or the "Two Pieces after Suetonius," gain by being considered in this light.

"Clearly about You" (145) and "Lullaby: Exercise in Human Charity and Self-Knowledge" (146) are connected, as Strandberg observed, by their epigraphs. The epigraph for the former is an inscription—"Bene fac, hoc tecum feres"— from a "tomb of Roman citizen of no historical importance"; the epigraph for "Lullaby" is the greeting by which Walter Winchell used to begin his radio broadcasts, "Mr. and Mrs. North and South America, and all the ships at sea, let's go to press." Strandberg notes that both "emphasize the basic theme of anonymity, of lack of identity," since those Winchell addressed "must cover millions of 'citizens of no historical importance'" (*A Colder Fire* 256); he notes as well that the theme of "lack of identity" evident in the first poem "continues to constitute the central problem in the second" (*A Colder Fire* 255–56). The question of identity is particularly evident in the "Whoever" and "whatever" of the poems' first lines: "Whoever you are, this poem is clearly about you" ("Clearly about You") and "Sleep, my dear, whatever your name is" ("Lullaby").

Yet this common theme is developed in opposite ways in the two poems. The speaker in "Clearly about You" hectors "you" into admitting to "your" identity, as if he knew in some detail what it was:

> You won't look in the mirror? Well—but your face is there
> Like a face drowned deep under water, mouth askew,
> And tongue in that mouth tastes cold water, not sweet air,
> And if it could scream in that medium the scream would be you.
>
> Your mother preferred the more baroque positions.
> Your father's legerdemain marks the vestry accounts.
> So you didn't know? Well, it's time you did. . . .

By contrast, in "Lullaby" he speaks soothingly and professes ignorance of his listener's identity: "Sleep, my dear, whatever your name is. . . . [W]hatever your face is, / Fair or brown, or young or old . . . / whatever your sex is, / Male or female, bold or shy." He is not even sure of his own: "Whoever I am, what I now bless / Is your namelessness." In the first poem, the speaker asserts that "this poem is clearly about you" and implies that "you" could discover "your" identity by simply looking in the mirror. In the second poem, "all will be clear" with regard to "your" identity not by a sudden discovery but, in a more gradual process, through "the inner logic History will unfold." In that unfolding, "you to yourself, at last, appear / Clearly."

The "sweet air" that the speaker in the first poem denies his listener in the line "And tongue in that mouth tastes cold water, not sweet air" becomes in the second poem a sweet vapor intimately associated with the listener: "your sweet identity / Fills like vapor, pale in moonlight, all the infinite night sky." It returns in the third poem, "Man in the Street" (147), in a way reminiscent of its appearance in the first, where it pointedly could not be tasted by the tongue: "God's sweet air is like dust on my tongue." These words are said by the person the speaker addresses, a man in the street who turns out to be Jesus Christ—as we have reason to anticipate from the poem's epigraph, which asserts that he can be found in the least likely places: *Raise the stone, and there thou shalt find Me, cleave the wood, there am I. / The Sayings of Jesus.* The poem's speaker addresses three questions to what might on first reading appear to be three different people:

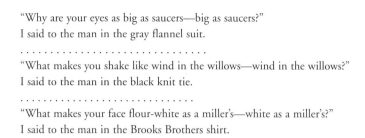

"Why are your eyes as big as saucers—big as saucers?"
I said to the man in the gray flannel suit.
. . . .

"What makes you shake like wind in the willows—wind in the willows?"
I said to the man in the black knit tie.
. . . .

"What makes your face flour-white as a miller's—white as a miller's?"
I said to the man in the Brooks Brothers shirt.

But then we are led to see that these three attributes belong to the same individual, "Wearing gray flannel suit, knit tie, and Brooks Brothers shirt." Similarly, in "Lullaby," three identities are proposed for the person the speaker addresses:

> But are you she, pale hair wind-swept,
> Whose face night-glistened in sea fog?
> Or she, pronouncing joy, who wept
> In that desperate noontide by the cranberry bog?
> Or only that face in the crowd, caught
> And borne like a leaf on the flood away, to which I gave one perturbed
> thought?

The third in its anonymity anticipates the man in the street. But the speaker rejects them all: "No, no, dearest, none of these— / For I who bless can bless you only / For the fact our histories / Can have no common bond except the lonely / Fact of humanness we share."

The reason the man in the street felt that God's sweet air was dust on his tongue is his dismay at what he sees of today's sinful humanity: "Users, abusers, . . . / Fat windbags . . . / Pickers and stealers, / . . . killers." The reason we might reasonably conclude (with all due allowance for irony in a poet who was never a real believer) that he is Jesus, bearing in mind the epigraph from the apocryphal Gospel of Thomas, is that he expresses verbatim the Savior's assurance of eternal life in John 14:2 (though with some additional, unbiblical words): "And I go to prepare a place for you, / For this location will never do." Thus this poem performs a reversal on the one that precedes it. In "Lullaby," the speaker blesses his listener; here, his interlocutor blesses him.

In "Switzerland" (148), the speaker once more issues a blessing, or, rather, he prays that God grant it: "O God . . . / Let down Thy strong hand to all whom their fevers destroy / And past all their pain, need, greed, lip-biting, and spasm, / Deliver them all, young and old, to Thy health, named joy." In "Switzerland," Warren combines elements from the two previous poems. From "Lullaby" he borrows the situation of a speaker concerning himself with, and issuing a blanket blessing to, a multitude of persons, in particular to "young or old" ("Sleep, my dear, whatever your face is, / Fair or brown, or young or old"), paraphrased in "Switzerland" by the "young and old" he asks God to bless with health. From "Man in the Street," he takes the theme of recurring identity, of a stranger suddenly turning out to be someone the speaker already knows—the man in the street revealing himself to be Jesus. In "Switzerland," this phenomenon takes the form of seeing the same old acquaintances wherever one goes: "Here are many old friends you have known from long, long back, / Though of course under different names and with different faces . . . the aging alcoholic . . . the lady theologian . . . the sweet young divorcée. . . . [T]hey all here re-enact / The acts you'd so shrewdly remarked at the very start, / When in other resorts you first met them." It is for all of these recurring characters and their avatars that the speaker wishes God's blessing of joy. One upshot of this phenomenon of recurrence is that "there's little difference, one finds, between different places," a statement that echoes interestingly with the blessing Jesus promises the speaker in "Man in the Street": "I go to prepare a place for you, / For this location will never do"—for the value of the promise is predicated on there being a difference between one place and another.

The concern with health expressed at the conclusion of "Switzerland" ("Deliver them all . . . to Thy health") continues in the beginning of "A Real Question Calling for Solution" (149): "Don't bother a bit, you are only a dream you are having, / And if when you wake your symptoms are not relieved, / That is only because you harbor a morbid craving / For belief in the old delusion in which you have already believed." The cherished "delusion" parallels the "favorite fallacy" seen among the resort guests in "Switzerland": "After lunch take the half-destroyed bodies and put them to bed. / For a time a mind's active behind the green gloom of the jalousie, / But soon each retires inside the appropriate head / To fondle, like childhood's stuffed bear, the favorite fallacy." The "delusion" in "A Real Question" appears to be that of having an identity, for the speaker assures his listener that he has none, that he is only a dream he is having. The speaker does not argue against the truth of "the thought that, on your awaking, identity may be destroyed" but only says that it is one "you" should "avoid," along with "Night air, politics, French sauces," and "autumn weather." By way of positive advice, he recommends: "There is only one way, then, to make things hang together, / Which is to accept the logic of dream." The "fallacy" fondled by the resort guests is not so readily identifiable, but their identity, like that of the "you" of "A Real Question," is if not destroyed at least questionable, given that despite different names and faces they are each somebody else.

Yet that questionableness, based as it is on the speaker's power of recollection, of seeing an old acquaintance in a new face, is itself brought into question by the assertion the speaker in "A Real Question" makes that memory is itself a delusion: "memory / Is nothing, is nothing, not even the memory of smoke / Dispersed on windless ease in the great fuddled head of the sky, // And all recollections are false."

The passage continues: "and all you suffer / Is only the punishment thought appropriate for guilt / You never had, but wish you had the crime for, / For the bitterest tears are those shed for milk—or blood—not spilt." This allusion to sought-after but unmerited guilt prepares the way for "The Letter about Money, Love, or Other Comfort, if Any" (150), which is a veritable catalogue of crimes committed by one seemingly guilt-free individual. The "you" in question, to whom the speaker must hand deliver a letter, has left an apartment in Nashville with "rent in arrears, your bathroom a sty" with "milk rotting in bottles inside the back door"—echoing the "milk . . . not spilt" that would have been a crime in "A Real Question" had it been spilt. In Dubuque, he had left his dog to starve to death; he made a suicide attempt in Italy, "but someone smelled gas at the door / in the nick of time, and you fooled with the female Fulbrights / at the Deux Magots and the Flore." Joseph Blotner writes that this "life itinerary suggests Warren's own" (333). Warren went to college in Nashville and attempted suicide there (not in Italy), he traveled in France and Italy, and, as Strandberg points out, the allusion to Dubuque could be "a reference to Warren's teaching stint at the University of Iowa in 1941" ("Whatever Happened to 'You'?" 149). In "A Real Question," the speaker likewise provides a list of things "you" have done, and these too have the flavor of autobiography: "there was the year when every morning you ran / A mile before breakfast—yes, and the year you read / Virgil two hours just after lunch. . . . // When you slept on a board . . . / When you took the mud baths . . . / When you slept with another woman you found that the letter / You owed your wife was a pleasure to write, gay now and teasy."

"A Real Question" and "The Letter about Money, Love," in both of which a list is provided of what "you" have done, are followed by "Arrogant Law" (152), which inverts this into a series of questions beginning "Have you . . . ?": "Have you crouched . . . // Have you lain by your love . . . // Have you stood beside your father's bed . . . ?" The first four lines are particularly rife with reference to the immediately preceding "The Letter about Money, Love": "Have you crouched with rifle, in woods, in autumn, / In earshot of water where at dawn deer come, / Through gold leafage drifting, through dawn-mist like mist, / And the blue steel sweats cold in your fist?" That "blue steel" recalls the way the water "glints / blue steel to sky" in the place where the speaker will leave the letter for "you." "The

Letter" ends at dawn (in first dawn's drench and drama"); "Arrogant Law" begins there. The question, "Have you crouched . . . ?" inverts the prediction the speaker makes that "you . . . / will crouch among the black boulders" when, having been chased from the society of men for his crimes, this "you" will have to hunt animals for food; it recalls as well an earlier moment in "Letter . . ." when "you'd been caught / crouched in the dark" singing to a teddy bear (itself a reminiscence of the "childhood's stuffed bear" to which the "favorite fallacy" was likened in "Switzerland").

"Arrogant Law" and "The Self that Stares" (153) were originally parts (a) and (b), respectively, of the same poem, appearing under the latter title in the *Virginia Quarterly Review* (as Burt notes in the *Collected Poems* 678–79n). Traces of that original unity are evident in the recurrence of the line "Time unwinds like a falling spool," which is the last line of each of the three stanzas of "Arrogant Law," as the ninth line of "The Self that Stares"; and the latter poem continues the questioning "Have you . . . ?" with which each of the former's stanzas begin. The first stanza of "The Self that Stares" begins: "Have you seen that brute trapped in your eye / When he realizes that he, too, will die? / Stare into the mirror, stare / At his dawning awareness there."

"The Self that Stares" is the last in the sequence "Garland for You," and with this question about looking into the mirror, it symmetrically recalls the first, "Clearly About You," in which there was likewise a face in the mirror that served as a harbinger of mortality, and in which "you" were also dared to look there : "You won't look in the mirror? Well—but your face is there / Like a face drowned deep under water." In the *Virginia Quarterly Review* version, there was another stanza in part (b), preceding what is now the first stanza in "The Self that Stares." It began: "Have you seen that fool that is your foot / Stray where no angel would follow suit?" and went on to speak of a straying hand and heart (679n). Its removal allows "The Self that Stares," as it appears in the book, to focus entirely on the reminder of one's death to be found in the mirror, the second (and now final) stanza not issuing a new "Have you . . . ?" question but serving as a conclusion to those, in both poems, that have preceded it.

This more restricted focus also allows the poem to more tellingly prefigure the next, "Apology for Domitian" (154), the first of two under the title "Two Pieces after Suetonius." For "Apology for Domitian" is also focused on the realization that one is going to die: "He was not bad, as emperors go, not really— / Not like Tiberius cruel, or poor Nero silly. / The trouble was only that omens said he would die, / So what could he, mortal, do? Not worse, however, than you might, or I." Even the mirror reappears, with its hint of another's presence (recalling the "brute" seen in the mirror in the preceding poem): "He would wander his hall of moonstone, / Mirror-bright so he needn't look over his shoulder to know that he was alone." And so does "you," as the speaker once more, as in "The Self that Stares," reminds "you" of his mortality: "Let's stop horsing around—it's not Domitian, it's you / We mean, and the omens are bad, very bad."

In "Apology for Domitian," "music, at sunset, faint as a dream, is heard from beyond the burdock." The burdock is likely growing on American, not Roman, soil, and the speaker is at this point addressing "you" and not the emperor; nevertheless, soft music at twilight is likewise heard in "Tiberius on Capri" (155): "*All is nothing, nothing all:* / To tired Tiberius soft sang the sea thus, / Under his cliff-palace wall" as he "stares past the dusking sea-pulse / Yonder, where come, / One now by one, the lights, far off, of Surrentium." The two poems are already linked by virtue of being "Two Pieces after Suetonius"; in addition, the protagonist of the second is mentioned in the first: Domitian was "Not like Tiberius cruel." We have seen why, given that Warren decided to write a poem about each of these two emperors, Domitian comes first—so that he obsession with the foreknowledge of his death would echo the foreknowledge the speaker of "The Self that Stares" tries to impart to "you," an attempt the speaker of the Domitian poem repeats.

As for why Tiberius comes second (apart from as a consequence of Domitian coming first), that will emerge from reading "Tiberius on Capri" in tandem with "After Night Flight Son Reaches Bedside of Already Unconscious Father, Whose Right Hand Lifts in a Spasmodic Gesture, as Though Trying to Make Contact: 1955" (156). This, however, would seem a risky venture, given that "After Night Flight," the first of the "Mortmain" series devoted Warren's father, is so magnificent a poem in its own right that it would seem almost sacrilege to view it in light of another, and even more so to view it in light of its place in a sequence (*You, Emperors, and Others*) that in many respects it towers above—or to view it in that larger sequence which, as John Burt notes, is "widely considered to be" one of Warren's "low points" ("Introduction," *Selected Poems of Robert Penn Warren* xix), when it is already part of another distinguished, if smaller, sequence, the five poems of "Mortmain." Yet interestingly, the poems Burt calls out for praise in the book are precisely these: "but even *You, Emperors, and Others* is graced by 'Tiberius on Capri,' in which even the emperor's debaucheries cannot free him from the sense that 'all is nothing, nothing all,' which he hears the sea singing to him; and by 'Mortmain,' Warren's powerful elegy for his father" ("Introduction" xix).

It will not be a question of comparing Robert Franklin Warren to Tiberius, but rather the speaker in one poem to that in the other; both are even more obviously than usual Robert Penn Warren. In the second of the two sections of "Tiberius on Capri," Warren recalls standing, on the eve of World War II, where Tiberius stood watching the gathering dark:

There once, on that goat island, I,
As dark fell, stood and stared where Europe stank,
Many were soon to die—
From acedia snatched, from depravity, virtue,
Or frolic, not knowing the reason, in rank
On rank hurled, or in bed, or in church, or
Dishing up supper,
Or in a dark doorway, loosening the girl's elastic to tup her,
While high in the night sky,
The murderous tear dropped from God's eye.

And faintly forefeeling, forefearing, all
That to fulfill our time, and heart, would come,
I stood on the crumbling wall
Of that foul place, and my lungs drew in
Scent of dry gorse on the night air of autumn,
And I seized, in dark, a small stone from that ruin,
And I made outcry
At the paradox of powers that would grind us like grain, small and dry,
Dark down, the stone, in its fall,
Found the sea: I could do that much, after all.

His "forefeeling" and "forefearing" of the death to come parallels Domitian's in the poem before, with the difference that the emperor was thinking of his own. Warren's response echoes the emperor's rage at the predicted fate; both felt the urge to strike out. "Suppose from long back you had known the very hour— / 'Fear the fifth hour'" and knew it could not be avoided. "Then wouldn't you have to strike something at least?" Domitian pulled the wings from flies; Warren threw a small stone into the sea: "I could do that much after all."

The downward movement of his hand anticipates the downward movement of his father's that is at the center of "After Night Flight." In the title, it lifts, but in the poem

Like an eyelid the hand sank, strove
Downward, and in that darkening roar,
All things—all joy and the hope that strove,
The failed exam, the admired endeavor,
Prizes and prinkings, and the truth that strove,
And back of the Capitol, boyhood's first whore—
Were snatched from me, and I could not move,
Naked in that black blast of his love.

Warren "seized" the stone; his father's hand had risen to "claw" and "clutch" at a star. "Dark down," the stone fell; "Downward" and in a "darkening" roar the hand sank.

What his father's death does to Warren recalls what he foresaw happening to the victims of the coming conflict. "All things . . . / Were snatched from me"; those about to die would be "snatched" from life. The list of things that were snatched from him—joy, hope, failure, endeavor, success, truth, sex behind the Capitol— echo, not least as a list, the things from which the war's victims would be snatched: acedia, depravity, virtue, frolic, supper, sex in a doorway. "All is nothing," as Tiberius learned; all becomes nothing as "All things" are "snatched from me."

The remaining poems of "Mortmain" are similarly connected by recycled elements. The dying fall of the father's arm is followed in "A Dead Language: Circa 1885" (157) by the repeated rising and falling of his arms in the strength of his youth as we see him "Cutting crossties for the first railroad in the region, / Sixteen and strong as man—was a man, by God!— / And the double-bit bit into red oak . . . and the axe swung." The next year he works in a general store, where the hand that "could not / Reach" the star it clawed at in "After Night Flight" "reached out and / Took the dime from the gray-scaled palm of the Negro plowhand's hand." He had succeeded in learning some Greek in those days, and when Warren was a boy would regale his son with John 1:1 in the original as he was shaving, waving "the bright blade like a toy." In "Fox-fire: 1956" (157), Warren finds his father's old Greek grammar, yellowed with age, and we see him with his own son, "among his toys . . . / Bright images, all, of Life's significance" as well as an echo of the "bright . . toy" of his father's blade when he remembered his Greek. The blade returns in "In the Turpitude of Time: n.d." (158), no longer a bright toy but the "razor edge" on which "Hope dances." In "Fox-fire," "all night . . . the constellations grind," while a "stone, night-long, groans to divulge" its secret in the other poem. He speaks in "In the Turpitude of Time" of "How cause flows backward from effect / To bless the past occasion, and / How Time's tongue lifts only to tell, / Minute by minute, what truth the brave heart will fulfill," and in "A Vision: Circa 1880" (159) gives an example of that phenomenon, or rather the attempt to make it happen. In that poem, he has a vision of his father as a boy emerging from the woods: "And staring, I know who he is, and would cry out. / Out of my knowledge, I would cry out and say: / *Listen!* Say: *Listen! I know—oh, I know—let me tell you!*" That is, he would like cause to flow backward from effect, to travel as if in a time machine to 1880 to speak to that boy who would grow up to be his father. "I strive to cry across the dry pasture, / But . . . my tongue makes only the dry, / Slight sound of wind on the autumn corn-blade," the tongue that in the poem before would lift "to tell . . . what truth the brave heart will fulfill."

That Warren chose to follow the sequence devoted to his father's death with "Fatal Interview: Penthesilea and Achilles" (159) may seem puzzling. It does send us back to antiquity, which is where we were in the two emperor poems that preceded the "Mortmain" series, but to a more distant antiquity, an event from the Trojan War not recounted in Homer though told in Apollodorus. Penthesilea was an Amazon who fought for the Trojans and whom Achilles killed in battle, but with whom he fell in love when it was too late: "woe is my soul that it's this sweet blood I spill now, / For this is my True Love." From the very first line of the poem, Warren dares us to see Penthesilea in the place of the father from the poem before: "Beautiful, bold, shaking the gold glint of sun-foil, / Which light is." For in the first line of "A Vision," he had presented his father in the same way, first glimpsed in a shower of gold: "Out of the woods where pollen is a powder of gold / Shaken from pistil of oak," his "brow bearing a smudge of gold pollen." What he has done is to pose us a riddle, the answer to which lies in Achilles' desire, paralleling Warren's in "A Vision," to go back in time: "oh, darling, except for mishaps, / You had lain on a bed far softer than this while I mammocked those paps!" When he first saw her breasts, after stripping her corpse of its armor, he felt immediate pangs of regret. "His life went like dust on his tongue; he wept, for he knew he had botched it." When Warren gazed "Down the tube and darkening corridor of Time / That breaks, like tears, upon that sunlit space," where his father, as a boy in 1880, stood, he felt dryness on his tongue too: "my tongue makes only the dry, / Slight sound of wind on the autumn corn-blade" (and we recall that the tongue is a metaphor in "In the Turpitude of Time" for the attempt to go back in time: "we do not know / How cause flows backward from effect / To bless the past occasion, and / How Time's tongue lifts only to tell, / . . . what truth the brave heart will tell"). The dryness in both poems includes the earth as well: "the pasture parched" in "A Vision," parched earth that Penthesilea thought her arrows would "unparch" by making Greek blood flow.

Achilles also boasted of his prowess in battle, specifically of having "spilled buckets of blood, like water." This theme returns in the form of a water bucket that is by contrast not spilled in "Ornithology in a World of Flux" (161): "I came from the spring with water, across the rocky back-pasture, / But so still I stood sky above was not stiller than sky in pail-water." The water reflecting the sky itself reflects the closing lines of "Fatal Interview," in which the slain Penthesilea's "blue eyes . . . , puzzled, stare up at blue sky they lie under." That is, in their blueness her eyes take on the blueness of the sky they take in, as the water in the pail takes on the stillness of the sky as well as reflect it. "One crow beats up past Scamander, / And will pluck the blue eyes." Similarly, a bird is intimately related to the stillness of the water in the pail reflecting the sky, because "It was only a bird call at evening, unidentified" that makes the speaker stop in his tracks and stand "so still" that the water in the pail was no less still than the sky: "Years pass . . . / And I stand in a far land, the evening still, and am at last sure / That I miss more that stillness at bird-call than some things that were to fail later."

"Ornithology in a World of Flux," the first of a series of six under the title "Some Quiet, Plain Poems," is followed by "Holly and Hickory" (161), where the idea of water so still it can reflect the sky is inverted into water so unstill that it cannot reflect the stars: "water moving in wheel ruts, star-glintless." Yet stillness returns in "The Well House" (162), where the speaker alludes to his "old knack / Of stillness," and the "glintless" water of "Holly and Hickory" is answered by water that does glint, "the water's dark-glinting floor" seen when the speaker stares into the well. In returning to the well, the speaker risks being moved by the memory of what once happened there: "Your tears might mean more than the thing you wept for but did not understand." The theme of understanding only later what something meant recurs in "In Moonlight, Somewhere, They Are Singing" (162): "My young aunt and her young husband / From their dark maples sang, and though / Too young to know what they meant I was happy and / So slept, for I knew I would come to know." Their voices "like vine, climbed up moonlight," recalling "The clematis that latches the door / Of the ruinous well house." Those two voices are answered by two other answering voices in "In Italian They Call the Bird *Civetta*" (163): "This small owl calls from the moat now. / That other owl answers him" (the owl from the moat is heard in Italy; the other owl is remembered from his Kentucky boyhood). This situation is reversed in "Debate: Question, Quarry, Dream" (164), when one voice seeks but does not receive a response. The speaker remembers as a boy "Squatting in the canebrake where the muskrat will come. / *Muskrat, muskrat, please now, please, come soon.* / He comes, stares, goes, lets the question resume. / He has taken whatever answer may be down to his mud-burrow gloom."

"Debate" closes with Warren thinking of his son safe asleep, "under a tight roof, clutching a toy," an image that is horribly transformed in "Ballad: Between the Boxcars (1923)" (164) into a fatal failure to hold on. A fifteen year old whom Warren knew in his youth was crushed to death because he did not heed the advice to "go for the grip at the front, not the back, of the boxcars." It was a "hot clasp" in which "He spilled, as boys may, too soon."

Violent death is the focus as well of "Two Studies in Idealism: Short Survey of American, and Human, History" (167), in which the reader enters into the mind of a Confederate (in "Bear Track Plantation: Shortly after Shiloh") and a Union soldier (in "Harvard '61: Battle Fatigue"), both of whom die in battle. The Rebel begins by remarking, "Two things a man's built for, killing and you-know-what."

Sex and killing are rough equivalents in his estimation, in that "what happens under the cover / Or at the steel-point" is worth remembering because in both there is "that look in their eyes." He has had his share of women but complains that Jefferson Davis promised him ten Yankees and he has only killed three before "that Blue-Belly caught me off balance." The boy who fell off the boxcar lost his balance, too, not getting a good grab on the proper grip; and Warren laments that he died too young to make use of his exceptional sexual aura: "the way he was built / Made the girls in his grade in dark stare, and finger the quilt" (that "quilt" returns as the "cover" the Confederate will speak of). But "Like a kid in his first brothel, / In that hot clasp and loveless hurly-burly, / He spilled, as boys may, too soon, between the boxcars." In these lines, the clasp and the spilling refer equally to the sex he missed and to the way he died, to both premature ejaculation and premature ejection from life. That equivalence is paralleled by the equivalence the Rebel soldier will make between sex and death. In "Ballad," Warren regrets being unable to remember "whether he got off his yell / Before what happened had happened between the boxcars." The Confederate soldier the Union soldier remembers killing in "Harvard '61," however, did get off his: "He uttered his yell, he was there!—teeth yellow, some missing," as he suddenly came into sight and the Harvard graduate pulled the trigger.

Meditation on death continues in "Nocturne: Traveling Salesman in Hotel Bedroom" (169), which begins with the observation that "The toothbrush lies in its case, / Like you in your coffin when / The mourners come to stare / And the bristles grow on your chin." This poem and the two "Studies in Idealism" that precede it show three contrasting attitudes toward idealism in light of one's eventual demise. The Rebel soldier makes a point of having no idealism, claiming to live only for the thrill of provoking "that look in the eyes" of the other whether it be "under the cover / Or at the steel-point." For "it's something to save from the mess, / No matter whatever else you never got done. // For a second it seems like a man can know what he lives for." It is a way of establishing identity: "then you know who you are." He hopes he did not give, through the look in his own eyes at the moment of death, the impression of having had any other reason to fight. "Did that look mean then / That I'd honed for something not killing or you-know-what? / Hell no." In stark contrast, the Union soldier is so obsessed with "dying for Right" that he is angry to see "others die who simply haven't the right. // Why should they die with that obscene insouciance? / They seem to insult the principle of your own death." In the traveling salesman Warren depicts a man who regrets having neither idealism nor a strong sense of self. "Far off, in the predawn drizzle, / A car's tires slosh the street mess"—recalling the "mess" from which the Southern soldier hopes to have something to save—"And you think, in an access of anguish, / It bears someone to happiness, // Or at least to a destination / Where duty is clear, and sleep deep, / And the image of self, in dark standing, / Does not pluck at the hangnail, and weep."

The salesman's loneliness is matched by that of Mr. Moody in "So You Agree with What I Say? Well, What Did I Say?" (170), whose "orbit revolved / Between his Bible and the cobbler's bench." Like the traveling salesman, he is glimpsed alone in his room, at night: "once, when he'd lighted his lamp, we spied in the shack / To see him eat beans, then over his book bend his head." The salesman had recourse to the same book, though he approached it in a different spirit: "Take a slug of Old Jack neat, / Try a chapter in the Gideon, / Then work on the sales sheet."

Although surrounded by family—a daughter, her daughter's husband, her own husband—the unnamed woman in "Prognosis: A Short Story, the End of Which You Will Know Soon Enough" (171) is, though unwillingly, as locked in solitude as Mr. Moody. She has just learned she has cancer, and when she tries to talk about it with each of those three, she finds it impossible. Her daughter is too busy washing her hair to listen; the son-in-law might have lent an ear, but dinner guests arrive at the moment she begins to speak; in bed that night, she does tell her husband, but he "made no reply, / For as though provoked at her words, there was sudden essay / Of old force that she long had thought spent," as he makes love to her against her will. Between his Bible and his cobbler's bench, for Mr. Moody "all human complexities" were "resolved / In that Hope past deprivation, or any heartwrench. // Or so it seemed" to the poet and the friends of his youth. The woman in "Prognosis" has no such certainty, though she begins to yearn for some hope: "and God, God, somewhere, *she said,* are lilies, in a field, white, / and let me guess where, where they are, but I don't know, and a slight / wind moves them slow."

That slight wind is replaced by the "Sail-bellyer" the speaker in "Autumnal Equinox on Mediterranean Beach" (173) longs for, to blow all the summer's trash away. "Come howl like a prophet the season's righteous anger. . . . / Snatch the laundry off the line, like youth away . . . / Come swirl old picnic papers to very sky-height." The woman in "Prognosis" comes to terms with death: "I do not grieve to be lost"; the speaker in "Autumnal Equinox" welcomes the end too, but in an angry way: "time to pay the piper, // And be glad to do it, for man's not made for much pleasure, / Or even for joy." Yet the woman still yearns for that: She "wept for joy" at her dream of a field of lilies slowly moving in the wind and envies the grain of sand that can say "I know my joy, I know its name."

The first thing the speaker in "Autumnal Equinox" asks of the wind is to "come bang / To smithereens doors." That wind, like death, brings an end—and knocks: "Come howl like a prophet . . . / And knock down our idols with crash, bang, or clangor." The first of the "Nursery Rhymes" that follow,

"Knockety-Knockety-Knock" (174), begins as the traditional "Hickory-dickory-dock— / The mouse ran up the clock," but Warren then adds a knock at the door (to which the title alludes): "Someone's at the door . . . / A knockety-knockety-knock / That walks in at the door / As I lie on the floor." Victor Strandberg explains that the intruder is "death," who "comes to take the little boy's mother. Since 'the strange foot came in,' she who had 'held me tight' is now 'deader than mackerel'" (*A Colder Fire* 270).

Death comes again, as the title reveals, in "News of Unexpected Demise of Little Boy Blue" (175); so too does the "dock" of the traditional rhyme: "Hurry up, Little Boy, or I'll dock your wages." The little boy in the poem before recalled that "When I'd wake in the night, / Mother held me tight . . . / Then dreams were just dreams, / And not, as it now seems, / A knockety-knockety-knock / That walks in at the door." But now mother is dead. Similarly, Little Boy Blue is informed by the ill-tempered speaker that "Nobody will come when you have a bad dream," at least not unless he blows his horn.

In a gentler way than the one who demands of Little Boy Blue "come blow your horn," the speaker in "Mother Makes the Biscuits" (176) calls for children to make music: "Clap hands, children, / Clap hands and sing!" Little Boy Blue was supposed to blow his horn because of what the animals were up to: "The sheep's in the meadow, the cow's in the corn." Likewise, the children are asked to sing because of what certain other animals are doing: "Clap hands and sing . . . // For the green worm sings on the leaf, / The black beetle folds hands to pray."

Stars disappear in this poem—"all night we have stared / At the black miles past where stars are / Till the stars disappeared"—and "The Bramble Bush" (177): "I now saw past the fartherest stars / How darkness blazed like light . . . // The stars were gone."

Stars persist into the beginning of "Short Thoughts for Long Nights" (178), where (in "Nightmare of Mouse") a mouse refuses to believe that death, in the form of a predator, was lurking: "It was there, but I said it was only a trick of starlight." Stars hid from him that unpleasant truth. In "The Bramble Bush," it was when the "stars were gone" that "I heard the joy / Of flesh singing on the bone," as if their disappearance were necessary for that revelation. The stars' disappearance is "like petals from a wind-torn bough / In furious beauty blown," a hopeful counterpart to the near-despair with which the wind in "Autumnal Equinox" is urged to blow. Indeed, the four "Nursery Rhymes," in addition to what echoes they make within their own sequence, also work together as a single poem in relation to "Autumnal Equinox" in the echoing sequence of the book as a whole. Thus even the command issued to Little Boy Blue to "come blow" is another version of the command the speaker in that poem issued to the wind:

"Blow the cat's fur . . . / Blow the hen's tail feathers . . . / Come blow up old women's skirts." The "Short Thoughts" function in this manner as nine parts of the same poem, referring back to "Nursery Rhymes" through the speaker's allusion to "the death of my mother" in "Nightmare of Man," recalling the revelation in "Knockety-Knockety-Knock" that "Ma's deader than mackerel." Echoes of Little Boy Blue come with the "Little boy" addressed in "Little Boy on Voyage" and "Little Boy and General Principle" and with the "trumpet *toot*less" of "Joy."

CHAPTER 5

"THE HEART CRIES OUT FOR COHERENCE"

TALE OF TIME:

NEW POEMS 1960–1966

Tale of Time appears at the beginning of the volume *Selected Poems: New and Old, 1923–1966*. It opens with a section titled "Notes on a Life to Be Lived" containing ten poems: "Stargazing," "Small White House," "Blow, West Wind," "Composition in God and Red-Gold," "Little Boy and Lost Shoe," "Patriotic Tour and Postulate of Joy," "Dragon-Tree," "Vision Under the October Mountain: A Love Poem," "Chain Saw at Dawn in Vermont in Time of Drouth," and "Ways of Day." All but three ("Patriotic Tour and Postulate of Joy," "Dragon-Tree," and "Ways of Day") would reappear in *Or Else—Poem/Poems 1978–1974*. The order of their appearance there bears no discernible relation to their order in *Tale of Time*. In a note in *Or Else*, Warren would write:

> This book is conceived as a single long poem composed of a number of shorter poems as sections or chapters. It is dated 1968–1974, but a few short pieces come from a period some ten years before, when I was working toward a similar long poem. After a time, however, I was to find that that poem was disintegrating into a miscellany, and so abandoned the project and published the pieces that I wished to preserve under the title "Notes on a Life to Be Lived." More lately, working on this book, I have decided that all except three of those early pieces have a place in the thematic structure of this poem. (709)

In Warren's estimation, "Notes on a Life to Be Lived" was not an organized sequence but the remnants of a failed attempt to construct one. With that in mind, and because I will discuss the seven sequences he includes in *Or Else* in my chapter on that volume, I will not do so here.

Tale of Time continues with "Tale of Time" (185), a poem in six parts about the death of Warren's mother. In the face of that tragedy, "the heart cries out for coherence" (187), a task even God finds difficult: "my mother / Died, and God / Kept on, and keeps on, / Trying to tie things together, but // It doesn't always work" (185).[1] It may not have worked in the larger poem that disintegrated into a miscellany, nor in "Notes on a Life to Be Lived" if those poems are merely what he wished to preserve out of that failed effort. Yet beginning with "Tale of Time" and continuing to the end of the larger sequence bearing the same title, Warren attempts to do precisely that.

"Tale of Time" is related to its neighbor, "Homage to Emerson, On Night Flight to New York" (194), in several ways:

1. In "Tale of Time," the narrator hears a plane passing overhead: "Now, far from Kentucky, planes pass in the night, I hear them and all, all is real" (186). In "Homage to Emerson," he is a passenger in just such a plane. In fact, Warren almost invites us to imagine that it could be the same plane, for from it, in "Homage to Emerson," he can see where Kentucky is: "To my right, far over Kentucky, the stars are shining" (196). The planes pass at night, within sight of Kentucky yet not directly over it, in both poems. More to the point, in "Tale of Time" the plane is presented as evidence that "all is real," while in "Homage to Emerson" it is because he is in the plane, because he is so far removed from the earth's surface, that he has precisely the opposite impression, that all is *not real:* "At 38,000 feet Emerson // Is dead right." In the plane he had been reading Emerson claiming, "There is / No sin. Not even error" (194).

2. Emerson's "smile / Was sweet as he walked in the greenwood. / He walked lightly, his toes out, his body / Swaying in the dappled shade" (194). In "Tale of Time," the "sun-dappled dark of deep woods" (185) is something Warren thinks about in the "interim" between the moment the dirt falls on his mother's coffin and the "full realization" (185) of her loss, which he expects will come after midnight. The extent of the repetition is worth savoring: not only the dappling but also the equivalence between "dark" and "shade." The contrast between the son made numb by his mother's death and the untroubled transcendentalist is made the more telling by Warren's having them walk the same forest path. In that dappled shade, Emerson's "smile never withered a violet. He // Did not even know the violet's name, not having / Been introduced, but he bowed, smiling, / For he had forgiven God everything, even the violet" (194). Violence, not violets, is what the orphaned son thinks in that forest: "You think of . . . / The sun-dappled dark of deep woods and / Blood on green fern frond, of / The shedding of blood, and you will doubt / The significance of your own experience" (185).[2] The reason he doubts it is that he cannot yet weep: "You stare at your face in the mirror, wondering / Why now no tears come. . . and so / You think of copulation, of . . . / Water deeper than daylight, of / The sun-dappled dark" (185). By contrast to the

poet who doubts the significance of his own experience, "Emerson thought that significance shines through everything" (195). On the basis of these two poems (in which Warren does not disclose that Emerson too suffered painful grief, including the loss of a son) one could reasonably conclude that the significance the Concord Sage found was too easily won.

3. In the interim between the "public ritual" of his mother's burial and the "private realization" he awaited, Warren goes with his father and brother to visit a dying woman who had been, as John Burt put it, his "black mammy" (*Robert Penn Warren and American Idealism* 79). Our attention is focused on her hand: "Her hand rises in the air. / It rises like revelation. . . . / The hand touches my cheek. / The voice says: *you.* // I am myself. // The hand has brought me the gift of myself" (188). One is reminded of the dying father's hand in "Mortmain." Randy Hendricks notes as well that the "gift" she gives recalls the mysterious gift in "I Am Dreaming of a White Christmas" that the father forbids the son from opening ("*No presents, son, till the little ones come*" [*Collected Poems* 278]) and the line in "Billie Potts" in which the father's murdering blow is phrased as a gift: "What gift—oh, father, father—from that dissevering hand?" (Hendricks 57; *Collected Poems* 89). Later in "Tale of Time," the poet imagines his real mother as a child to whom he, now grown, extends his hand: "I . . . / Reach out, saying: 'Your hand— / Give it here, for it's dark . . . I'll take you back home'" (192, 193). In "Homage to Emerson," the focus is again on the poet's hand, in the context of a revelation about himself that another old black inhabitant of Guthrie gave him:

> When I was a boy I had a wart on the right forefinger.
>
> At 38,000 feet you had better
> Try to remember something specific, if
> You yourself want to be something specific, I remember
> The wart and the old colored man, he said, *Son
> You quit that jack-off, and that thing go way.*
> And I said *Quit what,* and he giggled *He-he,* and he
> Said, *You is got white skin and hair red as a ter-mater, but
> You is human-kind,* but
>
> At 38,000 feet that is hard to remember. (194)

Like what the black woman's hand gave him, this knowledge too is a kind of "gift of myself," having the specificity that "You yourself" require. The two passages are further united through the myth by which Warren persistently identifies himself with the Perseus who traces his origins to an inseminating golden liquid, somehow both urine and semen—as revealed in *A Place to Come To,* where the protagonist's father may have been engaged in what the old black man accuses the poet of doing (an intentional ambiguity that leaves room for his having simply been urinating). The passage in "Homage to Emerson" is about semen, while the equivalent scene in "Tale of Time" reeks of urine: "light / Lay gold on the roofs of Squigg-town . . . and / The room smelled of urine." Afterward, "My brother says: *The whole place smelled of urine*" (188, 189). Warren makes clear that the old black woman whom he went to visit in that room was, as he described her to Floyd Watkins, a "second 'mother.'"[3] Like a mother, she "had held me in her arms, / And I had cried out in the wide / Day-blaze of the world" (187). As a figure for Danae, his mother in his personal myth, it makes sense that her room would smell of urine. It likewise makes sense that the black man who instructs him in the etiology of warts should address him, in a fatherly way, as "Son."

Emerson's untroubled saunter through the greenwood finds a problematic counterpart in "Shoes in Rain Jungle" (198), a poem of protest against the War in Vietnam, where progress through a forest is considerably more difficult: "Shoes rot off feet before feet / Rot, and before feet / Stop moving feet / Rot, rot in the rain, moving. // . . . an army / Marches on its feet. If / It has them. / If the feet have shoes." The poet's speedy travel across the country at thirty-eight thousand feet, so cut off from reality that he can imagine Emerson being right about there being neither sin no error, is brought back to earth, too, by this slow and risky going.[4] The erroneous notion that the world is free from sin and error is countered in "Shoes in Rain Jungle"—the "juxtaposition" of which to "Homage to Emerson," as James A. Grimshaw Jr. observes, "suggests an irony" (*Understanding Robert Penn Warren* 140)—by the assertion that "History" is not so easily ignored, being "what you can't / Resign from."

The feet that disappear in "Shoes in Rain Jungle," having rotted off, return in the form of what is missing from an "amputee's / Stump" in "Fall Comes in Back-Country Vermont" (199). The death of a member of a small community is felt like a "Twitch" in what remains. The amputee may "wonder / How that which has gone off and set up / As a separate self is making out, and whether // It repents of its rashness." It is as if the missing part—and the citizen who died—had voluntarily resigned from the whole of which it had been a part. The metaphor is thus an ironic reversal of the terms of the assertion in "Shoes in Rain Jungle" that history is something you can't resign from. For by "history" Warren means the realm of time, which includes the inevitability of death. That inevitability is something you can't resign from either, though you can, as Warren does, speak of death as if it were itself a voluntary withdrawal.

The rain that in "Shoes in Rain Jungle" causes feet to rot reappears as Vermont rain that makes the speaker "wonder about the drainage // Of the cemetery" where the man is buried whose death is likened to the missing part of a limb. The man was a cancer victim. His widow leaves town, "for here winter's / Not made for a woman lone, lorn, and slow-foot" (200), a reminiscence of the slow-footedness of soldiers with rotting shoes. A pair of young people make love in the abandoned house, on the "raw mattress" of the bed where he died. The girl has a sudden realization: "'But here—it was here— / On this bed that he died, and I'll catch it and die'— / But does not, comes back, comes back until snow flies, / And many years later will be the last person / To remember his name." That fascination with the bed where someone died is played out again in "The Day Dr. Knox Did It" (202), in which the speaker of the poem—Warren as a nine-year-old boy—is fascinated by the place in the hayloft where a man blew out his brains with a shotgun:

> That summer I'd played
> there in that loft, and so knew how
> if you lay on your back in the hay, all
> you could see was the twilight of spider-web
>
> hung from the rooftree, or maybe one wasp
> cruising slow. . . .
> . . . .
> That man—how long had he lain, just looking?
>
> That was the thing that stuck in my head.
> I would wonder how long he had lain there, first. (204)

After the event, he revisits the spot with the son of the man who had killed himself there. "I stared" and "kept thinking about how the place looked clean. / I kept wondering who had cleaned up the mess" (205). The room where the man died in Vermont had been similarly sanitized: "the bed // Is stripped to the mattress, and the bed pan / Washed with ammonia and put on a high shelf" (200). It was on this mattress that the girl thought she would be exposed to some contagion.

The narrator flees the loft: "But ran from such wondering as I ran / down the street . . . / and the dust rose white in plops round my feet / as they ran toward that stream that was silent and silver" (206). He lay in the stream and let the water flow over him, and "the world / would flow, flow away, on forever." In "Elijah on Mount Carmel" (207), the first of two biblically based poems comprising "Holy Writ," a similar flight takes place, as King Ahab, frightened by Elijah's ability to call down fire from heaven when the priests of Baal could not, "had nothing to run to / But . . . Jezebel: that darkness wherein History creeps to die." In the stream, the nine-year-old boy "would lie / with my eyes shut" (206), holding his breath as he let the water, and the world, flow over him; likewise, in his escape from reality Ahab lay in Jezebel's arms, with "Eyes shut, breath scant" (208). Jezebel embraces her husband as the stream enveloped the boy.

"Elijah on Mount Carmel" is based on 1 Kings 18. Warren sets the scene in a prefatory note: "Elijah, after the miraculous fall of fire on his altar, the breaking of the drouth, and the slaughter of the priests of Baal, girds up his loins and runs ahead of the chariot of Ahab to the gates of Jezreel, where Jezebel waits" (207). "Saul at Gilboa" (209), its companion piece in "Holy Writ," is based on 1 Samuel 9, 10, and 28. Samuel, speaking from the grave, recalls anointing Saul to be king and recalls not telling Saul what would later transpire: that he, Samuel, would later anoint David to be king in the place of Saul, and that later still Saul would ask the Witch of Endor to call up the ghost of Samuel, who would tell him that the Lord had rejected Saul as king because he had disobeyed his command. Warren departs from both biblical accounts in order to make his two poems more congruent with each other, as well as be congruent with, and to some extent repeat and reenact, the poems in the sequence that precede and follow them. We have just seen how the boy's flight in "The Day Dr. Knox Did It" anticipates Ahab's flight, and how Ahab's "Eyes shut" in Jezebel's arms echo the boy's "eyes shut" in the stream where he takes refuge from the awful truth of what happened in the barn. We will see how Warren also alters the Elijah story so that it would become more congruent with, repeat, and reenact the Perseus myth that runs throughout his poetry, specifically the golden liquid by which Zeus impregnated Danae.

Such an interest in congruence, repetition, and reenactment is itself congruent with the opening lines of the Elijah poem: "Nothing is re-enacted. Nothing / Is true. Therefore nothing / Must be believed, / But / To have truth / Something must be believed, / And repetition and congruence, / To say the least, are necessary" (207–8). The argument appears to be that in reality—in real life, in history, in time—no event actually reenacts another, but that if we are to have truth, some reenactment, some degree of repetition and congruence, is required. This, then, would be the relation of Warren's poetry to reality, to create congruence and reenactment where there was none before, for the sake of belief, in the interest of truth.

At the conclusion of "Elijah on Mount Carmel," Warren focuses on King Ahab, who, panic-stricken by the display of Jehovah's power that Elijah staged, takes refuge in Jezebel's arms. This is the scriptural basis for the scene: "And Ahab rode, and went to Jezreel. . . . And Ahab told Jezebel all that Elijah had done, and withal how he had slain all the prophets with the sword" (1 Kings 18:45, 19:1 [KJV]). Here is how Warren renders it: "How could he ever tell her? Get nerve to? / . . . / Yes, how could he tell her? When he himself / Now scarcely believed it? Soon, / In the scented chamber, / She, / Saying, 'Baby, Baby, / Just hush, now hush, it's all right,' / Would lean, reach out, lay a finger / To his lips to allay his infatuate gabble" (208). The episode of Saul and the Witch of Endor is based on the following passage from 1 Samuel 28. The ghost of Samuel, conjured up by the Witch at Saul's command, has just told Saul that his doom is certain:

> Then Saul fell straightway all along on the earth, and was sore afraid, because of the words of Samuel: and there was no strength in him; for he had eaten no bread all the day, nor all the night. And the woman came unto Saul, and saw that he was sore troubled, and said unto him, Behold, thine handmaid hath obeyed thy voice, and I have put my life in my hand, and have hearkened unto thy words which thou spakest unto me. Now therefore, I pray thee, hearken thou also unto the voice of thine handmaid, and let me set a morsel of bread before thee; and eat, that thou mayest have strength, when thou goest on thy way. But he refused, and said, I will not eat. But his servants, together with the woman, compelled him; and he hearkened unto their voice. So he arose from the earth, and sat upon the bed. And the woman had a fat calf in the house; and she hasted, and killed it, and took flour, and kneaded it, and did bake unleavened bread thereof. And she brought it before Saul, and before his servants; and they did eat.
> (1 Sam. 28:20–25 [KJV])

Here is Warren's version: "She lifts him, gives him to eat. / She feeds him, morsel / By morsel, he like a child" (212). Although the witch asks Saul to take "a morsel of bread" in the scriptural passage, she does not feed him herself, "morsel / By morsel," as if he were a child. Actually, in the poem's first publication (*Yale Review*, Summer 1966) she did not do that either, for as John Burt notes in his edition of *The Collected Poems* (697n), the last two of the three lines quoted here ("She feeds him, morsel / By morsel, he like a child") did not appear in that version. Nor in that publication was "Saul at Gilboa" accompanied by the Elijah poem. Warren added those lines for the version that would appear in *Tale of Time,* where it would immediately follow "Elijah on Mount Carmel," in which Warren has Jezebel talk to Ahab as if *he* were a child: "Saying, 'Baby, Baby, / Just hush, now hush, it's all right'" (208). That addition is compelling evidence that he meant for the two poems of "Holy Writ" to parallel each other to this degree, that he sought such a congruence. The parallel between Ahab and Saul, both of them kings of Israel who face defeat because God has turned against them, was already there in the Bible; Warren enriches it by finding a way to make the Witch of Endor resemble Jezebel.

To Ahab, the wild-eyed Elijah "smelled like a goat." It was to escape the prophet's revelation of God's power and Baal's impotence that Ahab took refuge in Jezebel's arms, where he prayed: "Dear God, dear God—oh, please, don't exist!" (208). The goatish Elijah's revelation to Ahab of an inescapable reality is presaged in "The Day Dr. Knox Did It" by something from a goat that becomes the narrator's only connection to reality: after telling us how he fled from the hayloft to lie in the stream with his eyes shut as the world flowed away, he tells us how years later on Telegraph Hill in San Francisco he "watched fog swell up from the sea . . . and blot me out / from all relation but to the dry // goat droppings that beneath my feet / pressed the thin soles of my sneakers" (206). He was as cut off from reality as he had been when he was thirty-eight thousand feet above the earth in "Homage to Emerson," a vantage point from which the transcendentalist's denial of reality seemed dead right. Emerson walked lightly on the earth, barely in touch with reality: "He walked lightly, his toes out, his body / Swaying in the dappled shade" (194).

Ahab fled to Jezreel on his chariot, while Elijah ran ahead on foot. "His thorn-scarred heels and toes with filth horn-scaled / Spurned now the flint-edge and with blood spurts flailed / Stone, splashed mud of Jezreel" (208). "Saul at Gilboa" will share this focus on feet. Elijah's heels are "thorn-scarred"; Saul's ankle is "Scarred by thorn" (209). It is through the eyes of Samuel, who was to anoint young Saul king, that we see this; he exclaims, alluding to Saul, "How beautiful are the young, walking / On the fore-part of the foot. . . . / Toward me he walks, I am old. / Dust of desert on him, and thorn-scar, he / Walks" (209, 210). In the following passage, Samuel continues to focus on Saul walking, while revealing that he is to him as a father—but there is something strangely goatlike about Samuel himself: "He comes walking who will make Israel / One among the nations. He walks / In his youth, which is the sweet affront / Of ignorance, toward me, and I / Smile, feeling my face, even in that smile, go stiff as / Fresh goat hide, unflayed, set in sun, goes" (210). Given that Elijah, who revealed the reality of God's power to Ahab, for whom it was an unwelcome truth, reminded him of a goat, and that the feel of goat droppings under his feet were the poet's only "relation" to reality in the poem before, we might expect Samuel's comparing his skin to a goat's to have some poetic justification in relation to those two earlier allusions. And it does, for Samuel foresees that after his own death he will return as a ghost, conjured up by the Witch of Endor to tell Saul the painful truth that, having fallen out of favor with God, he will lose his kingdom and be slain (1 Sam. 28). Like Elijah, Samuel will speak the unpleasant truth to the king. Like Elijah (and the goat droppings on Telegraph Hill), he represents a reality that cannot be evaded. Saul will not know that Samuel once felt his face resemble a goat's, nor know that Ahab thought Elijah smelled like a goat, nor know that the poet telling these stories was once connected to reality only through the goat dung he could feel through the soles of his shoes. But the reader of these poems can know that.

Besides the recurring reenactments from poem to poem, there is the recurring myth of the golden fluid, which has already appeared in the poem "Tale of Time" in the poet's visit, beneath a haze of gold light from the sky, to the urine-smelling home of the alternate mother. It reemerges here in the "spilled gold of storm" (208) by which Elijah's God makes a display of his power. Before that storm broke, the prophet taunted the priests of Baal, who were unable to draw down any fire from the sky: "Has your god turned aside to make pee-pee?" (208). This is how Warren renders what is given in the King James version of 1 Kings 18:27 as "Elijah mocked them, and said, Cry aloud: for he is a god; either he is talking, or he is pursuing, or he is in a journey, or peradventure he sleepeth, and must be awaked." Warren, though, was evidently relying on something closer to the Revised Standard Version: "Cry aloud, for he is a god; either he is musing, *or he has gone aside,* or he is on a journey, or perhaps he is asleep and must be awakened." For in a note on the galley proofs of *New and Selected Poems 1923–1985* that did not find its way into the published text he considered justifying his interpretation: "Some commentators interpret the phrase 'turned aside' as rendered here" (695n). No doubt he did find some commentators who interpret the phrase in that way. Intriguingly, he felt the need to justify his peculiar reading, which serves so well his ulterior aim of equating Jehovah with the Zeus of the inseminating gold.

In "Saul at Gilboa," Samuel, after meditating on what will happen to Saul, returns to the present. He is about to anoint Saul as king (the episode of the Witch of Endor is far in the future). He concentrates once more on the young man's feet: "The toes of his inordinate sandals / Turned inward somewhat . . . / Of the great toe, the nail / Was blackened. Bruised, / In the desert, by stone" (213).[5] The poem concludes with Samuel expressing yet again his delight in the way Saul walks: "How beautiful are the young, walking! // If I could weep" (214). The next poem in *Tale of Time,* "Into Broad Delight," the first of several poems within the series titled "Delight," will resume that theme in its opening lines: "Out of silence walks delight. / Delight comes on soundless foot" (215). Though the speaker there asserts that "*Your . . . hand . . . can never seize on / Delight,*" yet in the poem that follows, "Mediterranean Beach, Day after Storm" (215)—which is actually first "Vignette" within the poem "Love: Two Vignettes"—"your hand" is invited to participate in that delight: "Give me your hand" (216).[6] There is, however, a difference between the "you" of "Into Broad Daylight," the nonspecific "you" equivalent to everyman (as in "Delight will prepare you never" [215]), and the "you" addressed in "Mediterranean Beach," who seems to be a specific person, probably a lover (as the title "Love: Two Vignettes" suggests). In "Deciduous Spring" (216), the second "Vignette," the same "joy" that could be felt in the waves crashing on a Mediterranean beach is discovered in a forest, setting off the same sounding *-angs.* In "Mediterranean Beach": "How instant joy, how clang / And whang the sun"; in the second, "the world / All gabbles joy like geese, for / An idiot glory the sky / Bangs." Leaves "are / Bangles dangling and / Spangling, in sudden air / Wangling."

In "Deciduous Spring," the speaker commands: "Keep still, just a moment, leaves. // There is something I am trying to remember." This anticipation of "something," which occurs in the last two lines of the poem, introduces "Something Is Going to Happen" (216), although the speaker in that poem will make an association between being still and something happening that is the opposite of what the leaves were told: "Something may happen today if you don't sit still." That is, in "Deciduous Spring" keeping still will make it possible for something to be remembered, while in "Something Is Going to Happen," it is necessary *not* to keep still for something to happen. The speaker gives us a list of things that will happen, though they are hardly surprising events: "The way the wind blows is the way the dead leaves go"; "the sun rose in the east"; "feet move fastest down the old track they know." He reserves the surprise for the end: "to prepare you there's one more thing I must say: / Delight may dawn, as the day dawned, calmly, today."

"Dream of a Dream the Small Boy Had" (217) seems to grow out of one of the things that "happen" in "Something Is Going to Happen": "The way the wind blows is the way the dead leaves go." For the dream the boy had is of becoming something like the leaves that the wind blows away: "I didn't know where the wind went, which was bad, / For I was bright-colored like leaves in the blow-away time, / And wind blew me away." Then, in the dream, "my bones, / They hang in the tree, shaped like me, and they burn." The brightly colored leaves and the burning bones hanging in the tree where the leaves had been are transformed in "Dawn" (218), the first part of "Two Poems About Suddenly and a Rose," into brightly colored paper that burns: "Christmas— // Remember, remember!—and into flame / All those gay wrappings the children fling, then . . . while / Flame leaps, they, in joy, / Scream. Oh, children, // Now to me sing." That singing echoes as well from the dream, in which "I . . . hear my own heart / Off somewhere singing. . . . my heart a bird singing."

That the "Two Poems" are both "About Suddenly and a Rose," despite their titles—"Dawn" and "Intuition" (219)—comes into focus when we examine how they begin and end. The first word of each is "Suddenly." Their last lines are "The rose dies, laughing" ("Dawn") and "The rose dies laughing, suddenly" ("Intuition"). Both poems deal with the relationship of the present to the past: "Now not what was *not,* / But what is. From nothing of *not* / Now all of *is*" ("Dawn"); "life / Is what you are living, not / What you thought you had lived / All your life, but suddenly / Know you had not" ("Intuition").

In "Intuition," when the sudden happens "Suddenly / Life takes on a new dimension, and old pain / Is wisdom." Wisdom reappears in "Not to Be Trusted"

(219), only to be undone: "You // Cannot trust delight. / As I have told you, / It undoes the ambition of the young and / The wisdom of the old." Delight's unexpectedness continues in "Finisterre" (219), which speaks of endings that may yet prove not to be final. Looking out over a misty bay, the speaker declares that "it's hard to tell in this northern place / If this, now, is truly the day's end, or // If . . . / The light may break through yonder / To stab gold to the gray sea, and twist / Your heart to a last delight—or at least, to wonder." Absent for the preceding three poems, "delight" reappears in these last two.

"Delight" and "joy" alternate in the "Delight" poems, synonymous in this context. In no single poem do they both appear. Their distribution, if we count the poems as nine, reading "Love: Two Vignettes" and "Two Poems About Suddenly and a Rose" as four, is 1. delight, 2. joy, 3. joy, 4. delight, 5. joy, 6. joy, 7. neither, 8. delight, and 9. delight. If, however, we respect Warren's roman-numeral numbering, and count "Two Vignettes" and "Two Poems" each as a single poem, the distribution would be I. delight, II. joy, III. delight, IV. joy, V. joy, VI. delight, and VII. delight—so that one of the two appears in every poem.[7] Realizing now how interchangeable they are, we can see the relevance of Samuel's words, in a passage I had not yet quoted: "How beautiful are the young, walking! // I closed my eyes. I shuddered in a rage of joy" (213). This is an even tighter connection to the first line of the first "Delight" poem—"Out of silence walks delight"—now that we can see that "joy" and "delight" are the same thing, each being associated with walking.

Unlike "Delight" and "Holy Writ," "Tale of Time," "Homage to Emerson," and "The Day Dr. Knox Did It" function in the echoing structure of the sequence as a single poem, and that is how I have analyzed them here. Though composed of individually titled poems, these three unite those individual poems within a single overarching narrative: the death of the poet's mother, his encounter with Emerson, the suicide of Dr. Knox—as well as the effect of each of these on the poet. They are already too unified to give Warren the opportunity to demonstrate how "repetition and congruence" (208) can appear within disparate contexts. The contexts of the "Delight" poems are not quite as different from one another as the two "Holy Writ" narratives are and almost constitute a borderline case, somewhere between the "Holy Writ" model and that exemplified by "Tale of Time," "Homage to Emerson," and the "Dr. Knox" poems. Basically, each celebrates sudden delight or sudden joy in different contexts.[8] Yet the context itself of sudden delight or joy does not differ from poem to poem.

CHAPTER 6

"ALL // ONE FLESH"

INCARNATIONS:
POEMS 1966–1968

Dear Red,

    I have put off writing to you about the fine suite of poems enti-
tled "Ile de Port Cros" until I have time to do a little rereading and
meditation. Anyway, though they can stand a great deal more reading
and I am far from having digested them, I mustn't put off any longer
telling you that I think they are magnificent. I have at the moment
my favorites among the individual pieces, of course, but there is not a
weak link in the chain, and what really bowls me over is the impact of
the whole group taken as one beautifully interlaced and very rich,
massive, long poem.

    I have just said that the different parts are beautifully and intri-
cately laced together, but the reader doesn't have any sense of studied
design; the effect is that of natural growth, richness, and vitality. . . .

Yours,
Cleanth[1]

"ISLAND OF SUMMER"
1. "WHAT DAY IS"

Joseph Blotner records that in 1966 Warren and his family summered on the Île
de Port-Cros, off the coast of southeast France, near Toulon. Many, or perhaps all,
of the fifteen poems in the sequence "Island of Summer" were written there under
"a fig tree in a ruined garden far from the hotel."[2] This tightly interwoven
sequence is full of cross-references from poem to poem. So, too, is the first of the
poems, "What Day Is" (223)—as if the interrelationship of its stanzas could serve
as a guide to reading the poems to come. That interrelationship is based on a fun-
damental sequential structure in which each stanza anticipates the next, though
not excluding other, more distant connections.

The ancient past is evoked in both of the first two stanzas, but in contrasting ways. As James Justus explains, the "enterprising Phoenicians, Celts, and Romans who constructed" in the first stanza are followed in the second by "'Monks, Moors, murderers' who later destroyed" (83). The Romans left "Hewn stone" that may have served for irrigation channels; by contrast, the alliterative list of destroyers who came later "cut / Down olives, plucked vines up, burnt / The chateau."

Stanza three presents destruction of a different sort, no longer human but natural:

> All day, cicadas,
> At the foot of infinity, like
> A tree, saw. The sawdust
> Of that incessant effort,
> Like filings of brass, sun-brilliant,
> Heaps up at the tree-foot. That
> Is what day is.

The monks, Moors, and murderers cut down olive trees; the cicadas chew away at some unnamed tree. The Romans left "Hewn stone, footings," anticipating the sawing the cicadas will perform "at the tree-foot." The "handful of coins" bearing the image of "a late emperor" will give way to bright brass filings of sawdust. A Hegelian thesis-antithesis-synthesis process is at work, as the constructiveness of hewed footings is replaced by the destructive cutting down of trees, followed by something that combines parts of both: destructive activity performed on a tree, but at its "foot" (and leaving brasslike remnants that recall the wealth the Romans left behind). Indeed, the activity in the third moment, the synthesis, is both destructive and constructive, as it is part of a natural cycle of life. The cicadas are finding nourishment in the tree, while the olive tree destroyers and the vine pluckers were cutting off sources of nourishment. The necessarily destructive nature of the struggle for existence, and the poet's regret that it should be so, will be quite possibly the most important motif of the entire sequence. "This is the design of incarnations," writes Victor Strandberg, commenting on the last poem in the sequence, "The Leaf," "a running sacrifice of the world's flesh that the one life may continue" (*The Poetic Vision* 100). It is, Strandberg asserts, the "grief" that afflicts the poet in "The Leaf," bringing him to lie down in a high place on a bed of animal bones, past prey of the hawk circling above.

"That / Is what day is," the poet asserts at the end of stanza three, referring to the heap of sun-brilliant sawdust and to the "incessant effort" of the cicadas that produces it. Day's brightness is the bright sawdust; day as the passage of time is the incessant work that creates it. Days eat away at infinity as the cicadas eat away at the tree: "All day, cicadas, / At the foot of infinity, like / A tree, saw." The sun-brilliance that comes out of the harm done the tree is followed in stanza four by the sun's brilliance conceived as itself harmful: "Do not / Look too long at the sea, for / That brightness will rinse out your eyeballs. // They will go gray as dead moons." The sun's light on the sea will do to your eyes what the cicadas, which are "what day is," do to the tree.

2. "WHERE THE SLOW FIG'S PURPLE SLOTH"

While sunlight is destructive, both to the eyes of those who gaze on the sea and, through the cicadas that with their sun-brilliant product are "what day is," to the tree in the first poem, in the second poem just the opposite happens. In "Where the Slow Fig's Purple Sloth" (223), the sun sacrifices itself for the sake of the tree, or its fruit: "for the fig's bliss / The sun dies." The sun's light passes into the fig, imbuing it with a strange radiance: "When you / Split the fig . . . // It fills / The darkening room with light." It's another version of what happens in "What Day Is." There, the sun's light passes into the "filings of brass, sun-brilliant" that came out of the tree (not only because it shines on it but also because the cicadas' incessant sawing is what day is); here, the sun's light is miraculously (a miracle due to the sun's self-sacrifice) reincarnated in the "Flesh like flame" of the glow-in-the-dark fig. The sawdust is the first tree's strange fruit, analogous to the fig produced by the second; it is therefore fitting that the fig should be "imperial" ("the fig, / Motionless in that imperial and blunt / Languor of glut"), for the "filings of brass" in the third stanza of "What Day Is" recall the "handful of coins" bearing the likeness of "a late emperor" in its first (as the "Hewn . . . footings" the Romans left behind with the coins anticipate the "tree-foot" where the brass filings are heaped up).

3. "NATURAL HISTORY"

The thesis-antithesis-synthesis structure linking the first three stanzas of "What Day Is" likewise links the first three poems in the sequence. (1) Trees are damaged in the first poem, as "Monks, Moors" and "murderers" cut down olives and the cicadas saw away at the tree of infinity; (2) the tables are turned in the second poem, in which a tree is nourished by the death of its nourisher; and (3) in "Natural History" (224), the trace of earlier human presence is again evoked, as it had been in the first poem: Saracens slain in battle by Jean le Maingre. But this time that human presence, instead of destroying trees, contributes to their well-being: "the root / Of the laurel has profited, the leaf / Of the live-oak achieves a new luster." It is as if, in the great scheme of nature (hence the poem's title: "Natural History"), the men died for the trees, as the sun's death in the preceding poem brought bliss to the fig.

A relic of more recent human presence is a Nazi helmet with a bullet hole on either end:

> from left
> To right, entering at the temple, small and
> Perfectly round at the point of entry, neat, but
> At egress large, raw, exploding outward, desperate for
> Light, air, and openness after
> The hot enclosure and intense dark of
> That brief transit: this
> The track of the missile.

The "hot enclosure and intense dark" of the Nazi's head inside the helmet strangely recall the "Hot darkness" within the fig in "Where the Slow Fig's Purple Sloth." Strangely, for what could the two possibly have in common? As flesh, both recall the collection's title, *Incarnations.* They recall as well the first of the book's two epigraphs: "'Yet now our flesh is as the flesh of our brethren.' —Nehemiah 5: 5." For the flesh of the German soldier is as the "Flesh like flame" of the fig in Warren's insistent restatements, each poem in sequence a reincarnation, a re-infleshment, of the one just read. That the bullet should pass "from left / To right," in an enjambment that forces us to remember that that is the way we read, makes us realize that that is also the way we read a sequence of poems. If it is not yet apparent that Warren is alluding to the left-to-right movement of reading, it will become so in the eighth poem in the sequence, "Myth on Mediterranean Beach: Aphrodite as Logos" (228): "From left to right, she leads the eye" in

> her transit.
>
> Commanded thus from left to right,
> As by a line of print on that bright
>
> Blankness, the eye will follow, but
>
> There is no line, the eye follows only
> That one word moving.

The "word," the "Logos" of the title, is a bikinied hunchback. But in the sequence "Island of Summer" there are words that transit from left to right, from poem to neighboring poem—words like the "hot" and "dark" that move from "Where the Slow Fig's Purple Sloth" to "Natural History."

Within a single poem that transit can also be seen. The "track of the missile" (the bullet) is soon followed by the "track of fume" from another kind of missile, the track of which is now vertical instead of horizontal, the "rocket" (quite literally a missile, though not named as such) that rises "From the next island, from its pad at / *Le centre de recherche d'engins spéciaux.*" "Island of Summer" is made up of such neighboring islands, whether we think of neighboring poems or of contiguous divisions within certain poems, such as "What Day Is." "Natural History" is another instance of that, clearly dividing itself into three distinct sections: (1) the evocation of the Saracens who died in the fight with Jean le Maingre and the reflection that the native flora (trees) and fauna (the mullet) profited from the carnage; (2) the Nazi helmet with the trace of the bullet's transit; and (3) the rocket seen rising from the next island. Sections 1 and 2 both feature remnants of war; sections 2 and 3 both feature a missile (Warren's term for the bullet).

But there are more connections than that. The bullet emerges by "exploding"; the rocket rises after "the expected explosion." The bullet is "desperate for / Light . . . after / The . . . dark" of its enclosure; the rocket "Rises beyond the earth's shadow, in / Full light aspires." That is, like the bullet that yearns for the light, is "desperate" for it, the rocket "aspires" to the "Full light" above the dark of earth's shadow (it was launched "at dusk").

Section 3 recalls section 1 as well, in at least two ways. Both are partly in French, italicized in Warren's text. "*Et les Sarrasins / se retirèrent en une isle*" and so forth for a total of six lines in section 1, the "*centre de recherche d'engins spéciaux*" in section 3. More significantly, perhaps, the conclusion drawn in section 1 that the dead gave "new luster" to the live-oak is paralleled by the assertion in section 3 that "Beauty / Is the fume-track of necessity." Though to the extent that beauty is merely an accidental byproduct of necessity, this is a reformulation of the conclusion drawn at the end of section 2: if the Nazi died a quick death it is because "history, / Like nature, may have mercy, / Though only by accident."

In the description of the rocket's flight, the way "The glitters / Of flame fall, like shreds of bright foil, ice-bright" recalls "The sawdust / Of that incessant effort, / Like filings of brass, sun-brilliant" from two poems earlier, "What Day Is." The shreds and the filings, the metallic quality of the foil and the brass, and the parallelism of "like ———— of ————" followed by a hyphenated adjectival construction pairing "bright" with "brilliant"—all this compels us to see just how close the two passages are to each other, and to realize that when Warren says that "Beauty / Is the fume-track of necessity," he is thinking not only of the fume-track of the rocket but also of the sawdust at the foot of the tree of infinity. He further alludes to "What Day Is" through the "fume-track" itself where beauty lies, as it recalls in an almost punning way the "flume-line" there that is "now not easy / To trace." This would be the irrigation channel to which the "Hewn stone footings" bear witness. There is something like a flume-line to trace as we align this one with the "track of the missile" that moved from left to right through the Nazi's flesh and the "track of fume [that] now feathers white" restated as "the fume-track of necessity." And we suddenly realize that the narrator's attempt, in the first stanza of the first poem of *Incarnations,* to trace what he knows must be there, parallels our own attempt to make sense of the text: to trace, from stanza to stanza and from poem to poem, half-hidden connections.

4. "RIDDLE IN THE GARDEN"

"My mind is intact," the narrator begins, as if in contradistinction to the Nazi with a bullet hole on either side of his helmet, "but the shapes / of the world change." Yet the more they change, the more they stay the same. For the shape he first considers in "Riddle in the Garden" (225) is the peach: "how the hot sweet- / ness of flesh and the juice-dark hug / the rough peach-pit." While the shape may change from fig to brain to peach as we move from poem to poem, the hot dark- ness remains: in the fig of "Where the Slow Fig's Purple Sloth" the "fibers relax with a sigh in that / Hot darkness, go soft." In "Natural History," the bullet is "desperate for / Light, air, and openness after / The hot enclosure and intense dark." Thesis, antithesis, synthesis:

1. The fig is in bliss, content to relax in its inwardness;

2. the bullet in the brain, by contrast, is desperate to get out;

3. the peach-flesh repeats the desperate yearning of the bullet, but what it yearns for is what the fig-flesh blessedly enjoys, to remain in its hot darkness. By contrast to the Nazi soldier, who avoided suffering because "Death / Came quick," the peach in its "suicidal yearnings . . . wants / to suffer extremely."

The second shape to be considered is the plum, which by contrast to the pit- hugging peach, intent (like the fig) on its inwardness, expands outward. On its sur- face is a "Gray bulge of fruit-skin of blister" that the narrator urges us (or himself) not to touch, for "it will burn you, a blister / will be on your finger, and you will / put the finger to your lips for relief." Relief is precisely what is sought in "Natural History," and found in the realization that beauty is the fume-track of necessity. "This thought / Is therapeutic. // If, after several / Applications, you do not find / Relief, consult your family physician." It's the realization of what the world is like, announced in the opening lines of "Natural History," that makes relief need- ful: "Many have died here, but few / Have names, it is like the world, bodies / Have been eaten by dogs, gulls, rodents, ants." And the leaf of the live-oak has gained a new luster. That beauty can come out of it is some consolation. In "Riddle in the Garden," the world and one's relation to it are very much at issue. If you touch the plum's blister you will break the skin, and "exposing that inwardness will / increase your pain, for you / are part of the world." That beauty is only an accidental con- sequence of necessity, as "Natural History" affirms, that if history or nature seems to show mercy, it is only by accident, is another way of saying what "Riddle in the Garden" declares in its final line: "The world means only itself."

5. "PAUL VALÉRY STOOD ON THE CLIFF AND CONFRONTED THE FURIOUS ENERGIES OF NATURE"

The world may mean only itself, as each poem in the sequence may mean only itself, but there is always the risk of rupture when contact is made. The plum will expose its inwardness if a finger touches its bulging blister, and a similar blister will appear on the finger that dares make contact. You may "think / I am speaking in riddles" (as the narrator says concerning the plum), but in these highly self-referential poems we touch here on the enigma of their intricate structure. The world as Warren sees it, in other words, is incarnated in these poems.

The narrator in "Riddle in the Garden" began by reporting that his "mind is intact," as the plum would remain intact if one refrained from touching it. "Paul Valéry Stood on the Cliff" (226) concludes with a report on the state of that poet's mind. It appears that his is not unaffected by his confrontation with nature (with "the World" in an earlier version of the title [701n]): "in the bright intricacies / Of wind, his mind, like a leaf, / Turns. In the sun, it glitters."

As the blister on the plum makes a blister on the finger that touches it, the world's "glitter" makes Valéry's mind glitter too. Unlike the narrator's at the beginning of "Riddle in the Garden," but like his finger if, as seems likely, he speaks from experience in his warning concerning the plum, Valéry's is no longer entirely intact. The glitter that infects his mind had appeared in stanza three: "Surf, on the Pointe du Cognet, / Boomed, and clawed white, / Like vine incessant, up / That glitter and lattice of air." The poem, like Valéry's mind, is hardly intact either, as we can see infection from "What Day Is" in "incessant" (recalling the cicadas' "incessant effort") and from "Natural History." The "clawed white" repeats the "feathers white" of the description of the track of fume the rising rock leaves; the upward movement of the surf repeats the missile's; the "glitters / Of flame" reappear in the "glitter and lattice of air."

In the next stanza, Valéry looks "far down, below / The stone where his foot hung" in a recombination of two elements from "Hewn stone, footings for what?" in "What Day Is." In this stanza and the next, the cicadas' continual sawing returns as a gull's continual scything:

> below
> The stone where his foot hung, a gull
> Wheeled white in the flame of
> Air. The white wing scythed
>
> The bright stalks of altitude
> Down, they were cut at the root,
> And the sky keeps falling down,
> Forever it falls. . . .

The stalks correspond to the tree, the root to the "tree-foot," "Forever" to "incessant," the gull to the cicadas, the scything to the sawing.

A more proximate repetition is that of the burning the plum in "The Riddle in the Garden" can cause in one who contemplates the world too directly ("do not / touch that plum, it will burn you") in the burning that afflicts Valéry's eyes after having gazed at the furious energies of nature from that cliff: "His eyes, they fly away, / They scream like gulls, and // Over Africa burn all night." He had, of course, not heeded the warning given at the beginning of the sequence: "Do not / Look too long at the sea."

6. "TREASURE HUNT"

This brief poem (227) alludes both to its immediate predecessor and to the one to which that predecessor so insistently refers: "Hunt, hunt again. . . . But . . . it / Is not under the stone at the foot / Of the garden." In "What Day Is," he came across "Hewn stone, footings"; the allusion to "Paul Valéry Stood" is more extensive, recalling not only "stone" and "foot" but also the question of what is under them: "far down, below / The stone where his foot hung, a gull." What the gull is doing beneath the stone is scything the bright stalks of altitude, repeating, as we have just seen, the work of the cicadas in "What Day Is." As the poet's attempt in that poem to trace the flume-line of which the hewn stone footings are the trace parallels the reader's attempt to trace the flume-lines and fume-tracks that crisscross the sequence, so too does the fact that he has looked "under the stone at the foot" ("I tell you this much to save you trouble, for I / Have looked, I know") parallel our looking to see what we can find under the same repeated "stone" and "foot." We have just looked there, as did Valéry, and what we found was the same thing we found at the foot of the tree in "What Day Is": day itself, nature's incessant effort in which some suffer for the sake of others, whether by cicadas or vine.

At this transition point in the sequence, it is time to start to look somewhere else. And that is precisely what the poet is about to do.

7. "MOONRISE"

For in "Moonrise" (227) the narrator for the first time speaks of other human beings occupying the same space and time as he (as opposed to the long-departed Saracens, Romans, and Moors). The scene is set on the terrace of the island's café. The "faces" of the café's clients "lift up. From the shadow / Of sockets, their eyes yearn, and / The faces, in that light, are / Washed white as bone." These people have in common with the treasure in the poem before the condition of being unknown: "We do not even / Know the names of one another." In "Treasure Hunt," the narrator had said, "I / Have looked. I know." But all he knows is where the treasure is not; he does not know where it is. Knowing will persist as a theme for two more poems. "[W]atching" the bikinied hunchback in "Myth on Mediterranean Beach," "we feel the slow knowledge grow"; in "Mistral at Night," the narrator observes that the world is like wind and leaves clashing in it, and that "This knowledge / Is the beginning of joy."

What causes the eyes of the café denizens to look up is the moon which has suddenly risen from behind a ridge: "Light, . . . / Silver, pours at us. We are / In that silence, stunned." The moon is presented as something menacing. "Some" of the café's customers "have shown more judgment. / They loll in the shadow of laurel," where they appear to have escaped the baleful effect of the moon, which "Washed white as bone" those caught in its glare. The sun in "What Day Is" has a similar laving effect; its "brightness will rinse out your eyeballs."

8. "MYTH ON MEDITERRANEAN BEACH: APHRODITE AS LOGOS"

The moon's role as the sudden cynosure of all eyes is taken over in "Myth on Mediterranean Beach" by "Aphrodite as Logos" (228): "the eye follows only / That one word moving . . . all faces turn. Look!" As the moon took away the flesh of its gazers, leaving their faces "Washed white as bone," the bikinied hunchback, "passing, draws their dreams away, / And leaves them naked to the day." Those bereft of their dreams are "the lovers, one by one," whom she passes on the beach, including "the French lad / Who exhibitionistically had // Been fondling the American college girl" but now "Loses his interest." In an earlier version of the poem, he had lost "his erection" (701n), which makes it all the more clear that in addition (because she emerges from the waves in "Botticellian parody") to being Aphrodite she is also Medusa, or an anti-Medusa who instead of turning men to stone makes them lose their hardness. Her sexuality, such as it is, is apparent: "under the belly-bulge, the flowers // Of the gee-string garland the private parts." Not only gazed upon, she gazes. "Her pince-nez glitter like contempt // For all delusion"—and it is under the force of that gaze that the French lad loses his interest. Like Medusa in the force of her gaze, she is also like her in that for a moment at least we see only her head (I am alluding to Perseus's beheading of the monster). When she reemerges from the sea that head is all we see, and then as she approaches the shore progressively the rest of her body appears: "She lifts her head, looks toward the shore. // She moves toward us, abstract and slow, / And watching, we feel the slow knowledge grow." Doubtless she is a kind of Aphrodite, emerging from the foam in a parody of the etymology of the goddess's name (from *aphros,* "foam") and of the Botticelli painting, as Warren makes explicit. But knowledge as well of her incarnation of Medusa, who haunts Warren's work because it is an integral part of his personal poetic mythology, dating back at least to the peculiar attraction of golden beeches in "Gold Glade" in *Promises* and apparent even before that in the beech-father symbol in *World Enough and Time* (see *The Taciturn Text* 114–21): the poet as Perseus, born of Danae, conceived through the gold that was Zeus's concealment, Perseus who would grow up to be the hero who successfully confronted Medusa.

Medusa for Warren represents the mother, as it does for Freud: "[I]n the myth [of Medusa] it is the genitals of the mother that are represented."[3] Freud notes that the "terror of Medusa . . . occurs when a boy . . . catches sight of the female genitals, probably those of an adult, surrounded by hair, and essentially those of his mother."[4] Indeed, if a son must kill both parents to achieve maturity, Warren's heroes slay their father by reincarnating Oedipus, beginning with Perse (as in Perseus) Munn, who finds himself at the crossroads near Thebes, Kentucky, and do in their mothers by becoming a Medusa-slaying Perseus. Warren's guilt for his mother's death is quite real and is repeatedly explored in heart-wrenching poems from the 1930s to the end of his career.

A curious but telling detail about the bikinied Medusa is her artificially gold hair: "an old / Robot pince-nez and hair dyed gold." In the only other instance of gold so far in the sequence, in "Where the Slow Fig's Purple Sloth,"

The air

> Is motionless, and the fig,
> Motionless in that imperial and blunt
> Languor of glut, swells, and inward
> The fibers relax like a sigh in that
> Hot darkness, go soft, the air
> Is gold.

The air is gold because this is a reenactment of the primal scene of the poet's conception as Perseus. The fig is, as it is in Dante (*Inferno* 25: 1–3), the cunt—or, with reference to the poet's mythological origin, the womb. Warren's fig is intensely feminine and sexual: "the fig exposes, / To the glaze of afternoon, one haunch / As purple-black as Africa." The sun who "dies" for the fig's bliss, the sun to whom she enticingly exposes her haunch, is the sky god Zeus, whose golden light is what the fig, which swells like a waiting female organ, so languorously desires. Just before this moment, the air had been motionless and the fig was too, as if they were two lovers about to embrace.

When the narrator picks up the fig and splits it open ("When you / Split the fig, you will see . . . / Flesh"), he is gazing upon what Freud thought was so petrifying about Medusa, that her frightening face, ringed by hair, is the mother's genitals. For Freud, Medusa's serpentine locks were representations of the male organ:

"The hair upon Medusa's head is frequently represented in' works of art in the form of snakes. . . . [H]owever frightening they may be in themselves, they nevertheless serve actually as a mitigation of the horror [of castration represented by the decapitation of Medusa's head], for they replace the penis, the absence of which is the cause of the horror" ("Medusa's Head" 212). By making the hunchback's hair as gold as the air that makes love to the fig (and after the swelling of sexual arousal in the vulva, what else could the sigh of the fibers' relaxation be but the moment of climax?), Warren has collapsed one episode in Perseus's story onto another, his conception and his encounter with the monster. The hair as serpents in representations of the myth and the hair as dyed gold in Warren's version (in "Myth on Mediterranean Beach") are both signs of penile potency, since for Warren gold is code for the inseminating gold from Zeus.

"Myth on Mediterranean Beach" seems almost a retelling of *Promises*' "Foreign Shore, Old Woman, Slaughter of Octopus" (122), which is yet another account of seeing an old woman on a Mediterranean beach, even if the woman is not bikinied but dressed in "peasant black." She, too, is "barefoot" and "follows her slow track . . . and does not look back" as the hunchback "turns now to take the lifeward track . . . and does not stop."

Remarkably, elements of Perseus's encounter with Medusa are present there as well, thanks to the recollection of what happened earlier that day on the beach: "All day there was picnic and laughter, / Bright eye and hair tossing, white foam and thigh-flash." Here we remember that Aphrodite was born from the waves, an event her hunchback version reenacts: "The last foam crisps about the feet. / . . . She stands complete // In Botticellian parody" ("Myth on Mediterranean Beach"). So that the thighs flashing in the foam recall that fact, while the bright eye and tossing hair may hint at the Medusa imagery to come. It will come in the slaughter of the octopus, who like Aphrodite emerges from the sea and like Medusa is uniquely horrible: "up from some cold coign and dark lair of water, / Ectoplasmic, snot-gray, the obscene of the life-wish"—obscene as Freud's interpretation is obscene, an interpretation Warren adopts and incorporates into another obscenity (at least he will in "Island of Summer" if not yet in *Promises*), that of the primal scene in which he sees himself as Perseus tracing his paternity to liquid gold, and finding to his horror (especially in "Island of Summer") yet another obscenity in the life-wish itself, for to live is inevitably to will the death of others.

"Sad tentacles weaving like prayer": here we see Medusa's writhing serpents, the hair Warren (in an earlier poem, dating after the death of his mother) saw, in a projection of guilt, piled upon his own head:

> And you have felt the live locks lift
> And coil, upon your crimeless head,

> And fled your own un-Gorgoning gift,
> As some young Gorgon might have fled
> Who, kindly yet and new in horror,
> By the dawn's first light had leaned to peer
> At love, and learned her mortifying power. ("Goodbye" 29)

The "un-Gorgoning gift" I interpret as the gift Perseus alone of all men had, the ability to un-Medusa Medusa, to ward off her gaze (by the mirror of Athena's shield) and destroy her. That the "mortifying power" is that of "love" suggests that for Warren even in 1941 (date of this poem's publication) Medusa's essence was sexual. Medusa in the *Promises* poem is shared between the old woman and the octopus in whom, as Victor Strandberg points out, she sees herself: "[T]he old woman in black . . . herself near death, sees in the slaughter of the octopus a portent of her own extinction: 'She knows, as the sea, that what came will recur'" (*A Colder Fire* 214).

The about-to-be slaughtered octopus has "eyes wide to glare-horror of day-wash, / The nightmare was spread out on stone. Boys yelled at the knife flash." We are not told who kills the octopus, but the knife suggests the blade with which Perseus put an end to the open-eyed nightmare that turned men into stone. To make the story personal, to set it within his private Perseid, Warren lets it unfold beneath a yellow sky: "Saffron-saddening the mountain, the sun / Sinks" (not unlike the golden light in which "The sun dies" in "Where the Slow Fig's Purple Sloth").

The black-garbed woman in the *Promises* poem is another instance of the mysterious passing stranger, as we have seen in realizing her continuities with the trespasser in "Dark Night of" (123). So too is the old woman on the beach in the poem in *Incarnations,* who after her immersion into and reemergence from the sea continues her solitary journey, treading "the track the blessèd know // To a shore far lonelier than this." The narrator watches her disappear as he did the tramp in "Dark Night of": "I stood there alone / To stare down the lane where he'd gone. . . . / On a track no man would have planned. . . . / He moves in joy past contumely of stars or insolent indifference of the dark air." In "Vermont Ballad: Change of Seasons" in *Rumor Verified* (467), the passing stranger is glimpsed again: "I go to the windowpane . . . // And stare up the mountain track / Till I see in the rain-dusk, trudging / With solid stride, his bundle on back, // A man with no name . . . / On an errand I cannot guess." The woman on the beach bears the hump on her back as a tramp his bundle: "Bearing her luck upon her back, / She turns now to take the lifeward track."

At the midpoint of the sequence, eighth of the fifteen poems in "Island of Summer," "Myth on Mediterranean Beach" is a veritable crossroads of intersecting Warren themes. The hunchback in a bikini is in addition to the mysterious stranger, Medusa, and Aphrodite Anadyomene (in earlier versions of the title [701n]), Logos: "That one word moving . . . in lonely // And absolute arrogance across the blank // Page of the world." The word on the beach recalls the footprints the young protagonist of "Blackberry Winter" liked to leave in the mud so that he could pretend it was Friday's footprint left on the beach and he was Robinson Crusoe (in a short story in which he would also encounter the mysterious passing stranger in the form of a menacing tramp with a knife). Though he cheated by making the marks himself, we can see that like the narrator of the poem he is eager to find a message to read on nature's blank page. As he is in "Aspen Leaf in Windless world," in *Being Here:* "Look how sea-foam, thin and white, makes its Arabic scrawl / On the unruffled sand of the beach's faint-tilted plane. / Is there a message there for you to decipher? / Or only the joy of its sunlit, intricate rhythm?" (430). Like the Arabic scrawl on the beach, the hunchback on the beach looks like writing: "From left to right she leads the eye / . . . from left to right, / As by a line of print on that bright / Blankness."

As I indicated when considering the precursor "Natural History" provides of this left-to-right transit (the bullet that pierced the Nazi helmet but which did not openly advertise its textuality in the way the hunchback does), that directionality imitates not only the way we read English (if not Arabic) but also the way Warren leads us to read "Island of Summer," following the word that moves from left to right, from poem to poem. The eye itself that is led from left to right in "Myth on Mediterranean Beach" is one of those left-to-right moving words, as the eyes of the people on the café terrace had had their attention caught by the sudden moonlight. As had their faces ("the faces . . . / From shadow lift up"), reappearing when the hunchback appears and "all faces turn."

9. "MISTRAL AT NIGHT"

Another word the sequence invites us to follow is "knowledge." Watching the hunchback arise from the waves, "we feel the slow knowledge grow // How from the breasts the sea recedes," and so on through the catalog of her emerging anatomy. In "Mistral at Night" (230), another kind of knowledge is presented for our consideration:

> the world
> Is like wind, and the leaves clash. Their knowledge
> Is the beginning of joy. I
>
> Tell you this as explicitly as I can, for
> Some day you may find the information
> Of crucial importance.

But how explicit is this telling? To understand the business about the wind and the leaves we will need to pay attention to what he says about them earlier in the poem: "In shadow / Of laurel the clash of the dry leaf." But even this seems less than helpful until we hearken to the echo these lines make to a passage from two poems before: "Some, / However, have shown more judgment. / They loll in the shadow of laurel" ("Moonrise"). Those with sufficient judgment to take refuge in the laurel's shadow appear to have escaped the moonlight and its power to wash faces white as bone. But "Mistral at Night" lets us know that there is no safety there either, for the wind's reach, if not the moon's (besides, in "Mistral at Night" the "moonlight" is "To tatters torn" by that wind), extends to the shadow of laurel.

That clash "is / In your sleep, and is as / Unforgettable as what is most deeply / Forgotten" ("Mistral at Night"). Warren's sequences are constructed in such a way that they can re-create in the reader a sense of déjà vu, that they can make the reader undergo the process of forgetting and remembering. Such phrases as "in the shadow of laurel" are planted in the reader's consciousness, then forgotten, then recalled a poem or two (or more) later, where they most likely engender the dimmest of recollections. Another way of putting it, a way Warren encourages, is to say that his sequences re-create the experience of dreaming in our sleep of what we think we remember: "In your sleep . . . that, oh, / Will be the last thing remembered, at last, in / That instant before remembering is over. But what / Is it? You must wait // To find out" ("Mistral at Night"). Another way of conceiving it, as he does in the lines above, is that it is like living a life as a gradually unrolling spool of memories, one after another, like what we see on a page as our eyes make their continuous transit from to left to right. The "instant before remembering is over" is one's last moment on earth. Warren will ask the question again in "Aspen Leaf in Windless World" (430):

> What image—behind blind eyes when the nurse steps back—
> Will loom at the end of your own life's long sorites?
> Would a sun then rise red on an eastern horizon of waters?
> Would you see a face? What face? Would it smile? Can you say?
>
> Or would it be some great, sky-thrusting gray menhir?
> Or what, in your long-lost childhood, one morning you saw—
> Tinfoil wrappers of chocolate, popcorn, nut shells, and poorly
> Cleared up, the last elephant turd on the lot where the circus had been?

Of the images proposed here, the first three seem some hoped-for revelation, something perhaps God could provide as an answer to the riddle of existence. But the last of these candidates for last image is something more consonant with what "Mistral at Night" had already proposed, not just an image but an image remembered. Moving forward while looking back is typically Warrenesque. That is how he arranged his four self-selected anthologies (the *Selected Poems* of 1943, 1966, 1975, and 1985), in what he appropriately termed "anti-chronological order" (724n), from most recent to earliest. In these collections, the "great, sky-thrusting gray menhir" of "Aspen Leaf in Windless World" reveals itself to be a remembered thing, too, the "cromlech . . . the taciturn tall stone" that looms up in what is consistently the last poem, and thus "the last thing remembered," in these self-selected anthologies, "To a Face in the Crowd."

10. "THE IVY"

Both "The Ivy" (231) and "Mistral at Night" are about sleep and dreams and what is going on outside one's bedroom window. The "wind-thrust" of the mistral does damage to moonlight and clouds and makes the laurel leaves clash; the ivy "assaults the wall," vowing to pull it down. "You sleep. What is your dream?" the narrator of "The Ivy" asks, echoing the question "What is it?" that the narrator of "Mistral at Night" asked, referring to the "last thing remembered" that "is / In your sleep, and is as / Unforgettable as what is most deeply / Forgotten." But what is also "In your sleep" is the class of the dry leaf in the laurel that the wind stirs up. It's as if the last thing remembered is somehow the same thing as what is heard during sleep, the force of the mistral. As Warren would later remark, in "Dream" from *Now and Then* (353), "I have read in a book that dream is the mother of memory." In "Dream of a Dream" (353), which follows "Dream" in that sequence, he speaks of how what is heard outside one's bedroom window influences what one dreams:

> Moonlight stumbles with bright heel
> In the stream, and the stones sing.
> What they sing is nothing, nothing,
> But the joy Time plies to feel
> In fraternal flux and glimmer
> With the stream that does not know
> Its destination and knows no
> Truth but its own moonlight shimmer.
> In my dream Time and water interflow,
> And bubbles of consciousness glimmer ghostly as they go.

The ivy in "The Ivy" is as single-minded as the stream that knows in truth but its own moonlit shimmer: "like the sea / it dreams a single dream, it / is its own dream. Therefore, // Peace is the dream's name." One could say that the ivy has the purity of heart that Kierkegaard defines as to will one thing. "Time / is nothing to the ivy" in the sense that it is infinitely patient and active, its long-term assault on the wall paralleling the "incessant effort" of the cicadas sawing the tree in "What Day Is" and the "incessant" ascent of the surf in "Paul Valéry Stood." Time is nothing to the ivy in another sense, that the ivy is just not in Time's realm, like the sea as defined in "Myth on Mediterranean Beach": "that realm where no Time may subsist." The bikinied hunchback goes into that realm when, "moved by memory in the blood," she "Enters that vast indifferency / Of perfection that we call the sea" and "lingers there / . . . , somnambulist." She becomes one with the vast indifferency of nature.

11. "WHERE PURPLES NOW THE FIG"

The harsh light of day returns, after two nighttime poems, and in some respects things are reversed. The stone in the poem before ("The Ivy") was impervious to the stars—"the stone, / where no stars may come"—if not to the ivy; but now nothing can stay the effect of the sun—"the sun, it would / Burn our bones to chalk" (231)—except the protection fig leaves might afford. As the skin may serve as protective integument against the force of the sun, the fig leaf protects the fig from both the sun and another kind of whitening: "a leaf hangs / Down, and on it, gull-droppings, white / As chalk, show, for the sun has // Burned all white." There is a parallel between this poem and the one that precedes it in that the ivy is to the stone wall as the fig leaf is to the fig and the skin to the bones it covers. In the same way that the skin keeps sunlight from penetrating to the bones, and the ivy keeps one whiteness or another from getting to the fig, the ivy that covers the stones keeps the starlight away: "all night the stone, / where no stars may come, dreams."

The reversal is that that which covers the stones thereby assaults them, while that which covers the bones affords them protection.

12. "THE RED MULLET"

The first words of "The Red Mullet" (231)—"The fig flames inward on the bough"—announce its continuity with "Where Purples Now the Fig," where our attention was drawn to "the fig, flame in / Its inmost flesh." As if still seeking to escape the denuding light of the sun, which only the frail integument of skin kept from burning our bones to chalk, the narrator now seeks out a place "Where no light may // Come," a striking restatement of the phrase "where no stars may come" that in "The Ivy" described the condition the stones were in on account of the ivy that covered them. The precision of the repetition lends weight, I think, to the parallel I proposed between ivy and leaf (and skin), stones and bones (and fig).

That lightless place is underwater, in the black shadow of the shoal where the mullet, "he the great one, like flame, burns." We briefly met him in "Natural History," where like the laurel and the live-oak he profits from the "Many" who "have died here" (his "mouth" was "agape"); now we get to know him better. He is "merciless as / Genghis, motionless and mogul," clearly male.

Yet he bears some resemblance to the bikinied hunchback, that "old / Robot with pince-nez and hair dyed gold," especially about the eyes. "Her pince-nez glitter like contempt // For all delusion." His eye is similarly stern: "he sees and does not / Forgive." Physically, there is some commonality as well: "the eye of / The mullet is . . . ringed like a target / In gold, vision is armor." The woman's eyes are ringed too, by her pince-nez, which, with its contemptuous glitter, counteracts the vulnerability to ridicule to which he would otherwise fall victim because of her appearance: "The breasts hang down like saddle-bags, / To balance the hump the belly sags." For her, as for the mullet, "vision"—her contemptuous, glittering gaze—"is armor."

Yet the mullet—"he, the great one"—is as male as the hunchback is female. Gold is the sign of the father's potency, and the mullet bears it around his eyes. The gold the hunchback has is not her own, for her hair is dyed. As Danae's, the mother, the stain of coloration could be conceived of as coming from the gold of the father; while the hair of Medusa, who the hunchback also is, is a coil of "live locks" (as in the poem "Goodbye" 29), writhing serpents incarnating the power to father.

13. "A PLACE WHERE NOTHING IS"

"I have been in a place where / nothing is" (232), and that place is evidently a version of where he has just been, the watery depths in which he had been conferring with the mullet. In this place "nothing- / ness presses on the ribs," which is not surprising as he had said in "The Red Mullet" that "I / . . . dive deep to develop my lung-case, I am / Familiar with the agony of will in the deep place . . . as oxygen fails." Of course, the nothingness that presses against his ribs is something more than water. It is, strangely, a place where "there are voices," a statement difficult to understand unless we keep it in mind when we read, two poems later in "The Leaf," that when the cicada ceases he can hear his father's voice. One poem helps us interpret another, and Warren is precise with his placement of words, especially when they are fairly close together in a sequence. I would suggest that there is a connection between the father's voice in "The Leaf" and the voices here, and that the reason this place is "populated with nothingness" is that it is peopled with the dead. The father glimpsed in the mullet is among them.

14. "MASTS AT DAWN"

In "What Day Is," the first poem of "Island of Summer," the narrator told us not to look too long at the sea. "A Place Where Nothing Is" concludes by contravening that admonition: "I retract my words, for / the brightness of that nothing- / ness which is the sea is / not nothingness, but is / like the inestimable sea of // Nothingness Plotinus dreamed." "Masts at Dawn" (233) continues this embrace of the sea: "When there is a strong swell, you may, if you surrender to it, experience / A sense, in the act, of mystic unity with that rhythm. Your peace is the sea's will." Such an acceptance of the sea's will may be at odds with the narrator's familiarity "with the agony of will" when diving underwater, but it is in harmony with his statement in "The Ivy" linking the sea with peace ("like the sea / [the ivy] dreams a single dream. . . . / Peace is the dream's name").

As in the poem that immediately precedes it, the sea in "Masts at Dawn" is a place where a certain nothingness is: "the bay-face is glossy in darkness, like // An old window pane flat on black ground. . . . It neither / Receives nor gives light." There has been no light in one way or another for three consecutive poems:

Where no light may come. ("The Red Mullet")

A lamp / by each bed burns, but / gives no light. ("A Place Where Nothing Is")

It neither / Receives nor gives light. ("Masts at Dawn")

The overlap is striking: "no light" in the first and second, "gives no light" / "nor gives light" in the second and third.

Given the many echoes in these poems, we listen intently when the narrator speaks of echoes, as he does in "A Place Where Nothing Is": "there is, in that / land of nothingness, / no echo, for the dark has / no walls, or if there is echo, / it is, whatever the original / sound, a laugh." That there are no walls in the land of nothingness will itself have an echo in *Incarnations,* in the line "The cans, they have no doors" ("can" here meaning latrine) that makes its own echo, appearing four times in the first poem in the next sequence, "Penological Study: Southern Exposure." Poems in a sequence have no walls to bounce anything off of if we forget that they are in a sequence (or, in this instance, in a book composed of sequences). But being in a sequence, the "no light" of one poem can be deflected by the "no light" of the one next to it.

In any case, the conversion in the land of nothingness of any echo into a laugh reminds us that whatever appears twice is never quite the same the second time as the first, indeed the second appearance may (as I show in *The Braided Dream*) ironize, even parody the first. The mullet, "he the great one" who, "like flame, burns" in the darkness of the shoal, gets transformed in "A Place Where Nothing Is" into "A lamp" that "by each bed runs, but / gives no light," which may mean he has lost any power to give off light. And in "Masts at Dawn" he is further degraded, when his "eye" which had been "round, bulging" and quite menacing in its unwillingness to forgive reappears as "a slight convexity only . . . like // An eyelid, in darkness, closed" formed on the bay's surface by the corpse of a drowned cat. While the lamp that like the mullet burns but which gives no light becomes the window pane on a black background that "neither / Receives nor gives light."

15. "THE LEAF"

In "The Leaf" (234), the eye, round and bulging in the mullet, the slight convexity of an eyelid when it was a drowned cat, is now the soaring hawk's, for whom "the world is a metaphor, his eye / Sees, white, the flicker of hare-scut, the movement of vole." The narrator sees this as he lies down, supine, on a "High place." Beneath his back are the remnants of what the hawk has preyed upon and eaten, "The clutter of annual bones, of hare, vole, bird, white / As chalk from sun and season, frail / As the dry grass stem." The comparison to chalk recalls the fear he expressed in "Where Purples Now the Fig" that the sun would burn our bones to chalk; the image of dry grass stems looks back to "Paul Valéry Stood," where the gull's wing "scythed // The bright stalks of altitude / Down," making them fall down with a "clatter like glass," that clatter anticipating the clutter of grass-fragile bones in "The Leaf."

His lying down in that place, almost like Prometheus chained to his rock awaiting the raptor that will tear out his liver, almost as if he were becoming one with the hawk's victims, awaiting the moment when the hawk will swoop down on him and make him a victim too, parallels his lying down in "Masts at Dawn": "I lie in my bed and think how, in darkness, the masts go white." There too, lying down was the enactment of the effort to accept the world as it is, the "try // To love so well the world that we may believe, in the end, in God."

That stunning line, which seems so conclusive and does conclude "Masts at Dawn," is shown by what happens in "The Leaf" to be a less than final word. There is a moment in "The Leaf" that comes close to replicating this desire to accept and love the world for what it is, but it appears not to have been very satisfactory: "I / Have opened my mouth to the wind of the world like wine, I wanted // To taste what the world is, wind dried up / The live saliva of my tongue, my tongue / Was like a dry leaf in my mouth." This is recounted in the past tense, in the second section of the poem; the other three sections are cast in the present. That second section is a retrospective look at what the narrator has been doing on this summer island. "I // Have watched the deployment of ants." (Does this refer to a poem that didn't make the final cut? The only other allusion to ants appears in "Natural History" in a list of the creatures who have eaten the many who "have died here."). "I / Have conferred with the flaming mullet in a deep place." Then he remembers going to the high place where he lay down on the remnants of the hawk's meals.

The concern that inhabits the greater part of "The Leaf" is guilt, shame, and the fear of exposure: "The hand, // To hide me from the blaze of the wide world, drops, / Shamefast, down. I am / What is to be concealed." There was a hint of this in "Masts at Dawn": "the stars . . . withdraw into a new distance, have discovered our unworthiness." But the stars are discreet; realizing our unworthiness, they have the grace to withdraw. The blaze of the world, however, shows no sign of going away.

The narrator is quite specific about the source of his shame: "To this spot I bring my grief. / Human grief is the obscenity to be hidden by the leaf." Strandberg identifies the grief as the sorrow that comes from the realization that one must kill to live in the world: "The major cause of grief . . . is the naturalistic evidence of death. . . . This is the design of incarnations—a running sacrifice of the world's flesh that the one life may continue" (*The Poetic Vision* 100). I agree. That realization is what the narrator learned from watching the ants, conferring with the mullet, and discovering the hawk's boneyard.

But there is another nuance to his shame, inescapable because the hand that covers it is a fig leaf like that with which our first parents covered their nakedness: "the leaf / Of the fig five fingers has, the fingers / Are . . . innocent—but of a hand." Warren intensifies the sexual undercurrent by projecting his personal poetic mythology onto the fig in "Where the Slow Fig's Purple Sloth," turning it into Danae brought to bliss by the sun's golden light. Consequently, when the poet tells us "I lurk / In the shadow of the fig. . . . // To this spot I bring my grief," he is taking refuge in his mother's arms.

In the third section of "The Leaf," we encounter liquid gold: "The world is fruitful. . . . / The plum . . . bursts . . . the gold ooze has striven / Outward, it wants again to be of / The goldness of air and—oh—innocent." The adverb "again" informs us that the gold ooze inside the fruit had originally come from the gold of air. This is entirely consistent with the interpretation I have been proposing, that the gold of air is Zeus's inseminating fluid. Warren makes the connection between the ooze's desire to return to its source to regain an original innocence and the narrator's desire to return to his ultimate origin quite explicit: "The world // Is fruitful, and I, too, / In that I am the father / Of my father's father's father."

It is an extraordinary resolution of the problem complained of in the first section of the poem. If the shame is the human grief at the obscenity of having been born into a natural world where one must profit from the dead in order to live (as have dogs, gulls, rodents, ants, fish, laurel, live-oak, and mullet), then how better to disinculpate oneself than to reverse the sequence of Time? It's like going back to Eden before the Fall.

Marshall Walker criticized this "principle of retroactive fatherhood" as being something for which "Warren does not adequately prepare us. . . . [H]is vision seems merely whimsical, unearned" (164). Yet Warren has been preparing us for it all along, by writing poems that continually cast a backward glance, and has been preparing us for it in the lines that immediately precede these, by speaking of the plum's gold ooze's desire to return to its origins and reclaim its innocence.

But there is another desire at work in the narrator's assertion of retroactive paternity. It is paternity itself that he desires, to outfather his father by becoming his father's ancestral progenitor. Calvin Bedient's comment on the line is relevant here: "the son is 'the father / Of [his] father's father's father': he has inherited the male principle. His one hope—mythic—is to become himself a hawk . . . faultlessly chaste in unexhausted potency" (168). "The hawk is both father and son, in a crackling synthesis" (167).

The narrator of "The Leaf" goes on to make another claim: "I, / Of my father, have set the teeth on edge." We are now two steps beyond the quest for lost innocence first expressed by the plum's ooze. The first of these was the assertion of retroactive paternity. The second is, far from a quest for innocence, an assertion of guilt. The reference is to Jeremiah 31:29: "The fathers have eaten sour grapes, and the children's teeth are set on edge." In that passage, those words are preceded by "In those days they shall no longer say:" and followed by "But every one shall die for his own sin; each man who eats sour grapes, his teeth shall be set on edge" (Jer. 31:29–30). But Warren rejects the prophet's new dispensation, preferring guilt to innocence, as long as it is guilt by blood—or, in his reversal of the father-child relation, by paternity.

"But / By what grape? I have cried out in the night." The guilt is real and anguishing. The son has hurt the father, in some unfathomable way. Not perhaps until the publication of Warren's *Portrait of a Father* in 1988 might we get some inkling of why. In that memoir of his father, he tells of his discovery of the poems his father had written in his younger years, before he started a family, and of his father's discomfort at the discovery; he tells, too, of showing one of his own first poems to his father, a poem he signed "Penn Warren," omitting the first name they shared. "Then . . . he asked me whether I did not like the name 'Robert.' With an instant of shame—it must have been shame—I remembered that he had once signed his full name" (63).

His cry in the night is answered. "From a further garden, from the shade of another tree, / My father's voice, in the moment when the cicada ceases, has called to me." These lines reach back to the poem before, "Masts at Dawn," to the calling of another voice: "It is long since // The owl, in the dark eucalyptus, dire and melodious, last called." The owl's voice is the father's, and not only because it called "from the shade of another tree"—the eucalyptus. Like the hawk, the owl is a raptor, appetite incarnate: "the last of night's voices is heard— / The owl's mystic question that follows his glut" (from "On Into the Night," in *Being Here* [415]). It is the father as desire, lacking the nobility of the high-flying hawk. When he calls in "Masts at Dawn" the owl is paired, through an anaphoric "long since," with those who satisfy their lust in other ways:

> It is long since
>
> The owl, in the dark eucalyptus, dire and melodious, last called, and
>
> Long since the moon sank and the English
> Finished fornicating in their ketches.

The interval in "The Leaf" in which the father's voice may be heard, "the moment when the cicada ceases," reaches all the way back to the first poem in the sequence, to the cicada in "What Day Is" whose effort was "incessant." That that "incessant effort " should finally "cease," if only for a moment, provides some closure to the sequence, allowing the last poem to revise the first. It's as if only the father's voice can break through the otherwise overwhelming song of the natural world.

"II. INTERNAL INJURIES"

"I. Island of Summer" is followed in *Incarnations* by "II. Internal Injuries," which is divided into two sequences, *Penological Study: Southern Exposure,* consisting of seven poems, and *Internal Injuries,* comprising eight. Thus the title of the second sequence is also the title of the whole. This is appropriate, as internal injuries are important in both: the ravages of the cancer growing inside the convict Jake in the first section and those suffered by the black woman hit by a car in the second. To minimize the confusion that can arise from the same title applying to two different entities, I will do what Warren does in the table of contents (but which John Burt does not do in his edition of the *Collected Poems*): give the titles of the sequences (*Penological Study* and *Internal Injuries*) in italics and refer to the title of the second section of *Incarnations* which is made up of these two sequences as "II. Internal Injuries" (though of course Warren did not include the quotation marks). The narrator of *Penological Study* is visiting a state penitentiary, for reasons not entirely clear. James Blotner writes that Brainard Cheney, to whom with Frances Cheney the poem is dedicated, had once witnessed an execution as a reporter (Blotner 543n). Blotner also records that Warren explained in a letter to Allen Tate that *Penological Study* is based on his recollection of a visit he made to the penitentiary in Eddyville, Kentucky: "I saw, in the infirmary, an old coot on the can. He was dying of gut cancer, I was told, but had the half-delusion that if he could crap it out he would be cured. So he spent all the time possible there, groggy with morphine" (Blotner 543n).

"Tomorrow Morning" (237), the second poem in the sequence, could be read as the narrator's vicarious living out of the moment of electrocution, as Strandberg does (*The Poetic Vision* 101), citing the lines "Truth will embrace you with tentacles like an octopus. It / Will suck your blood through a thousand suction cups." But Jake is not under any death sentence other than the one his illness will enforce. He has been imprisoned for "nigh forty years" already ("Keep That Morphine Moving, Cap" 236).

As Warren explained to Tate, Jake is glimpsed on the toilet, focused on what is "inside his gut," the "pumpkin [that] grows and grows." For his part, the narrator finds that "meaning / In my guts blooms like / A begonia"—a striking instance of sympathetic suffering, except for the fact that it takes place in response not to the convict's inner turmoil but to the internal injuries endured by the woman in the other sequence ("The World Is a Parable" 246).[5] But as the narrator of *Penological Study* asserts, "we are all // One flesh." The narrator in both sequences is of one flesh with the dying person who has accidentally come into his field of vision, though in both he tries to escape that fact. It is also a truth emblazoned as an epigraph to *Incarnations*: "Yet now our flesh is as the flesh of our brethren. — Nehemiah 5:5." Poetically, the two sequences presented under the title "II. Internal Injuries" approach the state of being of one flesh, too, given the parallels in their narrative outline and their shared images and language.

Apart from her race, relative age, and sex, the first detail the narrator gives of the traffic victim in *Internal Injuries* is "a sizeable hole (as / I can plainly see, you being flat on the ground) in / The sole of a shoe" ("The Event" 242). Early in the first poem of the other sequence, we are brought to see "A black hole" in Jake's white face which is the mouth from which the words kept coming, "Jest keep that morphine moving, Cap." A more extensive instance appears in the first poem of the first sequence and the fourth of the second. In "Keep That Morphine Moving, Cap," sweat drips from Jake's head "And each drop glittered as it fell. . . . // Each drop upon that gray cement / Exploded like a star." The glittering and exploding drops of perspiration are the objective correlative of his suffering, exuded from his body as he strains with the effort of expelling through excretion the cancer that is destroying him from within. They are paralleled in the other sequence by glittering and exploding screams from the injured woman that become, in the narrator's imagination, liquid: "The scream floats up . . . like a / Soap bubble . . . it glitters / Above the city . . . it / Explodes and over the city a bright mist / Descends of—microscopically—spit" ("The Only Trouble" 244).[6] There are screams, too, in *Penological Study*. A congress of long-haired comets "will be convened screaming" in "Night Is Personal" (240) and "metaphors will scream in the shared glory of their referents" in "Tomorrow Morning." The latter is an evocatively self-referential statement, for screams are shared among multiple referents—comets, the injured woman, and the metaphors themselves.

That metaphors will scream in the shared glory of their referents prompts the narrator in "Tomorrow Morning" to ask, "Does this suggest the beginning of a new life for us all?" He returns to that thought in the other sequence, in "The World Is a Parable": "There comes a time for us all when we want to begin a new life." We should note that it is not only the possibility of a new life that recurs, but the phrase "for us all" as well.

"Truth lives / Only in relation," as the narrator of the second sequence asserts in "Be Something Else" (246). What is this truth and what is the relation? In the immediate context of "Be Something Else," it is the relation between the narrator and the woman in the street. In the context of the two sequences titled "II. Internal Injuries," the relation is a complex and subtle interplay that sends us back and forth between the two, searching for what truth beyond the immediately anecdotal might emerge from their relation.

And then there is the larger context of the relation of these two sequences to *Incarnations* as a whole, including the "Island of Summer" sequence, in which the narrator encounters a combination of Medusa and Danae in the old hunchback on the beach. Remembering how those myths coalesced in that striking figure, we are in a position to understand the deeper truth hidden in the encounter with the old woman in *Internal Injuries*. She too is Danae—and Medusa.

As Perseus knew to look at Medusa only indirectly, through her reflection in Athena's shield, the narrator looks at the accident victim only through the eyes of other onlookers: "Sidewalk superintendents turn now / From their duties and at you stare, // While I, sitting in my taxi, / Watch them watching you" ("Her Hat" 243). Their eyes serve as an intervening reflective surface.[7] Yet in the lines that follow, he seems to protest too much, letting us know how much he is torn between wanting to look and the realization that he shouldn't: "for I . . . // Am no Peeping

Tom with my // Own face pressed directly to the / Window of your pain." The "with" is delicately ambiguous: is his face indeed pressed to the passenger window of his cab and yet he is no Peeping Tom? Or is he no voyeur because his face is not pressed to the window? He goes on to describe with such intensity what he would have seen had he been looking that it becomes increasingly likely he was looking—though through what protection the taxi's passenger window glass could afford: "to peer // Deep in your inward darkness, waiting, / With slack-jawed and spit-wet leer, // For what darkling gleam, and spasm, / Visceral and pure, like love." That "inward darkness" recalls the "inward . . . / Hot darkness" within the fig's flesh in "Where the Slow Fig's Purple Sloth" in "Island of Summer," the fibers of which relaxed in sexual bliss—flesh identifiable with both Medusa and Danae. It is thus both "visceral" and something "like love." In a section deleted from *Internal Injuries* before publication, we can glimpse a certain indecency in what the narrator sees: "why do you / Lie so indecently askew? / If only you would real- ize / How little aesthetic value's in rag garters and old black thighs."[8]

Even if he abandons the safety of others' eyes and thus departs from the mytho- logical model, there are other, more literal, mirrors that evoke the one Perseus used to escape being transfixed by what he saw. In "The Event," the first poem in the *Internal Injuries* sequence, the narrator addresses the woman: "look / In the mir- ror, that / Is you." When her scream turns into a glittering soap bubble floating above the city, it becomes a mirror: "on its bottom side all the city is / Accurately reflected, making allowance / For curvature, upside-down, iridescent as / A dream" ("The Only Trouble").

So the mirror from the myth is there, in more than one disguise. So, too, the decapitation—transformed into the detail of her hat, the very next thing to catch his eye after he stares at her inward darkness: "Look! your hat's right under a truck wheel. / It's lucky traffic can't yet move" ("Her Hat"). The misplaced hat, about to be destroyed, seems a substitute for the detachable head. Cutting a woman's throat, as Perseus did, is as it happens the very crime that put Jake in the pen. He "couldn't now remember why / He had cut her throat" ("Keep That Morphine").

In his novel *A Place to Come To* (1977) Warren will again transform an old woman knocked down on a busy street into Medusa, and this time the allusion could not be more explicit: "The motor traffic was heavy. . . . I was vaguely aware of . . . a female figure, clearly old, a classic shape. . . . I was almost unaware of the listing and heaving patch of blackness going forward, in and out of blackness. But suddenly, in the deepest patch of blackness, I did sense an agitation. . . . I saw the glint of a blade from the youth struggling for the purse" (386). He tries to stop the attacker and is wounded in the effort. "Then I was lying on the pavement, and my last vision, before fading out, just at the moment when traffic was halted by a light ahead, was of the taller of the two assailants . . . as he seemed to drift with ineffable, slow, floating godlike grace . . . to the hood of the nearest halted automobile to stand beautifully balanced there with the purse—like Medusa's head hanging from the hand of Cellini's Perseus" (387)

Many of the details are the same: the stopped traffic, the old woman as the essence of blackness (in the novel, she is "clad in black and topped by a shapeless black hat" [386], a moving "patch of blackness"; in the poem, her skin is black, and the narrator is drawn to peer deep in her "inward darkness"). Another similarity emerges from the aftermath. In the hospital, the woman dies under the illusion that the narrator is her son, who in reality is "in the pen somewhere" (389). So, too, is the son of the woman in *Internal Injuries:* "your son / Upriver, at least now you know / Where he is" ("The Event"). In the novel, the narrator does not disabuse her of her certainty that he is her son, as she dies clasping his hand. "The impression was still current [among the hospital staff] that the old lady was my mother, and I was rapidly approaching the stage of physical exhaustion and emotional confusion when I would plead guilty to anything, even sonhood" (388). In the absence of the actual son, "absent on business at San Quentin" (389), he will assume the filial duty of arranging for her funeral.

Putting these two stories together, as the intricate unity of Warren's oeuvre demands we do, compels us to see not only Medusa in the woman in the New York City street but also the mother. But of course for Warren, as for Freud, Medusa *is* the mother.

Medusa's long hair does not appear in the sequence about the traffic victim but does in *Penological Study,* in the form of the "screaming" comets with "Long hair" ("Night Is Personal"). Their screaming links them to the woman whose metronomic screams the narrator finds unbearable ("For God's sake stop that yelling!" ["Be Something Else"]). Screaming is shared, for "metaphors will scream in the shared glory of their referents" ("Tomorrow Morning"). In the next line (the one Strandberg reads as alluding to an electrocution), "Truth will embrace you with tentacles like an octopus" ("Tomorrow Morning"). In the immediate context, that "truth" is the one that is in the poem just before Jake had hoped would not be true ("only / In such a posture . . . can he / . . . half believe . . . / That the truth will not be true" ["Keep That Morphine"]), and the truth that emerges from relation here is what connects this octopus with the one in "Foreign Shore, Old Woman, Slaughter of Octopus" in *Promises.* That was the octopus that evoked Medusa's serpentine locks through its "Sad tentacles weaving like prayer," and that succumbed (like the old woman in black on the Chicago street in *A Place to Come To*) to a youth's "knife-flash."

Jake the convict is connected to his mother, in the peculiar focus Warren's narrator applies, through hair—though it is his own. In a flashback to his boyhood, he came to supper late, his hair still wet from swimming in the creek against her express command. "If out of a dire suspicion / She hadn't touched his hair and / Found it yet damp at the roots," she "might never have fetched him that / Awful whack" ("Wet Hair: If Now His Mother Should Come" 237).[9] Afterward, "She / Stood there and tried to think she / Was *somebody else*. But / Wasn't, so // Put him to bed without supper." But actually, in a subtle instance of self-referential metafictionality, Warren at this moment allows her to come very close to getting her wish, for in the other sequence the narrator implores the injured black woman to "Be *something else*, be something / That is not what it is" ("Be Something Else"). In ways beyond their knowing, the two women, one white and the other black, though both mothers (of penal inmates, as events develop), intersect, outside of time and circumstance but within the web of Warren's poem. They become for an instant interchangeable, each becoming somebody or something else—namely, each other.

Warren links them as well by setting up parallels between Jake and the man who knocked down the woman with his car. Each receives a punishing blow— Jake from his mother, the driver from a policeman for trying to leave the scene of the accident. "The spic has blood over one eye. He had tried to run away. / He will not try again, and in that knowledge his face is as calm as congealing bacon grease" ("The Jet Must Be Hunting for Something" 244). The focus on "his face" and the congealing grease recall details of the scene from Jake's childhood: "he was late, / With supper near over now . . . and grease / Gone gray on the forks." She "fetched him that awful whack. His face / In the lamplight was white" ("Wet Hair").

Like Medusa's victims who were transfixed by her gaze, so too is the narrator at risk: "Just now, when I looked at you," he addresses the traffic victim, "I had the distinct impression that you were staring me straight in the eye, and / Who wants to be a piece of white paper filed for eternity on the sharp point of a filing spindle?" ("The Jet Must Be Hunting for Something"). Hugh Ruppersburg reads this as if it were the woman who was transfixed on the spindle: "These are Baudelairean poems of city as nightmare . . . a place of annihilation which reduces the human essence to a statistic in the city bureau of records, 'a piece of white paper filed for eternity on the sharp point of a filing spindle.' The woman is virtually stripped of identity, and any human context" (110). But such an interpretation is possible only if the woman is stripped of the mythological context Warren has gone to such lengths to provide her. The narrator's reformulation a few lines later, by reminding us that that which is transfixed is white and adding the detail that that which transfixes is black, suggests that a white Perseus fully recognizes the danger present in a black Medusa's piercing gaze: "Nobody wants to be a piece of white paper filed in the dark on the point of a black-enameled spindle forever."

That mythological context includes Danae as well as Medusa. Given the gold in the air when the fig swelled in bliss in "Island of Summer" (in "Where the Slow Fig's Purple Sloth"), the bikinied hunchback's "hair dyed gold" ("Myth on Mediterranean Beach"), and the "gold ooze" in "The Leaf," it cannot be by accident that the accident in *Internal Injuries* could happen the way it did: "Wouldn't just *being* be enough without / Having the pee (quite / Literally) knocked out of / You by a 1957 yellow Cadillac . . . ?" ("The Event"). Though the pee is hers, it is there, evocative of the gold liquid by which Zeus made Danae pregnant with Perseus, whose primal scene this is, imaginatively re-created by the same poet who in "I Am Dreaming of a White Christmas" in *Or Else* (275) would dream of his parents' marriage bed covered with yellow dust, "that silken and yellow perfection of Time." Dust that is yellow for the same reason that the Cadillac is yellow and that Warren's last novel begins with the protagonist's father involved in a road accident brought about by an act of urination. Jed Tewksbury's father's hand was clutching his penis in death, after he had fallen off the wagon and been crushed by its wheels (*A Place to Come To* 3). What he was doing with it was the subject of some discussion at his funeral: "'and he ends like tryen to jack off' . . . 'naw, he must of been standen up to piss'" (*A Place to Come To* 7). The ambiguity serves Warren's purpose, for in the myth the golden liquid was what inseminated Danae.

Warren's own persona is deeply implicated in this double mythology, and not only through the first-person narration of *Internal Injuries* that invites us to see the poet in the narrator who reenacts the role of Perseus. Jake, the grizzled old man who is up "All night beneath that blazing bulb" and in whose gut the "pumpkin grows and grows" ("Keep that Morphine"), resembles the poet's father in "Reading Late at Night, Thermometer Falling" (310) in *Or Else,* up all night (reading, not excreting) "Under the bare hundred-watt bulb that glares / Like truth" as within him grows a "prostate big as a horse-apple. Cancer, of course"—as in Jake's case. In "One I Knew" (451) in *Rumor Verified,* the cancer in the father is a slowly blooming plant: "a large mysterious bud. . . . / The shimmering / White petal— the golden stamen— / . . . at last . . . / Divulged." Similarly, near the end of *Internal Injuries,* for the narrator "meaning / In my guts blooms like / A begonia" ("The World Is a Parable"). As if, despite the immediate cause being his concern for the accident victim's internal injuries, he were responding as well to those taking place within Jake (after all, the title "Internal Injuries" spans both sequences). That the narrator is father-obsessed is suggested by what he blurts out in an imaginary conversation with the Warden: "your father is not really dead, he // Is trying to get out of that box he thinks you put him in" ("Night Is Personal").

That persona is implicated in another way, in what is going on in the background as the traffic victim writhes in pain: "They are tearing down Penn Station" ("Her Hat"). The demolition impinges at times on the narrator's awareness:

> Pneumatic hammers
> Are at work somewhere ("The Scream" 243)

> I can see one cornice swimming
> High above the hoarding ("Her Hat" 243)

> Penn Station looks bombed-out. ("The Jet . . ." 244)

> Jack-hammers . . .
> Are trying to tell me something, they speak in code,
>   . . . those men in orange helmets,

> They must know it . . .
> . . . must know the message, know the secret names and all the slithery
>   functions of

> All those fat slick slimy things ("Driver, Driver" 247)

Why would the demolition workers know the functions of the body's internal organs and therefore know the message tapped out in the code of their pneumatic hammers? Could it be because the building they are disassembling bears the name of a human being, namely the author? It is a name he early chose to define his identity as an author, but with the result that he offended his father, as if he had been trying to renounce the first name they shared. He tells the story in *Portrait of a Father:*

> My father had known what it was to sweat over poems. I had long since seen the hidden book [in which Robert Franklin Warren had published three poems]. . . . I had begun to publish what I hoped were poems. . . . [O]ne of them, in some sort of reflex against the triple names of many nineteenth-century authors, was signed "Penn Warren." My father had read the poem and made a friendly but critical remark. Then, still holding the little magazine . . . he asked me whether I did not like the name "Robert." With an instant of shame—it must have been shame—I remembered that he had once signed his full name. (62–63)

Appropriately for its appearance as the place where the mother, Medusa and Danae, is the center of attention, Penn is his mother's maiden name.

Behind that coincidence there is another. Its homonym names the site where the events of the other sequence take place, a fact the first line of *Penological Study* makes clear right away: "Oh, in the pen, oh, in the pen, / The cans, they have no doors" ("Keep That Morphine"). That the two sequences could be said to progress from the pen to Penn Station is yet another indication of how tightly woven together they are.

Yet their individual poems are not braided together as tightly as those of "Island of Summer," as far as I can tell. It would seem impossible that they could be, for the contiguous echoes of that sequence go against the grain, in poems that, while sharing the same local geography, nevertheless have no immediate continuity. Each poem in "Island of Summer" focuses on a different object in that landscape: cicadas, a fig, a garden, a cliff. In *Penological Study* and *Internal Injuries,* by contrast, each poem contributes to telling the unfolding story; they are already linked by that narrative continuity. There are no differences for unexpected continuities to play off of, no new contexts in which sameness might surprise.

On the other hand, there are some intriguing instances of sameness between "I. Island of Summer" and the two sequences of "II. Internal Injuries." We have already seen that "the dark has / no walls" in "A Place Where Nothing Is," anticipating the absence of doors in the penitentiary latrine ("Keep That Morphine"). The "incessant effort" displayed by the tree-sawing cicadas in "What Day Is" finds a counterpart in the "Maniacal and incessant" noise of "the / Insects of summer" that "tore / The night to shreds" in "Wet Hair: If Now His Mother Should Come." The declaration in "Masts at Dawn" that "We must try // To love so well the world that we may believe, in the end, in God" finds two echoes, one in the exhortation in "Keep That Morphine" that "we . . . must try, / Like him, to tough it through," the other in the assertion in "Be Something Else" that "we love the // World." The "distinct impression" the narrator had that the black woman was "staring me straight in the eye" ("The Jet") recalls his remark in "The Red Mullet" that "The mullet has looked me in the eye, and forgiven / Nothing."

The most extensive parallel involves the notion itself of place. That "I have been in a place where / nothing is" in "A Place Where Nothing Is" is strangely like what the narrator says in "The World Is a Parable": "I / Must go somewhere where / Nothing is real, for only / Nothingness is real and is / A sea of light." He had spoken of the sea, too, in the earlier poem as a way of describing that nothingness: "the brightness of that nothing- / ness which is the sea is / not nothingness, but is / like the inestimable sea of // Nothingness Plotinus dreamed" ("A Place Where Nothing Is"). This place of positive nothingness is where the narrator of *Internal Injuries* wishes to escape from the burden of what he saw in the old woman in the street who was staring him right in the eye. But we saw how the same place when it was described in "A Place Where Nothing Is" sounded strangely like the place in the poem immediately before that one, "The Red Mullet": under the sea, where the ribs feel oppressed by nothingness and the absence of air, where there is "no light" despite a burning flame or lamp. There he could not escape being "looked . . . in the eye," because it was the red mullet's domain. The unforgiving mullet, "he the great one," is, we realized, the father. Warren's persona would rather risk his unforgiving stare than the mother's frightening gaze. The same preference is expressed in the opposition between his wanting the driver of the cab to take him away from where he has to look at the woman in the street and his willingness in "Where They Come to Wait for the Body: A Ghost Story" (239) to drive Jake home on his way to the airport.[10] He doesn't mind being with Jake in a car, and even imagines volunteering to do it, but in the other sequence he looks to a car as the way to escape the woman's presence.

"III. ENCLAVES"

Incarnations concludes with a brief section of four poems, two each in two sections; it may be more accurate to count them as two poems, each having two parts, even though each part bears its own title, because Warren in a note at the beginning of *Or Else* refers to the first of them, *The True Nature of Time,* as a "poem"— that is, as one poem, not two. They are (continuing the italicization practiced in the original volume's table of contents):

> *The True Nature of Time*
> 1. The Faring
> 2. The Enclave
>
> *In the Mountains*
> 1. Skiers
> 2. Fog

One might at first have thought that the narrator had succeeded in the desire he expressed in "The World Is a Parable," the penultimate poem of *Internal Injuries,* "to begin a new life" (a desire not all that new, we recall, since he had mentioned the prospect in the second poem of *Penological Study*), for the setting of "The Faring"(300) is worlds away from that of the preceding sequence, no longer New York but Normandy (in this poem "Eleanor [Clark] recognized the scene when she waited for Warren on the dock at Dieppe fifteen years before" [Blotner 378]). In "Driver, Driver," the last poem of *Internal Injuries,* he sought a new destination ("driver, listen now, I / Must change the address"); he appears to have found it. No longer burdened with the presence of a woman whose gaze he cannot bear, the narrator is now blessed with the company of the woman he loves, standing on the dock to greet him at he arrives on the Channel boat.

But by the time we arrive at the conclusion of this brief section, we will be where we were at the end of *Internal Injuries,* with a narrator obsessing over the terrifying mysteries of the body's innards. In "Driver, Driver" he wondered about "the secret names and all the slithery functions of / All those fat slick slimy things"; in "Fog" (248) he will speak of "The intricate secrets of / The lungs."

And even in "The Faring" Perseid imagery persists:

Roses. Yellow. . . .
Sea graying, but roses were yellow, climbing
The wall, it was stone. That last light
Came gilding a track across the gray water from westward.
It came leveling in to finger the roses. One
Petal, yellow, fell, slow.

At the foot of the gray stone, like light, it lay.

Yellow below, gold above. If yellow and gold are equivalent for Warren, as we may conclude they are from the yellow Cadillac in *Internal Injuries* (and from the fact that his daughter's hair in "To a Little Girl, One Year Old, in a Ruined Fortress" in *Promises* is alternately described as "yellow" and "gold"), then the wall-climbing roses are striving upward as the "gold ooze" of the plum in "The Leaf" (in "Island of Summer") "has striven / Outward" in its desire "again to be of / The goldness of air." One yellow petal then falls, as if disturbed by the gilding light that fingered it. It lies on the ground, "like light."

In "The Enclave" (301), which immediately follows, that last image recurs, transformed: "From the cock's throat, the cry, / In the dark, like gold blood flung, is scattered. / How may I know the true nature of Time, if / Deep now in darkness that glittering enclave / I dream, hangs? It shines." All that glitters it not gold, but here I think it is. The situation will recur in "Vision Under the October Mountain: A Love Poem" (301) in *Or Else,* where Warren will reprint "The Faring" and "The Enclave," placing them just before this poem because they "have a place in the thematic structure." That thematic structure, as so often in Warren's sequences, is undergirded by a sequential one, with the result in *Or Else* that the "glittering enclave" that "hangs" in "The Enclave" is immediately followed in "Vision Under the October Mountain" by a "gold mountain" that "hangs in gold air." I will argue in my reading of *Or Else* that the gold mountain is paternal, a floating presence above the narrator who is a not-yet-born fetus "in the // pulse and warm slosh of / that unbreathing bouillon" of his mother's womb. So that in "The Enclave" the hanging and glittering enclave is golden, and ultimately paternal. Paternal as well is the gold liquid flung on the ground, scattered like Onan's seed, in the manner of Jed Tewksbury's father in the opening pages of *A Place to Come To*—or perhaps no more onanistically than Zeus's, which reached its goal and fathered Perseus.

The ground may be littered with reminiscences of his origins, but Perseus here is no mere child trailing clouds of glory from the god who was his sire. He has confronted Medusa in *Internal Injuries;* now, in *The True Nature of Time,* he performs the next chapter in his heroic career, delivering Andromeda from her enchainment on a windswept shore. Perseus came flying toward her over the sea on Pegasus; similarly, the narrator of "The Faring" comes riding the waves on a boat that behaves like a horse: "Once over water, to you borne brightly, / . . . the Channel boat banging / The chop *like a shire-horse* on cobbles—thus I, / *Riding* the spume-flash, by gull-cries ringed, / Came." Andromeda stood naked on the rocky shore; the woman in the Normandy was clothed, but the wind did what it could to reveal her body: "Over / Your breast wind tautened the blue cloth, your skirt / Whipped, the bare legs were brown." In Warren's telling, the effect of the wind on her hair is insistent, appearing both in "The Faring": "Wind / Tugged your hair. It tangled that brightness"—and, by way of recollection, in "The Enclave": "Wind // Lifts the brightening of hair." This seems a reminiscence of a detail essential to the outcome in Ovid's telling: "She seem'd a Statue by a Hand Divine, / Had not the Wind her waving Tresses show'd."[11] He would not, that is, have recognized her for the maiden in distress she was (and who became his wife, as Eleanor Clark became Warren's).

The conclusion of "The Faring" retells its beginning, the light that "Came gilding a track across the gray water," repeating the narrator's arrival over the Channel. The yellow rose is the woman, Andromeda yielding to Perseus's touch as Danae did to Zeus. The son is becoming his father.

"Skiers" (248) tells a similar story, but from the perspective of one observing the arrival, not the one who arrives: "With the motion of angels, out of / Snow-spume and swirl of gold mist, they / Emerge. . . . / They slowly enlarge to our eyes." The "Snow-spume" serves to remind us of the "spume-flash" that the narrator was riding as he came closer and closer to the shore; the "gold mist" repeats the "gilding" light of "The Faring" and the "glittering enclave" of "The Enclave"— both, like the skiers, seen from some distance away. The skiers coming out of the spume and gold mist "Cry their bright bird-cries, pure / In the sweet desolation of distance," reiterating in a strange way the combination of bird-cry and goldness found in the "cock's . . . cry . . . like gold blood flung" in "The Enclave." Strange, but comprehensible, as bird-cries in the poems of "III. Enclaves" represent the father's voice. This is certainly apparent in the liquid gold of the cock's cry in "The Enclave." And just as much so in "Fog," where in the final lines of the book the narrator prays to hear the crow's voice once more: "What, in such absoluteness, /

Can be prayed for? Oh, crow, / Come back, I would hear your voice: // That much, at least, in this whiteness." Earlier in this poem he had been isolated, rendered totally alone by a fog that made him "contextless," cut off from the world by its blinding luminosity. The only thing he can perceive beyond himself is that "At fog-height, unseen, / A crow calls." Though that call "is only // A tatter of cold contempt," he will wish it back. Not all high-flying or -perched birds in Warren are hawks, but it would seem that more than just the hawks are the father.

At the moment of his greatest danger from the transfixing gaze of the black-enameled spindle, there is something like a bird in the sky, high up: "The jet is so far off there is no sound . . . / I do not know what the jet is hunting for" ("The Jet Must Be Hunting for Something"). Could it be the father, keeping watch over his son? Like the "gull" that "in the last light, hung" as the yellow petal fell in "The Faring"? The "glittering enclave" in the next poem (or in the same poem, if we follow Warren's lead and call *The True Nature of Time*, which is composed of "The Faring" and "The Enclave," a single poem) is the father, and it, too, "hangs."

"III. Enclaves" begins happily, with the reenactment of Andromeda's rescue, but ends in something close to desolation in "Fog" as the narrator feels reduced to being "an eye" that "Screams in the belly" and that "Sees the substance of body dissolving." Even in "Skiers," which precedes it as the first part of *In the Mountains,* there was a falling-off, as the skiers that looked like angels as they emerged from gold mist lost that quality when entered the "world, new and strange, of Time and / Contingency" at the bottom of the slope: "Now // On the flat where the whiteness is / Trodden and mud-streaked, not birds now, / Nor angels even, they stand." In "Fog" the narrator stands, too, not in mud-stained snow but in frightening invisibility: "My foot / Is set on what I // Do not see." The problem is that "all / Is here, no other where." This is the problem his fog-isolated heart, "contextless," faces, prompting the question, "how / Can you . . . now know / What you are?" But the question is not itself contextless, for the words "how / Can" and "What you are" had been spoken by the narrator of *Internal Injuries* to the woman lying in the street:

> If you insist on being
> > What you are, how can we
> > Ever love you, we
> > Cannot love what is—
>
> By which I mean a thing that
> > Totally is and therefore
> > Is absolute, for we
> > Know that the absolute is
>
> Delusion, and that Truth lives
> > Only in relation. ("Be Something Else")

He cannot love her if she, like his heart in "Fog," is contextless, absolute, is all that exists. That Truth lives only in relation: is this a truth the narrator of "Fog" has forgotten? Or is it that he knows it's true but suffers from there being no relation from which Truth could emerge? His heart may be contextless, but that context-lessness is not deprived of context. The context of *Incarnations* includes not only "Fog" but also "Be Something Else." The narrator of one sequence may not know what the narrator of another knows, but Warren's reader can know it.

That reader can know as well that the narrator's not knowing what his foot-ing is in the blinding fog—"My foot / Is set on what I // Do not see"—in this, the last poem of *Incarnations,* symmetrically answers (or restates) the question asked in the first stanza of the volume's first poem: "footings for what?" ("What Day Is"). We begin, with the cicadas, "At the foot of infinity" and end somewhere like it, floating with dangling feet in an immensity of blank, unknowable space. Somewhere between is the woman in the street who has been knocked off her feet: "having a sizeable hole (as / I can plainly see, you being flat on the ground) in / The sole of a shoe (the right one)" ("The Event"). But it turns out that the narrator has here (in the first stanza of the first poem of *Internal Injuries*) started off on the wrong foot, for three poems later we learn that she had "put the wrong shoe on the right / Foot, or vice versa" ("The Only Trouble"). This small detail of uncertainty fits into a larger picture, with the result that the poems of this volume may also proclaim, with the narrator (in "Night Is Personal"), that "we are all // One flesh."

CHAPTER 7
"THE WORLD / IN WHICH ALL THINGS ARE CONTINUOUS"
OR ELSE:
POEM/POEMS 1968–1974

"*Or Else—Poem/Poems 1968–1974* is conceived," Robert Penn Warren tells us in a prefatory note, "as a single long poem composed of a number of shorter poems as sections or chapters" (709). To what extent is the title's assertion—both *Poems* and *Poem*—a valid claim? James Justus writes of "the directions for reading this volume playfully handed over to the reader, who must decide is it a six-year collection of diverse poems . . . ? or is it a single poem conceived as a sequence? It is something of both" (97). Dave Smith finds that Warren "has caused his 32 poems to operate as something like panels which form a loose sequential movement. . . . In an especially canny but not unpredictable strategy—if one has noted Warren's long habit of binding poems into thematic sequences—Warren has constructed the poems of *Or Else* as reflectors, baffles, mirrors, and back-lights. . . . [I]t is through the juxtaposition and oblique continuities of remarkably varied poems that the form of *Or Else* creates a vision at once dynamic, complex, and emblematic."[1]

Or Else is actually composed of two intertwining sequences: twenty-four roman-numeraled poems with eight arabic-numeraled "Interjections" occurring after the first, fourth, fifth, seventh, twelfth, fifteenth, eighteenth, and twenty-first poems of the first group. The first of these "Interjections" is quite brief:

> "Interjection #1: The Need for Re-evaluation"
>
> *Is this really me?* Of course not, for Time
> Is only a mirror in the fun-house.
>
> You must re-evaluate the whole question. (271)

Is this really a poem, or merely a reflection on the poem it immediately follows, "The Nature of a Mirror" (271)? Is it just an interjectory remark on the mirror alluded to in the first poem's conclusion—"Time // Is the mirror into which you stare"? The "Interjections" to follow will prove more substantial than this one. But as the first of that second series, it may at least be announcing something of the structure of the sequences to follow,[2] for it could hardly show in any clearer way its continuity with its immediate predecessor. Shall we take that initial continuity as a harbinger of continuities to come?

The third poem in *Or Else*, "Natural History" (271), shows continuities with its roman-numeraled predecessor. In "Natural History," the "mother is counting her money like mad, in the sunshine." In "The Nature of a Mirror," the "sun / . . . sinks / Lower, larger, more blank, and redder than / A mother's rage." Both mothers are mad, though in different ways. The mother madly counting money in the sunshine is intelligible in the context of the myth of Danae's impregnation by Zeus that takes such forms in Warren as the gold fluid with which the novel *A Place to Come To* begins and the "carpet of gold": that "is Danae's lap lavished with gold by the god" in the poem "No Bird Does Call" (416). The shower is sometimes depicted in paintings as a liquid, and sometimes as a shower of gold coins (for example, in Tintoretto, Titian, and Van Dyck). It is with reference to the latter that we might regard the mother in "Natural History" who is "counting her money like mad, in the sunshine. / Like shuttles her fingers fly, and the sum is clearly astronomical." It is astronomical both in the sense of being a very large number and in that of being of celestial origin: "The money the naked old mother counts is her golden memories of love. / That is why I see nothing in her maniacally busy fingers." This scene recalls the moment in *Audubon: A Vision* when Audubon takes out his watch and dangles it before the woman in the shack:

> It is gold, it lives in his hand in the firelight, and the woman's
> Hand reaches out. She wants it. She hangs it about her neck.
>
> And near it the great hands hover delicately
> As though it might fall, they quiver like moth-wings, her eyes
> Are fixed downward, as though in shyness, on that gleam, and her face
> Is sweet in an outrage of sweetness, so that
> His gut twists cold. He cannot bear what he sees.
>
> Her body sways like a willow in spring wind. Like a girl. (256)

The parallel with the mother in "Natural History" is striking. It is as if the woman with the gold watch were, like the mother, recalling "her golden memories of love," for she becomes young again, "shy" and "sweet" and "Like a girl." The mother's fingers fly like shuttles; the woman's hands "quiver like moth-wings." By hanging the gold trinket about her neck, the woman gives a premonition of her end, when she is hanged and Audubon, seeing "Under / The tumbled darkness of hair, the face" that "Is, he suddenly sees, beautiful as stone, and // So becomes aware that he is in the manly state." The abundant hair, the beauty of stone, and the resulting hardness in the beholder all evoke the event to which Danae and Zeus's lovemaking led, her son Perseus's slaying of the Medusa, who in a Freudian reading of the myth is a figure for the mother. Warren lends support to Freud's argument by making the woman who was sent into such a reverie by Audubon's watch, and who in death became Medusa-like, so closely resemble the "naked old mother" in "Natural History."

What is the mother whose fingers fly like shuttles weaving? The other poem—the one that precedes it in the sequence if we for the moment abstract out the intervening Interjection as being of a different order, woven both in and out of the main sequence of *Or Else*'s poems—that other poem, "The Nature of a Mirror," does offer a possible answer in the form of a texture that may be maternal: "the sun, / . . . sinks /. . . redder than / A mother's rage, as though / . . . the first vagina / Had not had the texture of dream." This "first vagina" is probably in its most obvious sense the site of the narrator's first experience of intercourse. But on some other level it may be the original vagina, the one that in a later poem in *Or Else* is likewise a place where one dreams: "did we / once in the womb dream . . . ?" ("Vision Under the October Mountain: A Love Poem" 301). What we may have dreamed was of something golden, which I interpret, still in the context of Warren's reworking of the Danae myth, as the father's necessary presence: "Golding from green"—like the beech leaves in "No Bird Does Call," for this mountain's gold undoubtedly comes from its October-tinged trees—"gorgeous the mountain / high hangs in gold air . . . it is // the image of authority"—a paternal trait indeed. In the womb did we "dream / a gold mountain in gold / air floating, we in the // pulse and warm slosh of / that unbreathing bouillon. . . . did we / dream a gold mountain, did / it glow in that faceless unfatuous / dark . . . ?"

If that is the "first vagina," then "the sun, / Beyond the western ridge of black-burnt pine stubs like / A snaggery of rotten shark teeth" sinking "redder than / A mother's rage" may be a *vagina dentata*, frightening thought, but not far removed from the mother as Medusa, who was known not only for her serpentine hair but also her "huge teeth."[3] "The terror Medusa induces," wrote Freud, "is . . . a terror of castration that is linked to the sight of something. . . . [I]t occurs when a boy, who has hitherto been unwilling to believe the threat of castration, catches sight of the female genitals, probably those of an adult, surrounded by hair, and essentially those of his mother" ("Medusa's Head" 212). Teeth, trees and castration are brought together elsewhere in *Or Else*: "the saw's song . . . glee of steel and the / Sun-shriek, the scream of castration, the whirl-tooth hysteria / Of *now, now, now!*" (286; italics in the text) in "Chain Saw at Dawn in Vermont in Time of Drouth." If the teeth through which something like a mother's rage is seen in "The Nature of a Mirror" evokes Medusa, so too is the mirrored Gorgon evoked in "Natural History" when the mother's "smile sways like daffodils reflected in a brook." The teeth may be detected in that smile, or just beneath its surface; regardless, the mirror the brook affords reflects "the mirror into which you stare" in "The Nature of a Mirror," the mirror that is Time.

The father, too, appears in "Natural History":

> In the rain the naked old father is dancing, he will get wet.
> The rain is sparse, but he cannot dodge all the drops.
>
> He is singing a song, but the language is strange to me.
> . . . .
> The song of the father tells how at last he understands.
> That is why the language is strange to me.

The song and the language in which it is sung are strange to the son, but such it has always been in Warren's world. It is the taciturn text, the message the father leaves for his son to interpret in all the novels and in some very interesting poems. The poems in Warren's first and last sequences reenact that father-son relationship, each poem trying to make sense of its predecessor, reading that inherited text and trying out a new context for its fragments. Here, in addition to the snaggle-tooth mad mother seen in Time's mirror recontextualized as the brook-reflected smile of a mad money-counting Danae (did Perseus see his mother in the mirror when he slew the Gorgon?), we have the father who understands and the son who does not understand that understanding in one poem, which may be the recontextualization of an evidently more complete understanding: "The sky has murder in the eye, and I / Have murder in the heart, for I / Am only human. / We look at each other, . the sky and I. / We *understand* each other" ("The Nature of a Mirror").

I think that sky is the father. Zeus, the source of the gold translated here (in "Natural History") as "the sum . . . clearly astronomical," is the sky god par excellence. In "Time as Hypnosis" (272), the next poem in the sequence, gold—the inseminating, paternal essence in the Danae myth evoked in the "golden memories of love" the mother counts "like mad"—returns in the eyes of the predator that swoops down from the sky, bringing death to a field mouse:

> Have you ever seen how delicately
> Etched the print of the field mouse's foot in fresh snow is?
> I saw the tracks. But suddenly, none. Nothing
> But the wing-flurried snow. Then, small as a pin-head, the single
> Bright-frozen, red bead of a blood-drop. Have you ever

> Stared into the owl's eyes? They blink slow, then burn
> Burn gold in the dark inner core of the snow-shrouded cedar.

The eyes that here "Burn gold" anticipate the dreamed-of gold mountain of which the poet asks, "did / it glow in [the] dark?" Warren will return to this scene of the owl in the cedar in "On Into the Night" (416) in *Being Here:* "taciturn, / The owl's adrowse in the depth of a cedar / To pre-enjoy the midnight's revel." As a "taciturn . . . owl," he enacts the father's role in Warren's symbolic world, like "the taciturn tall stone, / Which is your fathers' monument and mark" in the earliest poem to which he kept returning in his several *Selected Poems,* "To a Face in the Crowd" (61).

That the owl in the cedar is the father—"the golden image of authority" in "Vision Under the October Mountain"—is apparent from the way the cedar returns in the next poem, "Blow, West Wind" (273), where its association with the father is made explicit:

> . . . O, the cedar
>
> Shakes, and I know how cold
> Was the sweat on my father's mouth, dead.
> Blow, west wind, blow, shake the cedars. I know
>
> How once I, a boy, crouching at creekside,
> Watched, in the sunlight, a handful of water
> Drip, drip, from my hand. The drops—they were bright!

For three poems in a row, there have been drops. In "Natural History," the father is dancing in the rain and will get wet because he cannot dodge all the drops. In "Time as Hypnosis," the field mouse the father-owl has killed drips blood. In "Blow, West Wind," there are beads of sweat, very cold, on the dead father's mouth, and bright water drips from the son's hand. The son watches the water drip down "in the sunlight" and marvels at the brightness—a golden brightness, as he makes, in imitation of his father, his own liquid dispersal. These several sorts of drops reek of both life and death, the sweat on the father's mouth the temperature it is because his corpse is cold. They evoke the raindrops the father both dodged and danced in—a father that was supposed to stay in his grave. That father understood something but expressed it in a language the son did not understand; the poet's insistent returning to and reworking of the drop imagery over the course of these three poems may be his attempt to interpret it.

The Perseus myth offers another key. The owl is not only the father but the son, if the son is Perseus, for the drop of blood from the field mouse recalls the drops of blood from Medusa's head that fell on the ground beneath Perseus's flight as he carried away his prize through the air on winged feet. This seems likely, given that Warren alludes to it in *A Place to Come To*: "'Dugton,'" Jed Tewksbury's mother once said to him, referring to his home town, "'do you know how it came to be? . . . One time there was a pigeon big as the Rocky Mountain and he stuffed himself on all the pokeberries and cow patties this side of Pike's Peak and the bowel movement hit him about this part of Alabama and they named it Dugton'" (25). Later in the novel, Jed will see a purse snatcher leap to the hood of an automobile and "stand beautifully balanced there with the purse—like Medusa's head hanging from the hand of Cellini's Perseus. . . . I remember thinking how beautiful, how redemptive, all seemed. It was as though I loved him. I thought how beautifully he had moved, like Ephraim, like a hawk in sunset flight" (387). Like the owl, the hawk in such poems as "Mortal Limit" and "Red-Tailed Hawk and Pyre of Youth" represents the father; Ephraim is Jed's son. Being Perseus is evidently something passed down from father to son to the son's own son.

"Necessarily, we must think of the / world as continuous," we are told in "Interjection #2: Caveat" (274). Certainly the world in the opening poems of *Or Else* is, as we have seen in the persistent drops and the insistent returnings to the Perseus myth. Yet in "Caveat," the narrator asserts as well that "on- / ly in discontinuity, do we / know that we exist, or that, in the deep- / est sense, the existence of anything / signifies more than the fact that it is / continuous with the world." The case is made in "Caveat" that if you "fix your eyes firmly on / one fragment of crushed rock" at a highway construction site, that one piece of crushed rock will begin to declare its discontinuity from the world. It will start to glitter, and then vibrate and "all things" will "seem to / be spinning away from the universal center that the single fragment of / crushed rock had ineluctably become."

Each poem in a sequence like this demands to be the center of our attention, and may even, as the piece of crushed rock threatens to do, "scream // in an ecstasy of // being." But the sequence too makes demands on our attention. In the immediately following poem, "I Am Dreaming of a White Christmas: The Natural History of a Vision" (275), what the narrator stares at (as he speaks of staring at the piece of crushed rock) and what becomes the essence of staring—his dead father's missing eyes in this vision of an impossible return to Christmas morning in Guthrie—has an occult relation to the object of his gaze in "Caveat," a relation that is only there when these two poems appear in sequence:

> The eyes
> Are not there. But,
> Not there, they stare at what
> Is not there.

> Not there, but
> In each of the appropriate twin apertures, which are
> Deep and dark as a thumb-gouge,
> Something that might be taken for
> A mulberry, large and black-ripe when, long back, crushed,
> But now, with years, dust-dried. The mulberries,
> Crushed and dessicated, each out of
> Its dark lurking-place, stare out at
> Nothing.

Nowhere else has the word "crushed" appeared in *Or Else* (nor will it)[4] but here and in the crushed rock that wants so much to declare its independence from the world's continuousness. Yet, alas! it is ineluctably continuous with these father's eyes, and Warren, it would appear, willed it so. For when he reprinted "I Am Dreaming" in the 1985 *Selected Poems,* he chose not to reprint "Caveat" (though had included it in the 1975 *Selected Poems*); contemporaneously, he removed the two instances of the word "crushed" from "I Am Dreaming" (Burt's textual note to this line, 711n). "Caveat" gone, these two erstwhile links to a now-vanished immediate predecessor had no longer any reason to exist. Like the father's eyes they once denoted, they are "not there. But, / Not there" perhaps they can "stare at what is not there."

Dave Smith notes that the scream in "Caveat" would soon be followed by another in "I Am Dreaming," which follows it in *Or Else:*

> in Bellevue,
> In a bare room, with windows barred, a woman,
> Supine on an iron cot, legs spread, each ankle
> Shackled to the cot-frame,
> Screams.
>
> She keeps on screaming because it is sunset.
>
> Her hair has been hacked short.

Smith asks, "[I]s it the scream that is an 'ecstasy of being'?" (53). This is just the sort of question Warren's sequential echoes make us ask. What might the screaming mental patient have to do with the screaming rock? The continuity between "Caveat" and "I Am Dreaming" with regard to continuity itself is readily apparent, for "Caveat" begins with the assertion that "we must think of the / world as continuous," and "I Am Dreaming" closes with this summing up:

> All items listed above belong in the world
> In which all things are continuous,
> And are parts of the original dream which

I am now trying to discover the logic of. This
Is the process whereby pain of the past in its pastness
May be converted into the future tense

Of joy.

If all things in "I Am Dreaming" belong in the same world of continuousness, then the screaming woman may not be just any mental patient, but someone, like the parents in the opening scene, from the poet's own life. Readers of Joseph Blotner's biography of Warren may be forgiven for seeing in her Cinina Brescia, the poet's first wife, who in May 1950 was "committed . . . to the psychiatric division of New York Hospital" (260).[5]

There is a tension in "Caveat" between the narrator's declaration that we must think of the world as continuous and his subsequent assertion, in the second stanza, that "on- / ly, in discontinuity, do we / know that we exist." The rock that first glitters, then vibrates, and from which "all things seem to / be spinning away" but which at the same moment becomes "the univer- / sal center" may be asserting, when it screams in an ecstasy of being, its discontinuity from the world. But whether it has achieved that discontinuity is not clear. On the one hand all things seem to be spinning away from it; but on the other, it has become the universal center.

Reading "I Am Dreaming" biographically, which Warren seems to invite us to do in the Christmas scene, we can imagine a similar tension between continuity and discontinuity in the scene of the screaming woman. The rock wanted to be discontinuous in order to know it existed (if we can read its screaming assertion of being as an exemplification of stanza two's assertion that only in discontinuity do we know that we exist); for the poet as he makes poetry of his own life, the woman on the cot was both in and out of his life. Blotner reports that Warren said of hearing of Cinina's death in 1969, at which time she had been out of his life for many years, "I didn't feel a thing," and that he said this with "a tone of muted wonder" (383).

More than the scream links the rock and the woman. After the rock starts to glitter and vibrate but before it screams, "At this point, while there is still time and will, / I advise you to detach your gaze" for "Not all witnesses / of the phenomenon survive unchanged." The fragment of rock assumes Medusan power, dangerous to look at. The reemergence of the Medusa theme at this point in the collection may have something to do with a detail in the scene of the screaming woman, one that almost appears added as an afterthought: "Her hair has been hacked short." Her threatening locks shorn, she is no longer quite the threat she was—appropriately so, for a piece of a rejected past that nevertheless belongs "in the world / In which all things are continuous."

The woman on the cot and the ghostly Christmas scene are connected not only for being pieces of the poet's personal past but also for their connections to the crushed rock of "Caveat," whose ties to the father's crushed-mulberry eyes and the woman's screams are now apparent. The poem's closing assertion challenges us to find other connections between the Christmas dream that occupies sections 1–8 and the Times Square (a place name evocative of the temporality haunting the poem) moments in sections 9–10 and the view from Nez Percé Pass in section 11.

The latter, though also important to Warren as the setting of *Chief Joseph*, may have some relation to the paternal nose in the Christmas dream, the "Nostril-flanges" of which have "gone tattered" in section 2, literally a "nez percé." Such an association seems bizarre, but we are dealing, as stanza 12 tells us, with the logic of dream, in a world where not only are "all things . . . continuous" but "are parts of the original dream which / I am now trying to discover the logic of." Equally bizarre, yet just the sort of thing dreams are made of, is the association that may arise from the "dry fabric" of the mother's dress in section 4 and the "drawers . . . drying stiff at the crotch" of the old men coming out of pornographic theaters in section 10. Though the dry fabric of the mother's dress "droops over breastlessness" it also "falls decisively away" from her knees and the viewer's attention is drawn to her crotch, to "the shrouded femurs that are now the lap," shrouded by that same dry fabric.

"Blow, West Wind" is not without its echoes (and reversals) in "I Am Dreaming," the poem that follows it in the roman-numeraled sequence. In the former poem, the dead cannot speak ("the last who might speak are dead"), while in the latter, they can: "*No presents, son, till the little ones come. / What shadow of tongue, years back unflexed, in what / Darkness locked in a rigid jaw, can lift and flex?*" (italics in the poem). Lines 5–8 of "Blow, West Wind"—

> I know how the kestrel hung over Wyoming,
> Breast reddened in sunset, and O, the cedar
>
> Shakes, and I know how cold
> Was the sweat on my father's mouth, dead.

—find multiple parallels in this passage from section 9 of "I Am Dreaming":

> Then,
> Of a sudden, know
>
> Times Square, the season
> Late summer and the hour sunset, with fumes
> In throat and smog-glitter at sky-height, where
> A jet, silver and ectoplasmic, spooks through
> The sustaining light, which
> Is yellow as acid. Sweat,
> Cold in arm pit, slides down flesh.
>
> The flesh is mine.

"I know" becomes "Then / . . . know"; the kestrel in the sunset sky becomes the jet in the sunset sky (sustained in a light the color and acidity of which suggest the golden mist of paternity); and the cold sweat on his father's mouth becomes the cold sweat on his own skin.

Though the last scene evoked in "I Am Dreaming" is of the "Nez Percé *Pass*" and in "Interjection #3: I Know a Place Where All Is Real" (282) the narrator speaks of "narrow and fog-laced *passes*," the latter poem is more strongly tied to the one that follows it, "Ballad of Mister Dutcher and the Last Lynching in Gupton" (282). This is typical of *Or Else*'s two intertwining sequences: the Interjections are echoed in one of the poems that adjoin them, but not necessarily both (the extremely brief "Interjection #1," for instance, comments exclusively on the mirror of the poem that precedes it but has no relation to the one following). The roman-numeraled poems, however, consistently rework elements of their predecessors in their series.

Access to the "Place Where All Is Real" can be gained only by escaping from murderous pursuers: "if you can manage to elude the natives of / intervening zones, who practice ghastly rites and have an appetite for human flesh." While there are no cannibals in the "Ballad," its story concerns a man trying to elude pursuers who are trying to kill him. They succeed, and the unnamed black man who had shot a clerk in an attempted robbery is lynched, thanks to the surprising expertise Mister Dutcher reveals about knotting a noose. The "you" in "I Know a Place Where All Is Real" was advised to "manage to" outrun his pursuers; the fleeing man in "Ballad" was not only unable to do so, but at his hanging unfortunately "managed never / to get a good, clean drop" and so suffered a drawn-out death. Of those who make it up to the high country "Where All Is Real," some come back down but may "die of an oppressive / pulmonary complaint" when they return to a lower elevation. A death, that is, from lack of breath—the fate met in another form in "the Last Lynching in Gupton."

At the heart of "I Am Dreaming" is the question, "Will I never know / What present there was in that package for me, / Under the Christmas tree?" The question remains unanswered, but the "Ballad of Mister Dutcher" reveals what lies hidden in another package, Dutcher's secret knowledge of knots, metaphorically presented as "that one talent kept, against the / advice of Jesus, wrapped in a napkin" (kept, that is, until the day of the lynching). That wrapping recalls the "wrappings" littering the hearth in the dream, "silver and crimson and gold, / Yet gleaming from grayness," the color that sums up Dutcher's outward appearance, whose face, smile, coat, and house were "gray." Of the three packages under the tree, the narrator was "wondering / Which package is mine," while Dutcher's napkin-wrapped talent is "something he can call truly / his own." That concealed talent "was what Mister / Dutcher, all the days, weeks, and years, / had known, and nobody'd known that he knew." Through the dream of his childhood Christmas, it is as if the narrator had been carrying it with him in all the years since then, like the mad killer's "treasure" in "Crime," the pursuing phantom in "Original Sin: A Short Story" (both in *Eleven Poems on the Same Theme* [68–70]), the "Nameless Thing" that walks the house after midnight in the poem of that title in *Rumor Verified* (456), or the manuscript of the Cass Mastern story that followed Jack Burden from one rented apartment to another in *All the King's Men*.

While the narrator of "I Am Dreaming" would like to know what he cannot know, and Mister Dutcher does not let others know what he knows until that fateful day, the narrator in the next poem, "Chain Saw at Dawn in Vermont in Time of Drouth" (285), would like to impart a certain knowledge to someone else, but must first discover it himself:

> I must endeavor to learn what
> I must learn before I must learn
> The other thing. If
> I learn even a little, I may,
> By evening, be able
> To tell the man something.

The two things to be learned are named a little earlier in the poem when the narrator lies in bed one summer morning thinking about a man he knows is dying: "I / Cannot tell him how to die because / I have not learned how to live." The victim of the lynching didn't know how to die, either, "for when the big / bread truck they had him standing on / drew out, he hung on with both feet / as long as possible" and consequently "managed never / to get a good, clean drop, which was, / you might say, his last mistake."

The dying man in "Chain Saw," reflecting on his life, "wonders / Why his boy turned out bad," a misfortune paralleled in the preceding poem, as Dutcher's son had "died / one cold winter night in jail, where / the town constable had put him / to sober up." This, in turn, suggests an intriguing parallel between Dutcher's son and the lynched man, in that both died while in the constable's custody, and through his negligence. Having on that earlier occasion allowed Dutcher's son to freeze to death in his cell, he now allows the lynching party to take possession of the prisoner without a fight. "The constable, it sort of seemed, / had car trouble, and there he was / by the road" with his head under the hood, when they caught up with him and his prisoner.

The parallel between the deceased son and the victim of Dutcher's knotting prowess is enhanced by a reemergence of *Or Else's* motif of the golden fluid and its echo a page later in a reflection on the death of Dutcher's son. When the bread truck was drawn away, the black man "keeled over, slow and head-down, in- / to the rope, spilling his yell out / like five gallons of fresh water / in one big, bright, out-busting slosh / in the sunshine." Spilling water in the sunshine is what the narrator recalls himself doing as a boy in "Blow, West Wind": "once I, as a boy, crouching at creekside, / Watched, in the sunlight, a handful of water / Drip, drip, from my hand. The drops—they were bright!" Dutcher sees his progeny, extinguished through the death of his only son, as a missing drop "with no / drop of his blood to persist in / that . . . / darkness that . . . is Time." It is surely no mere coincidence that on the preceding page the dying breath of the lynchee should be figured as a liquid spilled on the ground. Perhaps it is no coincidence, either, that at about the same time Warren was writing the "Ballad" (first published in 1974), he was writing the opening scene of *A Place to Come To* (published in 1977), in which a man also falls to his death as he stands on a moving vehicle, and as he spatters out a golden liquid. It's the narrator's father who does that in the novel, but we have now seen both father and son (the narrator as his father's child in "Blow, West Wind") perform that gesture in *Or Else*. "I Am Dreaming" begins with the narrator taking care not to stir up a golden shower, not to disturb the yellow dust on the bed where he was conceived:

> Saw
> It.
>
> The bed.
>
> Where it had
> Been. Now was. Of all
> Covering stripped, the mattress
> Bare but for old newspapers spread.
> Curled edges. Yellow. On yellow paper dust,
> The dust yellow. No! Do not.
>
> Do not lean to
> Look at that date. Do not touch
> That silken and yellow perfection of Time that
> Dust is, for
> There is no Time. I,
> Entering, see.

The yellow dust is Time's perfection, but because it is on the parents' bed it is surely also the father's trace. In "A Vision: Circa 1880" (from "Mortmain" in *You, Emperors, and Others*), Warren imagines his father as a boy, emerging "Out of the woods where pollen is a powder of gold" (159), which is another way of associating the father with a golden dispersal. In "I Am Dreaming," in a beautiful and appropriate blending of images, the father's trace, the residue of his fathering the child who would become the poet, becomes the mark itself of Time.

The drouth-stricken landscape of "Chain Saw at Dawn in Vermont in Time of Drouth," where the "The heel of the sun's foot strikes horridly the hill" and a "brook goes gray among boulders," is continuous with the landscape of "Small White House" (287), where "The sun . . . beats down," "hills shudder," and "The river . . . shrinks / Among the hot boulders." Apart from this, the situation is reversed. In "Chain Saw," the narrator is inside a house when he hears, in addition to the saw, a cry come from outside: "The crow, in distance, calls with the crystalline beauty / Of the outraged heart"; while in the other poem he is standing outside the small white house of the title when "a child's cry comes from the house." In a third point of comparison, the saw's "scream of castration," in which "the present / Murders the past," finds its equivalent in the only other event recounted in "Small White House": "the wax-wing's beak slices the blue cedar-berry, / Which is as blue as distance." In "I am Dreaming," the poet had told us that "His eyes / Had been blue," speaking of his father; they had become berries there too, "mulberries, / Crushed and dessicated." Crushed there, sliced here, the father's eye suffers. The chain saw's teeth ("the whirl-tooth hysteria / Of *now, now, now!* [italics in the poem]) that castrated the tree reappears in the form of a slicing beak (attacking, metonymically, a tree).

In "I Am Dreaming," the son recognizes that the flesh down which "Sweat, / Cold in arm-pit slides" is his own. That image reappears in "Chain Saw," suggesting a possible identification between the wielder of the castrating saw and the son: "under / Arm-pits of the blue-shirted sawyer sweat / Beads cold." In "Last Laugh" (366), in *Now and Then,* Warren would return to the idea of what a saw can do to a father, focusing on what twelve-year-old Samuel Clemens beheld as he peered through the keyhole at the results of his father's autopsy: "the head // Sawed through, where his Word, like God's, held its deepest den" (this peeping Tom would later, of course, invent the story of a boy Sawyer). That the sawyer is a figure for a father-murdering son is borne out by the saw's being characterized as "the present" that "Murders the past."

As the tree suffers, so too does the landscape, in both poems. In the line just after the one in "Chain Saw" in which the sun's foot smites the hill, "the stalk of the beech leaf goes limp." The beech is preeminently the father's tree, as we know from the extensive network of associations reaching back to *World Enough and Time* and ahead to "No Bird Does Call." In light of that, what happens to the stalk of the beech leaf sounds like paternal erectile dysfunction, particularly appropriate in a poem where the scream of castration is heard. Similarly, in "Small White House" the sliced blue cedar-berry (a part for the whole of the tree, as the stalk of the leaf may stand for the beech) is associated with the sun-smitten landscape there as well, in the internal echo between the third line, where the shuddering hills "withdraw into distance" and the seventh, where the cedar-berry "is as blue as distance."

"Interjection #4: Bad Year, Bad War: A New Year's Card, 1969" (287), like other Interjections, breaks the continuity of sequence in that it is connected to only one of the two poems it comes between, in this instance to "Forever O'clock" (288), which follows it. John Brown's favorite passage from Hebrews about there being no remission "without shedding of blood" is quoted in an epigraph preceding the Interjection. The poem is a meditation on blood and innocence, contrasting the War in Vietnam, the "bad war," with other wars, which "had been virtuous. If blood // Was shed, it was, in a way, sacramental, redeeming / Even evil enemies from whose veins it flowed, // Into the benign logic of History." The innocent sometimes must suffer "the paw-flick of / The unselective flame." The narrator adopts an ironic stance, praying God "To be restored to that purity of heart / That sanctifies the shedding of blood," to be restored to that time when, waging happier wars, "we, being then untroubled, / Were innocent."

"Forever O'clock" counters this nostalgia for innocence by beginning with instances of guilt—a criminal about to be executed, then what is apparently the narrator's own recollection of waking up in a hotel room with a woman not his wife. In the longest section of the poem, the narrator engages in a considerably longer and more detailed recollection; this time of innocence perceived, his glimpse of a two-year-old black child playing in the front yard of her house as he drives past.

The title alludes to the impending hour of death: "A clock is getting ready to strike forever o'clock." One can hear it getting ready to strike the way the convict about to be shot by firing squad can "hear the mind of the Deputy Warden getting ready to say, 'Fire!'" Like the remission of sin that can only be achieved through blood in the preceding Interjection, the sound of what is about to happen can only be perceived through one's blood: "The sound is one you hear in your bloodstream and not your ear."

The little girl's play, though innocent in itself, repeats in almost ritual fashion the representation in "Interjection #4" of war's destruction of the innocent as "the paw-flick of / The unselective flame." Only in the full sequence, however, which includes "Rattlesnake Country" (290), the poem after "Forever O'clock," does the full force of that parallel emerge:

> The naked child with plum-black skin is intensely occupied.
> From a rusted tin snuff can in the right hand, the child pours red dust over the
>   spread fingers of the left hand held out prone in the bright air.

The child stares at the slow-falling red dust. Some red dust piles precariously up
   on the back of the little black
fingers thrust out. Some does not.
The sun blazes down on the naked child in the mathematical center of the world.

The mathematical center she occupies is that of the three sequential poems, "In-
terjection #4," "Forever O'clock," and "Rattlesnake Country." It is by placing the
child in the center of the three that Warren makes it possible for us to see how the
red dust pouring down is a reincarnation of the flame, for in "Rattlesnake Country"
the girl's behavior is paralleled by that of a "boy"—the American Indian "Laugh-
ing Boy"—killing snakes. Specifically, he "keeps a tin can / Of gasoline" (recalling
the girl's "rusted tin snuff can") with which he will "Douse" rattlesnakes "with the
left hand" (while she held her tin can "in the right hand") and "with the nail of
the right thumb, / Snap a match alight. // The flame" will catch up with the rat-
tler before he reaches his hole, if Laughing Boy has timed it right. "The flame
flickers blue," and later, having tried this game himself and succeeded, the narra-
tor will "Remember / The blue-tattered flick of white flame"—as we should re-
member "the paw-flick of / The unselective flame" in "Interjection #4." If we do
remember it, then we can appreciate how the paw becomes the girl's hand and
then Laughing Boy's hand, and how the flame becomes red dust poured out of a
tin can, which itself becomes flaming gasoline poured out of another tin can.
Having already seen the interchangeability of a shower of gold liquid and a shower
of gold dust elsewhere in the interflow of *Or Else*'s images, we can see, too, that
the African American girl and the Native American Laughing Boy are repeating
not just the flick of the flame but also the golden shower enactments performed
by the narrator as a boy in "Blow, West Wind" and by the black lynching victim
in his life's last gasp in the "Ballad of Mister Dutcher."

   The "slow-falling red dust" of "Forever O'clock" is repeated by the "Ash" that
"sifts minutely down" on the landscape of "Rattlesnake Country." The ash, though
"gray," has its source in "the red eyes of fire" of a blaze on a neighboring moun-
tain. It makes its appearance on only one day of the several the narrator spends
there, thanks to "some secret, high drift of air" from that direction, which wafts
it down over his vanilla ice cream. This may be a self-referential moment in the
sequence, an indication of how dust from one poem can drift over and deposit
itself in the next.

   One more parallel resides in the fact that as the narrator in "Rattlesnake
Country" imitates Laughing Boy's flame-pouring, so too does the narrator in "For-
ever O'clock" re-create, if unintentionally, the flow of red dust. As his Studebaker
continues down the dirt road past the girl, "a plume of red dust now trails it
toward the horizon."

While "Interjection #4" flows into "Forever O'clock" but has no continuity with the poem that precedes it, "Small White House," in the latter poem the landscape "is brown-bright as brass, and like brass, sings with heat," while in "Forever O'clock" the "sky glitters like brass" as "The drouth does not see fit to stop even now." The poems are to some degree two versions of the same story, in which the narrator passes by a house where his attention is caught by a child, whom he hears in one poem and glimpses in the next.

"Rattlesnake Country" is followed by "Homage to Theodore Dreiser" (294), in which Dreiser's Indiana birthplace turns out to bear a strange resemblance (an ironic one, given the misnamed Terre Haute's mere 485-foot elevation) to a significant part of the former poem's high-country setting:

> Past Terre Haute, the diesels pound,
> . . . Deep
> In the infatuate and foetal dark, beneath
> The unspecifiable weight of the great
> Mid-America loam-sheet, the impacted
> Particular particles of loam, blind,
> Minutely grind.
>
> . . . .
>
> The particles, however minutely, vibrate
> At the incessant passage
> Of the transcontinental truck freight

Here loam is pounded by truck freight, while in "Rattlesnake Country" loam *was* truck freight: "Arid that country and high . . . but / One little patch of cool lawn: // Trucks / Had brought in rich loam. Stonework / Held it in place like a shelf." It is here that the snakes are set aflame as they disappear into the loam, there to perish, trapped in their holes.

A parallel event takes place within Dreiser's soul: "the screaming, and stench, of a horse-barn aflame, / . . . their manes flare up like torches." The rattlers and horses are both trapped where they live (the holes, the barn) by flames. The association of snakes and horses had already begun in "Rattlesnake Country," where the flame at the hole-mouth that "flickers blue" was anticipated by the faces of the wranglers driving horses down from mountain pastures "flickering white through the shadow" as "the riderless horses, / Like quicksilver spilled in dark glimmer and roil, go / Pouring downward." Warren intensifies the connection between this recollected scene and that of Laughing Boy and the snakes by saying that both are "nearer" but that the second is nearer than the first: "The wranglers cry out. // And nearer. // But, / Before I go for my quick coffee-scald and to the corral, / I hear, much nearer, not far from my window, a croupy / Gargle of laughter. // It is Laughing Boy." The Indian's method for exterminating rattlers is then recounted. The liquid horses prefigure both the gasoline Laughing Boy pours and the snakes disappearing down into the dark of their holes—indeed, prefigure the snakes and burning gasoline together "Pouring downward," like "quicksilver spilled in dark." The burning horses in the poem about Dreiser thus recall not just the burning snakes of "Rattlesnake Country" but the linkage already there established between horses and snakes.

Warren focuses on Dreiser's mouth—"Watch his mouth, how it moves without a *sound*"—as he had, in the poem before, on Laughing Boy's: "Sometimes, before words come, he utters a sound like croupy laughter." Both Dreiser and Laughing Boy have trouble getting out the utterance that boils within. Dreiser's mouth, where "Saliva gathers in the hot darkness of mouth-tissue," recalls the snake-hole as well, appropriately termed "the hole-mouth," where flames consume snakes in darkness, as flames consume horses inside his soul.

The narrator in "Rattlesnake Country" recalls that "you can see the red eyes of fire / Wink at you from / The black mass that is the mountain," anticipating the vision granted Dreiser in which "The world is a great ass propped high on pillows, the cunt / Winks" (where "ass" echoes "mass," and "Wink[s]," as in the preceding poem, begins a new line). Unable to sleep, and thinking "of the red eyes of fire that / Are winking from blackness," the narrator swims out across the lake in that direction, the moonlit water a "silvered and / Unbreathing medium" in which he feels undone, beyond all desire. The moon hangs down "like an old woman's belly." Moonlit lake is answered by moonlit river, both in the refrain of the song Dreiser and his brother wrote that is quoted at the beginning of the "Homage" and at the end, where the opening and closing of an eye is once again associated with the moon: "Have you ever / Seen midnight moonlight on the Wabash. . . ? / Have you ever thought how the moonlit continent / Would look from the tearless and unblinking distance of God's wide eye?" Here, moonlight and blinking are mutually exclusive; likewise in the other poem, where it is only in the moon's absence that the winking becomes visible: "If there is no moon, you can see the red eyes of fire / Wink."

"Homage to Theodore Dreiser" is followed by a poem about another novelist, "Flaubert in Egypt" (297). Of Dreiser, the narrator declares, "He will write a great novel, someday." That Flaubert would someday write one as well is alluded to when he discovers his heroine's name while gazing at the Cataract of the Nile: "Eureka—the name, it is Emma!" Each poem dwells on the novelist's sexuality, bringing him face to face with female genitals. For Dreiser, who was "Born with one hand in his pants" and who "moves in his dream of ladies swan-necked, with asses ample and sweet," the world "is a great ass propped on pillows" and a "cunt" that "Winks"; Flaubert spends one of his Egyptian evenings with a prostitute, finding "the *mons veneris* shaven, arse noble. / That night three *coups,* and once / performs cunnilingus. Fingers clutching her necklace, / he lies. He remembers his boyhood. Her fingers / and naked thighs twitch in sleep." Twitches and winks have a long association in Warren's network of imagery, especially in the novels. Whether Willie Stark winked or not at Jack Burden in chapter 1 of *All the King's Men* (16), for example, hinges on whether it was an involuntary movement—whether it was a twitch like that on the face of the hitchhiker Burden picked up in New Mexico that seemed to be the prelude to a wink.

Flaubert lying awake next to the sleeping prostitute is paralleled by the unnamed protagonist of "Interjection #5: Solipsism and Theology" (299), who "stared at the classic shut eyelids of his true love sleeping." The woman is hardly Flaubert's true love, but the gaze directed at the shut eyelids renews the theme of the feminine wink, as had the twitch of the thigh.

Gazing at the beloved without being seen by her, as does the man staring at his sleeping love, takes place too in "The True Nature of Time" (300), where the narrator tells his beloved that "I, unseen, saw. Saw / You." As his ship came in, she was standing on the pier, looking "toward that abstract of distance that I / Yet was." This event transpires where "Flaubert in Egypt" began, on the French coast of the English Channel, where Flaubert dreamed of the bright colors of the Egyptian desert, so different from what he saw here: "Off La Manche, wind leaning. Gray stones of the gray / city sluiced by gray rain." In "The Faring" (300), the first part of "The True Nature of Time," the narrator, approaching the French coast on a "Channel boat," can see "the gray city" with its "gray roof-slates." In "The Enclave" (300), the poem's second section, the "Wind leaning" "off La Manche" where Flaubert stood returns: "I . . . hear the wind off the sea heave. / Off the sea, it uncoils. Landward, it leans." The way the narrator nears the shore in "The Faring"—"The Channel boat banging / The chop like a shire-horse on cobbles—thus I, / Riding the spume-flash . . . , / Came"—parallels the way Flaubert nears the Sphinx: "rode hard at / the Sphinx . . . which / in that perspective and distance, lifted slow from / the desert, like a great ship." The images are intricately reversed: The narrator is "Riding" the waves on a ship that behaves like a horse, while Flaubert rides a literal horse as he approaches a figurative ship.

While Flaubert had to go to Egypt to find "sunlight . . . and new colors," the narrator of "The Faring" is more fortunate. Though the city is gray, as it was for Flaubert, sunshine brings out another color: "It was the gray city, but the gray roof-slates / Sang blue in the sun." And after the narrator is reunited with his beloved, the sun connects with another, more resonant hue: "The last light / Came gliding a track across the gray water from westward. / It came leveling in to finger the roses. One / Petal, yellow, fell, slow. // At the foot of the gray stone, like light, it lay." This avatar of the light Flaubert sought in the desert ("sunlight like murder, lust and new colors") is at the same time an avatar of the golden origins so persistent in *Or Else* (for example, in the naked old mother's "golden memories of love" that are a collection of coins in "Natural History" and in the "yellow . . . dust" on the parents' marriage bed in "I Am Dreaming of a White Christmas"). It is thus no accident that these roses are yellow ones ("Sea graying, but roses were yellow, climbing / The wall, it was stone"). The golden-shower effect visible in the sun-fingered yellow petal falling slowly to earth is visible too in "The Enclave": "From the cock's throat, the cry, / In the dark, like gold blood flung, is scattered."

The narrator hears the cock's cry from the darkness of his bed, and asks, "How // May I know the true nature of Time, if / Deep now in darkness that glittering enclave / I dream, hangs? It shines." The poem that follows, "Vision Under the October Mountain: A Love Poem" (301), reformulates this dream of a luminescence that hangs above the dreamer as a golden mountain that "high hangs in gold air." The bed where, the narrator of "The Enclave" tells us, "I lie // In darkness" becomes the "unfatuous dark" of prenatal existence: "did we once in the womb dream, dream / a gold mountain in gold / air floating . . . ?" The mountain, "Golding from green," gets its color from the leaves of October, about to fall, paralleling the yellow petals (of which one fell) that contribute to the other golden-shower effect, earlier in "The True Nature of Time." The yellow roses were "climbing / The wall, it was stone," the material of which the October Mountain is made: "how / can stone float . . . ?"

In the darkness of the womb, "we in the // pulse and warm slosh of / that unbreathing bouillon" could only dream the gold mountain, not see it, "floating / above our blind eyes with / no lashes yet, unbrined by grief yet, we / seeing nothing." Likewise, in "Stargazing" (302), the narrator is aware of the stars above his head but does not see them, not because he can't but because he won't: "And the girl is saying, 'You do not look / At the stars,' for I did not look at / The stars, for I know they are there, know / That if I look at the stars, I // Will have to live over again all I have lived." He speaks of having already lived, thereby situating the moment when he does not see the stars as just the opposite of the time *before* life begins when it was only in dream that we could see the gold floating above us, our blind eyes as yet "unbrined by grief." In both the pre- and postlife states, there is no breathing: in the womb we were in an "unbreathing bouillon"; in "Stargazing" the wind, a figure for the narrator who is reluctant to look at the stars, "is afraid / To breathe, and waits, huddled in / Sparse blackness" like the fetus huddled in the "faceless unfatuous / dark"; further, the absence of breath is invoked there as the indication that life is over, as the narrator in "Stargazing" recalls "moments when . . . the mirror / Showed no breath."

The stars are analogous to the golden mountain, but why? "Vision Under the October Mountain" and "Stargazing" provide an answer: in the former, the gold mountain "is // the image of authority, of reality," while in the latter, the narrator addresses the stars by the second (and only the second) of these terms: "to live over again all I have lived / In the years I looked at stars and / Cried out, 'O reality!'" Yet the narrator of "October Mountain" immediately puts into question what he has just said the mountain was the image of: "it is // the image of authority, of reality—or, is it?—floating / with no weight." I read the question as referring to the second of the terms. How, that is, can the high-hanging gold be the image of reality when it's not real? It floats with no weight, and is only what we may once have dreamed. The force of a multitude of images in *Or Else* and other Warren texts of golden spills and their traces, together with the elements of the Danae myth spelled out elsewhere in his work, lead inescapably to the conclusion that this floating presence sensed in the womb is the father's. It may be a dream, but it's an insistent dream—the dream of the persistent paternal presence, the trace of his authorship of one's (the narrator's and his doubles') being and of the taciturn texts Warren's fathers leave for their sons to read in his novels.

The stars in "Stargazing" are analogous to the golden mountain in "Vision Under the October Mountain" in the way that an element in one poem can be analogous to an element in a neighboring poem in the sequence, a certain sameness despite different contexts. In Warren's symbolic network the stars and the dreamed-of golden light represent different things, reality and authority, respectively. As the world's reality, the "arctic starlight" of "Stargazing" earlier appeared in "Interjection #5: Solipsism and Theology," where the protagonist "stared at the icy and paranoid glitter of winter stars. / He said: *They would grind me like grain, small as dust, and not care.*"

Yet something has happened in the interval, for in "Stargazing" the narrator asserts that "The stars / Love me," adding, "I love them. I wish they // Loved God, too. I truly wish that." If we can assume that the protagonist of "Interjection #5" is the poet's persona, the poem appears to represent him as he once was—"Wild with ego, wild with world-blame." Since then he has learned, among other things, that the glittery stars are not as indifferent as he thought, unless, that is, what he says in "Stargazing" about their loving him is meant ironically. As indeed it may be, for in the poem's first line he had said, "The stars are only a backdrop for / The human condition," and thus unlikely to love him.

Irony or no, his wish at the end of "Stargazing" that the stars "Loved God, too" is of a piece with the immediately following "Interjection #6: What You Some-times Feel on Your Face at Night" (302): "Out of mist, God's / Blind hand gropes to find / Your face. The fingers / Want to memorize your face. The fingers / Will be wet with the tears of your eyes. God // Wants only to love you, perhaps." Not only is the love of God present in both poems, but so too is blindness, willful blindness in the narrator's refusal to look up at the stars, complemented by God's inability to see the human face.

This in turn finds its complementary reversal in "News Photo" (303), when Robert E. Lee makes a spectral appearance: "There are tears in his eyes, or / at least would be, if / he had any." God is blind, so too the godlike Lee, who in other ways as well recalls the father of "I Am Dreaming of a White Christmas." Both see without their missing eyes, and both are presented in a half-decomposed state, with prominent skull (the father's "bald skin tight on skull," Lee "lifting the hat off . . . expos[ing] / the skull") and leathery skin ("Like old leather lacquered" [the father], "some leathery skin to face-bone" [Lee]). The tears in "Interjection #6" are on the face a blind God cannot see; in "News Photo," in the blind eyes of the gazing Lee.

The object of Lee's gaze is a man in a news photograph descending the courthouse stairs after being acquitted of a murder he did in fact commit. He had shot a civil rights worker, in the service, he believed, of the cause for which the Lee he idolized had fought, but the smile he thinks he sees on the general's face turns into bitter laughter. The fingers in "Interjection #6" with which God had wanted to memorize the face he loved, and which would be "wet with the tears of your eyes," find a ghastly counterpart in the murderous finger of the acquitted man, who "knows how precious flesh is, / having with his own hand, —finger, / rather— pump gun, finger on trigger of— . . . burst / flesh."

In "Stargazing," the narrator keeps his head down, refusing to look at the stars, in contrast to the girl by his side, who evidently does look at them, because she reproaches him for not giving them his attention. For him they are too painful to look at; they would remind him of what he would rather not think about. "I know they are there, know / that if I look at the stars, I // Will have to live over again all I have lived." The man in "News Photo," as he descends the courthouse steps,

> carries his face down. . . . His
> eyes turn inward. . . . [N]ow he
> moves toward the flash bulbs, his eyes
> inward on innocence. But the eyes
> of his wife, above him, to the left,
> stare out at the flash bulbs in
> outrage, for she hates the world.

The parallel is extensive, though it is surprising to find the narrator of "Stargazing," who appears to inhabit the poet's persona, metamorphosed into a rabid southern racist. The girl by his side becomes the wife by the racist's; the stars he won't look at but that she does become the flash bulbs the wife confronts but the husband won't. Those piercing lights represent the world she hates, as the stars represent a reality with which the poet's persona is in a complicated relation of both hatred and love.

The slowness and the care with which the man in "News Photo" descends the court house stairs—"carries it, the belly, carefully down // the stairs, and descending, lets it / down carefully, step / to step down, like an armful of / crockery"— are paralleled and reversed, respectively, in "Little Boy and Lost Shoe" (307) by the slow yet careless gait of the boy, who had lost his shoe in a field and "hobbled" home, "not caring." "I don't know why you dawdle and do not hurry," the narrator reproaches him in a parent's voice. "How dilatory can a boy be . . .?"

"Hurry, for the moon has bled"—as in the preceding poem Christ is said to have "bled for us all," and as in the next poem, "Composition in Gold and Red-Gold" (307), a chipmunk will bleed, for the sake of an artistic composition. The stillness of a golden autumn afternoon will be broken by the scream of the narrator's daughter when her cat suddenly kills it. "[O]ne can see / The faint smear of flame-gold at the base / Of the skull." But the golden light permeates all, both the blood's red, turned to "flame-gold," and the apples'

> golden
> The sunlight falls . . .
>   . . . in pitiless plenitude, and every leaf
> On the ruined apple tree is gold, and the apples all
> Gold, too, especially those
>
> On the ground. The gold of apples
> That have fallen flushes to flame, but
> Gold is the flame. Gold
> Goes red-gold.

The chipmunk, in life, "is / Golden in gold light." After the event, the "little girl"— an expression paralleling that of the "little boy" of the preceding poem (nowhere else in *Or Else* does either expression appear)—"weeps under / The powerful flood of gold light." The sun's "pitiless plenitude" parallels the moon's in "Little Boy and Lost Shoe," where "the moon has bled, but not like a heart, in pity."

The sun's golden light touches not only the little girl but the little boy as well: "Sunlight touched the goldenrod, and yellowed his hair." There is a difference, however, that while the girl (and the apples, the chipmunk, and the entire scene) is the passive recipient of this "powerful flood of gold light," the boy in the preceding poem creates the effect himself to some degree: "Home he hobbled, not caring, with a stick whipping goldenrod"—reenacting the original golden paternity, as the narrator as the dreaming narrator in "I Am Dreaming of White Christmas" keeps himself from doing, not wishing to stir up the yellow dust of time on the newspapers spread across the mattress where he was conceived. "Little Boy and Lost Shoe" may seem another version of "A Vision: Circa 1880" (in *You, Emperors, and Others*), where a boy (who this time is clearly the father) emerges "Out of the woods where pollen is a powder of gold / Shaken from pistil of oak minutely, and of maple" (159). What or who did the shaking? It is not exactly spelled out, but I think it was the boy: We see "In his hand a wand of peeled willow," anticipating the stick with which we see the boy in "Little Boy and Lost Shoe" "whipping goldenrod." The earlier boy's "brow bearing a smudge of gold pollen, lips / Parted in some near-smile of boyhood bemusement, / Dangling the willow, he stands." He is also "barefoot," while the one in the more recent poem is only half shoeless. The later poem may seem a version of the first, but they are not the same. The boy in "Little Boy and Lost Shoe" comes very close to his predecessor, but like a son coming close to being his father and not quite achieving it.

The "faint smear of flame-gold at the base / Of the skull" of the dead chipmunk is an "effect" that "Completes the composition"—that is, the "Composition in Gold and Red-Gold" that names the poem. The touch of red complements that of the apples lying nearby, the "fallen" ones whose gold "flushes to flame." This instance of sudden, surprising beauty is complemented by the possibility imagined at the end of the next poem, "Interjection #7: Remarks of Soul to Body" (309), of sudden glory: "But let us note, too, how glory, like gasoline spilled / On the cement in a garage may flare, of a sudden, up, // In a blinding blaze, from the filth of the world's floor." The complementarity is enhanced by the parallels between (1) the chipmunk corpse as detritus and the "filth," (2) the corpse being on the ground and the filth being on the floor, and (3) the "flame-gold" and the "flare" and "blaze."

In "There's a Grandfather's Clock in the Hall" (309), the narrator wonders if he "will ever have to wear false teeth," which continues the thoughts on aging expressed in the immediately preceding "Interjection #7" ("You've toughed it out pretty well, old Body, done / Your duty, and gratified most of my whims, to boot"), but "There's a Grandfather's Clock in the Hall" exhibits its closest ties with "Composition in Gold and Red-Gold." Beginning with the image of a grandfather clock, with "minute hand stands still, then it jumps," the poem is a meditation on mortality and time. The narrator remembers his last visit to his mother before she died. Though he knew her illness was terminal, knew that the false teeth by her bedside would never return to her mouth but by the undertaker's hand, yet he did not realize that her asking if he was wearing a new suit would be the last thing she would ever say to him. Death's sudden arrival is here equated with the abrupt movement of the clock's minute hand: "watch the clock closely. . . . / Nothing happens, nothing happens, then suddenly, quick as a wink, and slick as a mink's prick, Time thrusts through the time of no-Time." The death of the chipmunk came just as unexpectedly; when it happens, the daughter shrieks, and "the sky / Tingles crystalline like a struck wine glass"—a moment repeated in "There's a Grandfather's Clock" when "every / Ulcer in love's lazaret may, like a dawn-stung gem, sing." The glass and the gem resonate, not only when struck or stung, but also sympathetically, from poem to poem. Earlier in the sentence in which the gem sings, the narrator implores us (or himself) to "Seize the nettle of innocence in both your hands," which parallels the moment when "The little girl / Holds the cat in her arms, / Crooning, 'Baby, oh baby.'" The cat, though it has just killed the chipmunk, retains an infant's innocence in her eyes. Yet its lethal claws have something of the nettle about them.

"There's a Grandfather's Clock" recounts the mother's death; the father's is told in "Reading Late at Night, Thermometer Falling" (310). A subtler connection can be seen in the way in which the poet speaks of death-dealing Time. In "Grandfather's Clock," time seems immobile, then suddenly leaps forward. In "Reading Late at Night," it is presented as a slow-moving glacier:

> the past, great
> Eater of dreams, of secrets, and random data, and
> Refrigerator of truth, moved ·
> Down what green valley at a glacier's
> Massive pace,
>
> moving
> At a pace not to be calculated by the trivial sun, but by
> A clock more unforgiving . . .
> . . . The ice-mass
> . . . moves
> So imperceptibly that it seems
> Only more landscape.

The two versions of time work in opposite ways, one through an alternation of stasis and sudden movement, the other in an unstoppable inching advance; the movement of each is difficult to perceive, in one case because it is so slow, in the other because it is so quick. In "Grandfather's Clock," time's death-dealing "thrust" strikes only one person at a time; in "Reading Late at Night," time's glacier consumes everyone and everything in its path: "It looms. // The bulk of the unnamable and de-timed beast is now visible, / Erect, in the thinly glimmering shadow of ice."

A farmer on his way home happens to look up and see it and stares in "jaw-dropped awe." In "Folly on Royal Street Before the Raw Face of God" (315), a cat crosses a street in New Orleans, "Fish-head in dainty jaw-clench," before slipping from sight. In no other poem in *Or Else* does a hyphenated "jaw" appear. But though the farmer cringes before the impending doom of the ever-advancing glacier, the cat is oblivious to the portent the narrator senses:

<blockquote>

At sky-height—
Whiteness ablaze in dazzle and frazzle of light like
A match flame in noon-blaze—a gull
Kept screaming above the doomed city.
It screamed for justice against the face of God.

Raw-ringed with glory like an ulcer, God's
Raw face stared down.

And winked.

</blockquote>

In both poems, it is doom from on high: "At sky-height" the gull screams and God's face stares down; in "Reading Late a Night," the "beast, / From his preternatural height . . . lifts, / Into distance, // the magisterial gaze." The only discernible movement on the part of either God or the beast is in their eyes, the one to wink, the other to look elsewhere, "unaware of / The cringe and jaw-dropped awe crouching there below." Now we can understand why the narrator of "Interjection #5: Solipsism and Theology" complained that the "winter stars," in their "icy and paranoid glitter," "would grind me like grain, small as dust, and not care." The threat discerned in "Reading Late at Night" combines the stars' iciness with a glacier's power to grind to dust, and to do without caring, "unaware" of the earthlings in its path.

I argued in my reading of "Vision Under the October Mountain" that the narrator puts the "reality" of the floating and dreamed-of gold mountain into question but not its "authority," and argued as well that the stars represent reality while the golden light, so reminiscent of the paternal gold, represents authority (and that one important nuance of that word is the ability to author). We can see both elements in "Reading Late at Night" in the form of the father and the glacier, between whom there are some interesting parallels. In his mind's eye the narrator can see his father reading, his "forever / Marching gaze" translating "the perception of black marks on white paper into / Truth" as he progresses through book after book. In its unstoppableness, the father's "forever / Marching" advance resembles the glacier's advance timed to a clock that "Glows forever" (that clock is undoubtedly the one in "Forever O'clock" that is preparing to produce the stroke of doom). As a "forever // Marching gaze," it is echoed by the "magisterial gaze" of the beast in the glacier. That "The beast, / . . . lifts, / Into distance, // the magisterial gaze" parallels the narrator's recollection of a photograph of his father as a young man, "one hand out / To lie with authority on a big book. . . , eyes / Lifted into space"—as the beast's gaze was lifted "Into distance"—"And into the future." Earlier on the same page, in the narrator's imagining of the reading scene, neither the snap of a massive oak bough outside nor the groan of a beam within the house breaks his father's concentration: "But his eyes do not lift." In this too he resembles the glacier-beast, for both are oblivious to whatever is not their unending march.

The father's "authority"—a word that, significantly, appears in *Or Else* only in the photograph recalled in "Reading Late at Night" and in "Vision Under the October Mountain," where the father's presence above the fetus in the womb is the very "image of authority"—is genuine yet sadly problematic, for the future into which his lifted eyes stared "Had not been the future. For the future / Was only his voice that, now sudden, said: // 'Son, give me that!'" as he took back from the son the book in which his youthful poems had been published ("Not good," the narrator would later discover). The voice that would not let the son open the book suddenly reminds us of the moment in "I Am Dreaming of a White Christmas" when the son stretched out his hand to see which package was his: "But the voice: // *No presents, son, till the little ones come.*" The father's forbidding voice makes us realize that the unopenable package and the book containing his poems are clues to each other, and that the question posed in "I Am Dreaming"— "Will I never know / What present there was in that package for me?"—may find its answer in "Reading Late at Night."

Though the glacier consumes the father, as "the past, great / Eater of dreams, secrets, and random data, and / Refrigerator of truth" obliterates everything in its path, he reappears in "Folly on Royal Street" as a God more forgiving than the clock that governs the glacier's imperceptible progress. It turns out that the city may not be doomed after all, since God's raw face, the sun's "noon-blaze," after staring down upon a world that includes the narrator and his friends, all drunk and all shocked by the "glittering vacancy" around them, winks. That sign of forgiveness bears a direct connection to what is said in "Reading Late at Night" about how the glacier moves "At a pace not to be calculated by the trivial sun, but by / A clock more unforgiving."

Father and glacier, authority and reality, the trivial sun and forever o'clock are compared one to the other in these two poems. So too are father and son, as readers. The father read for truth ("I think I hear / The faint click and grind of the brain as / It translates the perception of black marks on white paper into / Truth. // Truth is all"), while the son, with his equally tipsy friends, "Mouthed out our

Milton for magnificence." The father read no Milton, and no poetry as far as we are told, but "Hume's *History of England,* Roosevelt's / *Winning of the West,* a Greek reader, / Now Greek to him . . . or / Some college text book, or Freud on dreams, abandoned / By one of the children. Or, even / Coke or Blackstone." Except for the Freud and possibly some of the Greek reader he could not read, these are reality-based texts, more likely to yield the kind of truth he sought. As for Milton, the narrator is of two minds about its value, on the one hand declaring "what is man without magnificence?" yet on the other immediately characterizing such hope of magnificence as "Delusion, delusion!" then countering that with "But let / Bells ring in all the churches. / Let likker, like philosophy, roar / In the skull. Passion / Is all. Even / The sleaziest." Victor Strandberg considers this last thought an endorsement of William James's assertion of alcohol's power "to stimulate the mystical faculties of human nature" and counteract society's "No" with an embracing "Yes" (*The Poetic Vision* 245). Strandberg also points out that the poem's first line— "Drunk, drunk, drunk, amid the blaze of noon"—parodies Milton's "dark, dark, dark, amid the blaze of noon" in *Samson Agonistes.* Milton, in other words, is not just what the narrator reads; it is what he rewrites. Father and son are compared in these two sequential poems not as readers alone but as poets too; the father having written poems he did not want his son to see, the son not only rewriting Milton into the poem we are reading but also alluding to his literary production in an auto-biographical aside at the end, having recounted the subsequent lives of his two friends: "As for the third, the tale / Is short. But long, / How long the art . . . !"

The narrator in "Interjection #8: Or, Sometimes Night" (317) finds the same "unsleeping principle of delight" in "the arc of the apple's rondure" as in "the subtly reversed curve" of "A girl's thigh" and in "The flushed dawn cumulus." Again and again, the reader of the sequence can undergo a parallel, though not identical, experience of finding the same thing in different places, for example, the apple. The narrator of the immediately preceding "Folly on Royal Street" tells of how C., one of the two friends with whom he quoted Milton, drunk, in New Orleans, was later to abandon his settled life and position in a bank to end his days in Mexico: "One morning was not there. His books, / However, were in apple-pie order." His sudden not-thereness evokes, strangely, the death of the narrator's father as related in the previous poem, "Reading Late at Night." More strangely, the apple is there too: "Who, aged eighty-six, fell to the floor, / Unconscious. Two days later, / Dead. Thus they discovered your precious secret: / A prostate big as a horse-apple. Cancer, of course. // . . . So disappeared. // Simply not there." Another site where that principle of delight can be encountered in "Or, Sometimes, Night" is in "a startling burst of steel-brilliant sun" that "makes / The lone snow-flake dance"—in which there lies an echo, unique in the collection, with the other of the two friends in the poem before. M. takes his boat out before dawn, cuts the engine, and instead of fishing, gazes at dawn's first light, which "is like / A knife-edge honed to steel-brightness." Though "steel" appears elsewhere in *Or Else,* "steel-bri . . ." does not. Finding sameness in difference, as does the narrator of "Or, Sometimes, Night," the reader of the sequence can see echoes of the narrator's father in C. and of the narrator himself in M., as one whose attention is caught by the sun's steel-brightness or -brilliance. The remaining site in "Or, Sometimes, Night" where the "unsleeping principle of delight" can be glimpsed is the "Timeless instant, glittering, between / Last upward erg and, suddenly, / Totter and boom" of a cresting wave; in "Folly on Royal Street," one finds "the shock of that sudden and glittering vacancy" in which the narrator and his two companions "rocked / On our heels"—a rocking evoked by the totter of the wave.

One can find sameness in difference, too, in the relationship between "Or, Sometimes, Night" and "Sunset Walk in Thaw-Time in Vermont" (317). In the former, the narrator finds the same principle of delight in "the arc of the apple's rondure" as in the "subtly reversed curve from / Buttock bulge to . . . under-knee nook"; in the latter, he speaks of "the bulge and slick twining of muscular water" in a stream, a metaphor that effects a juxtaposition parallel to that between the apple's arc and the muscular curve of the human female form. In another instance, the "startling burst of steel-brilliant sun" reappears in "Sunset Walk" as a "burst" that creates "startlement" (and nowhere else in the collection does any form of "startle" appear): "out of / The spruce thicket . . . it / Bursts. The great partridge cock . . . / Into the red sun of sunset, plunges. Is / Gone. // In the ensuing / Silence, abrupt in / Back-flash and shiver of that sharp startlement, I / Stand. Stare. In mud-streaked snow, / My feet are."

The parallels between "Folly on Royal Street" and "Sunset Walk," sequential in the roman-numeraled series, are even more extensive. There is a "burst" in "Folly" too: "spring, / Off the Gulf, without storm warnings out, / Burst, like a hurricane of Camelias, sperm, cat-squalls, fish-smells." The cat passes by with a fish in its jaw, then "Was gone. We, / In the shock of that sudden and glittering vacancy, rocked / On our heels." Compare this with what happens in "Sunset Walk": "it / Bursts. The great partridge cock . . . plunges. Is / Gone. // In the ensuing / Silence, abrupt in / Back-flash and shiver of that sharp startlement, I / stand." Specifically:

1. "[S]pring . . . / Burst" corresponds to "it / Bursts."

2. While it is spring that bursts in "Folly" but the partridge that does so in "Sunset Walk," the cat corresponds to the partridge in that both catch the narrator's eye; in addition, the cat and the fish in its mouth are in fact metonymies for the spring that bursts upon New Orleans "like a hurricane of / . . . cat-squalls, fish-smells."

3. "Was gone" corresponds to "Is / Gone."

4. The narrator's "shock" corresponds to his "startlement."

5. "[T]hat sudden . . . vacancy" corresponds to "the ensuing / Silence."

6. "[G]littering" corresponds to "Back-flash."

7. The focus on the narrator's feet in "We . . . rocked / On our heels" corresponds to that in "I / Stand. . . . In mud-streaked snow, / My feet are." Later, "I / Stand here with the cold exhalation of snow/ Coiling high as my knees."

There is doom in both poems (the only two where the word appears): The gull in "Folly" screams "above the doomed city"; in "Sunset Walk," the stream "heaves / . . . like / Doom."

A similar string of correspondences links "Sunset Walk in Thaw-Time in Vermont" with "Birth of Love" (319), where the partridge of "Sunset Walk" finds itself paralleled by the woman of "Birth of Love" who emerges from a woodland pool:

1. The partridge emerges out of a thicket of "Black spruce"; the woman rises from the pool, her white nakedness seen "Against / The . . . night of spruces," her "body, // Profiled against the darkness of spruces."

2. As the partridge flies up from the spruce boughs, it leaves behind the "Back-flash and shiver of that sharp startlement"; in rising from the water, the woman's "motion has fractured it to shivering splinters of silver." "Shiver" corresponds to "shivering," the flash of "Back-flash" to the splintering silver fragments of light visible on the water's surface, and the sharpness of the "sharp startlement" to the sharpness apparent in the "fractured . . . splinters."

3. The observer of the partridge's emergence stands there with cold feet: "I / Stand. Stare. In mud-streaked snow, / My feet are. . . . I / Stand here with the cold exhalation of snow / Coiling high as my knees"; the observer of the woman's emergence from the forest pool is "hanging / Motionless in the gunmetal water, feet / Cold with the coldness of depth." Here are two instances of echoes unique in *Or Else*. Only in these two poems are the protagonist's feet cold and do the words "with the cold[ness]" appear.

4. The next words after those just quoted from both poems focus on the observer's eyes: "In mud-streaked snow, / My feet are. I, / Eyes fixed past black spruce boughs on the red west"; "feet / Cold with the coldness of depth, all / History dissolving from him, is / Nothing but an eye. Is an eye only."

5. The partridge flies upward, to the sky: "Into the red sun of sunset, plunges." The woman rises from the water, and "With face lifted toward the high sky . . . / A white stalk from which the face flowers gravely toward the high sky," she ascends, "Moves up the path that, stair-steep," winds up the bank from the pool.

6. The partridge "Into the red sun of sunset, plunges. Is / Gone"; the woman, after ascending the steep bank toward the sky, "Glimmers and is gone." Nowhere

else in the collection, except for the next poem, "A Problem in Spatial Composition" (321), does the phrase "is gone" appear. Nowhere but in the poem that immediately precedes "Sunset Walk" in the roman-numeraled series, "Folly on Royal Street," does the singular of the verb "to be" appear with "gone" (the cat with fish in its mouth "Was gone")

"Sunset Walk" concludes with the narrator's thinking of his son fifty years after his own demise, and with the question "what / Blessing should I ask for him? . . . // For what blessing may a man hope for but / An immortality in / The loving vigilance of death?" "Birth of Love" concludes similarly, with the protagonist wishing he could reach out and protect his wife from all that might happen to her beyond his reach, as the narrator of "Sunset Walk" wished to "bless, / Forward into that future's future," his son: "in his heart he cries out that, if only / He had such strength, he would put his hand forth / And maintain it over her to guard, in all / Her out-goings and in-comings." And the question of "what / Blessing" he should ask and "what blessing" he may hope for is echoed by the last line of "Birth of Love," in which the protagonist sees the first star gleam above the trees where the woman had disappeared: "I do not know what promise it makes to him."

The body of the woman who emerged from the water in "Birth of Love" is metaphorized into a plant: "The body, / . . . is / A white stalk from which the face flowers gravely toward the high sky." Conversely, in "A Problem in Spatial Composition," the poem that concludes the collection, a plant is metaphorized into a human body:

> the stub
> Of a great tree, gaunt-blasted and black, thrusts.
>
> A single
> Arm jags upward . . .
>
> Then
> *Stabs,* black, at the infinite saffron of sky.

It is a body that "stabs," as the observer of the woman who has come out of the pool is stabbed by what he sees: "Sees // The body that is marked by his use, and Time's" (to which we might compare the "gaunt-blasted" look of the tree—not that she is gaunt, but that like the tree, her body shows the effect of Time) "grapple the pond-bank. Sees / . . . that posture of female awkwardness that is, / And is the stab of, suddenly perceived grace." The word "stab" appears only in these two contexts.

The last thing we see through the protagonist's eyes in "Birth of Love" is "The first star pulse into being," of which the narrator does not know "what promise it makes to him." The last thing we see through the narrator's eyes in the final poem is the hawk that suddenly glides down from the sky, hovers for an instant, then perches on the "topmost, indicative tip" of the upward-reaching arm of the tree. And then "The hawk, in an eyeblink, is gone." The star makes an indecipherable promise, unreadable to the narrator if not to the protagonist; yet we have every reason to believe that the protagonist *is* the narrator, the Robert Penn Warren whose woodland pool this was (and whose wife this was). This makes the star all the more like the hawk, for in Warren's poetic universe the hawk is the father, and the father—like Willie Stark in *All the King's Men*—at times winks at the son in an ambiguous way. It was ambiguous for Jack Burden in the novel because, as Willie said, maybe he just had something in his eye, and what seemed a wink was really an involuntary blink, like the "eyeblink" during which the hawk disappears from sight. The hawk and the eyeblink are inextricably connected in this concluding line to *Or Else*. God—*that* father—had just winked a few poems earlier in the sequence, in "Folly on Royal Street" ("God's / Raw face stared down. // And winked").

But, to speak of last words, the most striking are these: "is gone." In all the collection they appear only in the two immediately preceding poems: in "Birth of Love," where the woman from the pool disappears as she ascends the bank, through the trees: "Glimmers and is gone," and in "Sunset Walk," where the partridge plunges into the sunset and "Is / Gone." Thus the last words of the collection— "is gone"—are a concluding, and indicative, instance of the echoing words that illumine the sequence, particularly in its final poems. The echoes we have been tracing here are important enough to have the last word.

Except to say that reading *Or Else* with such attention to its continuities is, I think, a way to follow the practice of the father whose gaze kept progressing at a glacial pace. And that, read this way, the poems taken two by two betray a strange tendency to become the same poem—as, within "Reading Late at Night," the father who sought truth in his reading seems almost to become the glacier, the "Refrigerator of truth" that will consume him—as each poem, like the inevitable march of time, replaces its predecessor with itself.

CHAPTER 8

"EVERYTHING SEEMS AN ECHO"
CAN I SEE ARCTURUS FROM WHERE I STAND?
POEMS 1975

"Everything seems an echo of something else," Warren writes in "A Way to Love God" (325), the opening poem in *Can I See Arcturus from Where I Stand?*, the sequence of ten poems that begins *Selected Poems 1923–1975*. This line is placed just after two stanzas that illustrate the truth of that assertion, as they echo passages from *Eleven Poems on the Same Theme*. In the first of these, mountains in their sleep "remember . . . that there is something they cannot remember. . . . Theirs is the perfect pain of conscience, that / Of forgetting the crime, and I hope you have not suffered it. I have." So, too, has the "mad killer" in "Crime" (68), who "tries to remember . . . but he cannot seem / To remember what it was he buried under the leaves," most likely the victim of his crime. What Warren in "A Way to Love God" says he cannot remember may well be that his not being able to remember is itself a recollection of the mad killer's inability to remember in the poem from three decades before. Though it is more likely that he means just the opposite, that he remembers it very well indeed. In the second of these stanzas, "in *plaza, piazza, place, platz,* and square, / Boot heels, like history being born, on cobbles bang"—as they had in "Terror" (77), another of the *Eleven Poems:* "the blunt boot-heels resound / In the Piazza."

It is immediately after those boot heels bang on the cobbles that he writes of everything seeming an echo of something else, as if alluding to the echoes he had just made.

But there are several kinds of echoes in Warren's poetry:

1. that between one poem and another from a prior volume, as in these reminiscences of "Crime" and "Terror";

2. the very localized echo in "*plaza, piazza, place, platz,*" the same word echoing in different tongues in the same line;[1]

3. the one he is about to make in the next two stanzas after the remark about the pervasiveness of echoes: in the first, when the executioner held up the head of Mary of Scots, "the lips kept on moving, / But without sound"—this is followed in the second by a recollection of sheep whose "jaws did not move";

4. the persistent sequential echoes evident in most, though not all, of Warren's poetic volumes, linking one poem to the next, as the axe that cut off Mary's head is followed in "Evening Hawk" (326), the second poem in the *Arcturus* sequence, by the "honed steel-edge" of the hawk's wing that "Scythes down another day," cutting the "stalks of Time" and, in particular, "The head of each stalk";

5. the symmetrical echoes to be found in the *Arcturus* sequence but possibly in no other, linking the first poem with the last, the second with the next to last, and so forth, of which Mary's severed head also provides an example, for the gesture in which "by the hair, the headsman held up the head / Of Mary of Scots" is repeated in the last poem in the sequence: "Have you ever / Had the impulse to stretch forth your hand over / The bulge of forest and seize trees like the hair / Of a head you would master?" ("Old Nigger on One-Mule Cart Encountered Late at Night When Driving Home from Party in the Back Country" 333).

The intensity of these echoes, particularly with the addition of the symmetrical ones, amply justifies the remark that "Everything seems an echo of something else," as well as the declaration made in the first words of the poem (and of the sequence): "Here is the shadow of truth, for only the shadow is true." For an echo casts a shadow on what it echoes, and vice versa. For after reading "Evening Hawk," we cannot help seeing what happened to Mary of Scots in the shadow cast by the "honed steel-edge" of the hawk's wing which also severs heads.

In reading *Arcturus,* I will focus on types 4 and 5, though also pay attention to Warren's personal Perseid when it appears, as it does when the headsman lifts the head of Mary of Scots by the hair, for Perseus performs the same gesture in the Cellini statue to which Warren alludes in *A Place to Come To* (387).[2] The immobility of the sheep, whose "eyes / Stared into nothingness" and whose "jaws did not move" while shreds of grass "Hung from the side of a jaw, unmoving," might also recall the paralysis afflicting those who gazed on the Gorgon.[3]

As I argued in *The Braided Dream* (193–95), the hawk in "Red-Tail Hawk and Pyre of Youth" is the father, Laius slain by his son. The hawk in "Evening Hawk" is the father as the Titan Cronus with his castrating sickle, conflated with Father Time (Robert Graves writes, "The later Greeks read 'Cronus' as *Chronos,* 'Father Time' with his relentless sickle" [45]):

> The hawk comes.
>
> His wing
> Scythes down another day, his motion
> Is that of the honed steel-edge, we hear
> The crashless fall of stalks of Time.
>
> The head of each stalk is heavy with the gold of our error.

Warren tells the following story in *The Gods of Mount Olympus,* a book for children:

> Mother Earth . . . created out of herself a beautiful strong, gray metal [from which] she made a sickle with jagged teeth at the edge of the blade. Then she called the Titans together. "My children," she said, "you have a savage father. . . . Listen to me and I shall tell you how we can punish him for his wickedness." The Titans were afraid of what their mother proposed and shrank from it. Only Cronus . . . spoke up boldly. He agreed that Father Sky had begun the trouble and deserved to be punished for it. When night came on and Father Sky drew near to Mother Earth, Cronus leaped up and dealt his father a terrible wound. His blood ran out upon the earth and into the waters of the sea. (3–4)

Given his young audience, Warren could not spell out the nature of that "terrible wound," though he does return to it later, as if it held a fascination for him: "Some people believed that [Aphrodite] was a daughter of Zeus, but there is another and more interesting story of how she came to be. When Cronus wounded Father Sky with the sickle, some of Father Sky's blood spattered on the sea. From the foam which gathered round this blood a girl began to take shape" (33). Mother Earth's anger at her husband and the jagged teeth on the sickle recall the opening poem in Warren's last sequence, *Or Else,* where the sun, "redder than / A mother's rage," sinks "Beyond the western ridge of black-burnt pine stubs like / A snaggery of rotten shark teeth" ("The Nature of a Mirror" 271).

The blade of the hawk's wing recalls the executioner's axe (which itself recalls Perseus's blade) from the preceding poem, as it too cuts off heads. But this time it is the poet's own ("*our* error"), and the gold that weighs down that head is itself heavy with meaning, evident in *Or Else* and elsewhere (in such poems as "No Bird Does Call," "A Vision: Circa 1880," "I Am Dreaming of a White Christmas," and the opening scene of *A Place to Come To*). It is the gold to which the poet as Perseus owes his origin, but also an inseminating power he inherits from his progenitor. The gold, inherited from the father, will be visible in the father in "Red-Tail Hawk and Pyre of Youth": "Gold eyes, unforgiving, for they, like God, see all" (348). The "sunset hawk" in "Kentucky Mountain Farm," the evening hawk's predecessor, likewise had "gold eyes" (38). The evening hawk's eyes are not gold but like the Red-Tail's they are "unforgiving."

The heavy, gold-bearing stalk with a head is a penis, and that scythe can cut it off. We might have known this from the very beginning of the poem, seeing those hawk's "wings dipping through / Geometries and orchids that the sunset builds," for we should know that Warren plays on the etymology that traces the flower to *orchis,* testicles. In "Immanence" (from *Rumor Verified*), he does so by metonymy: "at night, // In bed . . . and a crusting on // Dong. Like an orchid, now darkness / Swells" (472). Darkness swells, but so does, at times, the dong. Thus the son's final gesture in "The Return: An Elegy" is a self-inflicted castration performed out of filial guilt for his mother's death:

> Could I stretch forth like God the hand and gather
> For you my mother
> If I could pluck
> Against the dry essential of tomorrow
> To lay upon the breast that gave me suck
> Out of the dark the dark and swollen orchid of this sorrow. (35)

In the third poem in *Arcturus,* "Loss, of Perhaps Love, in Our World of Contingency" (326), Warren associates being naked in his mother's presence with a loss almost too painful to contemplate. While that loss may be, as Victor Strandberg finds, "the former child-self's love of the world" (*The Poetic Vision* 112), in the context of the preceding poem's stalk-scything hawk it is also the loss of what disappears in castration:

> Shut your eyes, think hard, it doesn't really
>
> Matter which end you start from—forward from
> The earliest thing you remember, the dapple
>
> Of sunlight on the bathroom floor while your mother
> Bathed you, or backward from just now when
>
> You found it gone and cried out, *oh Jesus, no!* Yes,
> Forward or backward, it's all the same,
>
> To the time you are sure you last had it.

It is assuredly something he knew he had when his mother was bathing him, for he would have seen it then.[4] To establish the moment of loss, he must patiently retrace his steps, whether backward or forward from any point in the sequence of memory-images.

It is like reading Gibbon: "It does not matter where you begin. This is History. / Pick up any volume" ("Wind and Gibbon," in *Altitudes and Extensions* 580). It is also like reading Warren. For, as he writes in the "Afterthought" to *Being Here,* "The order and selection" of the poems in that volume (and, it appears, many of his other volumes of poetry) "are determined thematically, but with echoes, repetitions, and variations in feeling and tonality. . . . The thematic order—or better, structure—is played against, or with, a shadowy narrative, a shadowy autobiography" (441). Thus, if we may apply these words to the *Arcturus* sequence, the castrating powers of the scything hawk in the second poem are played against, or with, the possibility that that kind of loss is what the poet is alluding to in the third one. Thinking back to a time when he still had what he lost, in that third poem he recalls having the power to slice through the air that the father-hawk had in the second: "You again pass, cleaving the blue air." Birds like the hawk were also said to have that power in *Audubon,* where "they cleave" the air "With no effort" (Burt 266).

He still had it, apparently, in "Answer to Prayer: A Short Story that Could Be Longer" (327), in which he is with a woman to an "unlit room to enact what comfort body and heart needed." His heart had earlier been gratified when she "Looked up and grinned at me, an impudent eye-sparkling grin, as though / She had just pulled the trick of the week, and on a cold-flushed / Cheek, at the edge of the grin for an accent, the single snow- / Flake settled, and gaily in insult she stuck her tongue out, and blood rushed // To my heart." In "Loss, of Perhaps Love," the poet, talking to himself, had said: "Try to remember / When last you had it. There's always // A logic to everything, and you are a part / Of everything, and your heart bleeds far // Beyond the outermost pulsar." That bleeding in outer darkness echoes a leaking in lower darkness in the last lines of "Evening Hawk": "If there were no wind we might, we think, hear / The earth grind on its axis, or history / Drip in darkness like a leaking pipe in the cellar." And within "Evening Hawk," that leaking pipe recalls the bleeding member left behind by the "honed steel-edge" of the hawk's wing, the castrating "terrible wound" told in Warren's book on Greek mythology. This connection, which is encouraged by the assertion that there is a logic connecting all, suggests that the heart in "Loss, of Perhaps Love" and "Answer to Prayer" may be another organ as well, one to which blood also rushes. As Audubon and Cass Mastern put it, he was probably "in the manly state" (Burt 259; *All the King's Men* 166). The extruding tongue may have had something to do with it, too.

"Answer to Prayer" and "Loss, of Perhaps Love" are connected in other ways as well. Walking down a city street is difficult in both: "the night wind // Shuffles a torn newspaper down the street with a sound / Like an old bum's old shoe-soles that he makes // Slide on the pavement to keep them from flopping off" ("Loss, of Perhaps Love"). "In that bad year, in a city to have now no name"—but which John Burt suggests is "Minneapolis, probably" (812n)—"our feet / Unsteady in slip-tilt and crunch of re-freezing snow as if lame, / . . . down a side street // We moved" ("Answer to Prayer"). The look she gives him with a snowflake on her cheek repeats the look violets "under . . . snowdrifts" gave him when they "see / You again pass, cleaving the blue air" ("Loss, of Perhaps Love"). Cleaving the blue air has the paternal potency of the scything hawk; here, it anticipates the sexual potency the poet displayed that night in Minnesota.

The woman told him she had prayed that he might be happy, and "Her prayer, yes, was answered, for in spite of my meager desert, / Of a sudden, life— it was bingo! was bells and all ringing like mad, / Lights flashing, fruit spinning, the machine spurting dollars like dirt— / Nevada dollars, that is—but all just a metaphor for the luck I now had. // But that was long later." Burt explains the "Nevada dollars": "From slot machines, of course, but Warren has in mind Nevada as a center for divorce as well as for gambling" (812n). Joseph Blotner writes, referring to Warren's first wife, that "anyone who knew anything of his life with Cinina in Minneapolis would see her" (422) in this poem. He was granted a Reno divorce from her in June 1951 (Blotner 269). Hence Warren's remark that "one must be pretty careful how one prays."

That luck led to Eleanor Clark, who is probably the "you" to whom the fifth poem in the sequence, "Paradox" (328), is addressed, and whom he wed a year and a half later. But even though "Answer to Prayer" and "Paradox" are about different wives, and even though one is set on a snowy street and the other on a sandy beach, the second follows in the footsteps of the first—an activity that is also what the second happens to be about. The woman in "Paradox" was "Running ahead" ahead of him; he would gaze at her footprints in the sand, but when he reached one "There was only another in further flight." In "our more complex / Version of Zeno's paradox" he can never catch up to her; or "if I caught you . . . / You had fled my grasp, up and to go // With glowing pace and the smile that mocks / Pursuit." The poet and the woman in "Answer to Prayer" were making their way together with much less agility, "our feet / Unsteady in slip-tilt and crunch of re-freezing snow as if lame," but suddenly she stopped, told him to wait "And abrupt, was gone / Up the now-smeared broad stone to dark doors before I could restrain / That sentimental idiocy." Until that moment they had been walking with "two hands ungloved to clasp." In "Answer to Prayer," the woman escaped from his "clasp" and "was gone / Up" before he could restrain her; in "Paradox" the woman escapes his "grasp, up and to go."

The dark doors seem to have belonged to a church, for she emerged to announce that she had said a prayer for his happiness. "Then cocking her head to one side, // Looked up and grinned at me, an impudent eye-sparkling grin." This impudent grin (accompanied by the "insult" of the tongue) returns in "the smile that mocks" in "Paradox," first visible when "You turned and flung a smile, like spray. / It glittered like tossed spray in the sunlight." Both the smile and the grin are associated with wetness, the smile resembling sea spray, the grin having "for an accent, the single snow- / Flake" that settled on her cheek. The grin was preceded by a movement of the head to one side; the smile was preceded by a backward glance.

In "Midnight Outcry" (329), that smile is remembered in the poem's concluding lines: "The day wore on, and he would ponder, / Lifting eyes from his work, thinking, thinking, / Of the terrible distance in love, and the pain, / Smiling back at the sunlit smile, even while shrinking / From recall of the nocturnal timbre, and the dark wonder." Strandberg saw the woman in "Paradox" not as the second Mrs. Warren but as one of "various vanished girl friends . . . one he had chased down the beach without catching" (*The Poetic Vision* 110). But I think that "the sunlit smile" the poet at the conclusion of "Midnight Outcry" recalls is remembered from the immediately preceding poem in the sequence ("Paradox") and not from the poem in which he remembers it ("Midnight Outcry"), as Strandberg reads it: "the husband who hears his wife cry out in her sleep finds that nothing in her day-time life—her 'sunlit smile,' her 'Endearment and protest,' her tenderness toward 'the infant to whom she gives suck'—can assuage his separation from that part of her being which cried out" (*The Poetic Vision* 110). The "Endearment and protest" and the tenderness toward the infant do indeed appear in "Midnight Outcry," but the sunlit smile does not—though as a "smile [that] glittered . . . in the sunlight" it does appear in "Paradox."[5]

So too does a version of "the terrible distance in love" in the third line of the final stanza, quoted above. In "Midnight Outcry," it is the distance, as Strandberg writes, of "his separation from that part of her being which cried out" at midnight. The husband "fears to awaken and clasp her, lest / Their whole life be lost, for he cannot forget / That the depths that cry rose from might shrivel a heart, or member." (This association of heart with member justifies my assertion that the heart to which blood rushed in "Answer to Prayer" was also a member, as also the heart that bleeds in "Loss, of Perhaps Love.") This separation was anticipated by the distance that would forever separate the pursuer and the pursued in "Paradox," where the association of "clasp" with what might be "lost" in "Midnight Outcry" is anticipated by an association between what is "lost" and the poet's "grasp" (itself recalling the "clasp" in "Answer to Prayer"):

> That race you won—even as it was lost,
> For if I caught you, one moment more,
> You had fled my grasp, up and to go
>
> With glowing pace and the smile that mocks
> Pursuit down whatever shore reflects
> Our flickering passage through the years,
> As we enact our more complex
> Version of Zeno's paradox.

The passage through the years the poet and the woman share is further indication that this is not a brief fling but his life partner.

In "Trying to Tell You Something" (330), the poet again hears a nocturnal outcry, this time from an oak encased in ice. The oak "wants . . . to describe to you / What happens on a December night when // It stands alone in a world of snowy whiteness. . . . // It is ten below zero, and the iron / Of hoops and reinforcement rods is continuing to contract. // There is the rhythm of a slow throb, like pain." The wife's midnight outcry was likewise an expression of hurt: "he would ponder . . . the pain."

But in another regard the seventh poem in the sequence is just the opposite of the sixth. The poet in the latter was separated by a "terrible distance" from his wife's pain. He could not awaken and hold her in his arms "lest / Their whole life be lost"—for fear that what caused her that pain would come between them were it brought to the surface. He could engage in neither "Endearment" nor "protest" for the depths from which that cry arose were "Much deeper and darker than anything love may redeem." Yet unlike the spouse with whom he could not communicate, the tree wants to talk:

> The oak
> Wants to declare this to you, so that you
>
> Will not be unprepared when, some December night,
> You stand on a hill, in a world of whiteness, and
>
> Stare into the crackling absoluteness of the sky. The oak
> Wants to tell you because, at that moment,
>
> In your own head, the cables will sing
> With a thin-honed and disinfectant purity.
>
> And no one can predict the consequences.

Not only does it want to communicate, but it wants him to know that he will one day suffer the same pain.

Yet the prediction had already been made that he would suffer it—in "Midnight Outcry." For what the tree suffers is the result of shrinking, when in subzero temperature the iron encircling and reinforcing it "is continuing to contract." The poet in "Midnight Outcry" was twice in danger of contraction: first, when "he cannot forget / That the depths that cry rose from might shrivel a heart, or member," and then when "Smiling back at the sunlit smile, even while shrinking / From recall of the nocturnal timbre."

The brotherhood in pain the poet shares with the oak, which suffers what the poet will later suffer, and which wants to tell him that fact, is reexamined in "Brotherhood in Pain" (331), the eighth poem in the sequence. In place of an oak, "any chance object" will do, as long as you "Fix your eyes" on it: a falling leaf, a discarded piece of chewing gum, a sock on the floor, a single stone by a brook, or simply the first thing you see when you open your eyes after turning around three times:

In any case, you will suddenly observe an object in the obscene moment of birth.

It does not know its own name. The matrix from which it is torn
Bleeds profusely. It has not yet begun to breathe. Its experience

Is too terrible to recount. Only when it has completely forgotten
Everything, will it smile shyly, and try to love you.

For somehow it knows that you are lonely, too.
It pityingly knows that you are more lonely than it is, for

You exist only in the delirious illusion of language.

In a steady increase of pain through these last three poems, the poet in "Midnight Outcry" is distressed to see his wife in pain but does not suffer that pain himself; in "Trying to Tell You Something," he is told that he will suffer the same pain the tree endures; and in "Brotherhood in Pain," he not only suffers the same pain as the object, but does so to a greater degree, being "more lonely than it is."

The object that suffers in being born is followed in the ninth poem, "Season Opens on Wild Boar in Chianti" (331), by something that suffers in dying. But unlike the object in "Brotherhood in Pain," the boar can cause suffering in others as well: "Dead too, at the tusk-point, the best hound." One of the candidates for the suffering object in the eighth poem bears a curious resemblance to this dead dog: "the hunk // Of dead chewing gum in the gutter with the mark of a molar / Yet distinct on it, like the most delicate Hellenistic chisel-work." Like the dog, it is "dead," and like the chewing gum, the dog bears a tooth mark, that of the tusk that killed him. The "delicate" chiseling on the tooth and its mark is echoed by the boar's murderous yet "delicate, razor-sharp feet" (which might have also left their mark on the dog).

As the human beholder in "Brotherhood of Pain" shares the object's loneliness ("it knows that you are lonely, too") and pain (as we may presume from the title), Warren in "Season Opens" notes that he and the rest of humanity share the boar's ultimate doom:

> In the twilight and silence, now passing
> Our door, men pant with the heavi-
> ness of their destiny's burden,
> Each wondering who will be able
> To choose his own ground when the adversary
> Encounters him, red eye to red eye.

The boar chose his ground "in a cavern of rushes. / In front was only the whole world." Like the "best hound" to whose death Warren alludes in the line immediately preceding this description of the hunters bearing their prey, these men "pant" (and, as if to underscore the allusion, in the next poem in the sequence the "night pants hot like a dog"). That is, they have something in common not only with the boar but with the hound. Thus this poem also parallels the one before it in that they both offer the poet more than one piece of the world of reality (as opposed to the illusory linguistic one in which he sees himself existing) that has something important to tell him about himself.

If any of Warren's poems deserve to stand alone on their merits, "Old Nigger on One-Mule Cart Encountered Late at Night When Driving Home from Party in the Back Country" (333) would qualify. Yet its meaning also is enhanced by the connective tissue of its context in the sequence.

Calvin Bedient says of this "mighty" poem (129), this "star-climbing mono-lith" (186), that it "cultivates brotherhood but swerves away from it at the last" (129). What I think he means is that although near the end of the poem Warren addresses the old man of the title as "Brother, Rebuker, my Philosopher," instead of at that point talking about racial brotherhood he begins to meditate on death, seeing his own prefigured by that of the man in the cart:

> will you be with me when
> I arrive and leave my own cart of junk
> Unfended from the storm of starlight . . .
> To enter, by a bare field, a shack unlit?
> Entering into that darkness to fumble
> My way to a place to lie down.

As Warren pointed out to *New Yorker* editor Howard Moss with regard to the poem's first publication, the "shack" is the "grave" (quoted by Szczesiul 169). Evidently disappointed by Warren's seeming change of subject from correcting his politics to thoughts of his own death, Bedient complains of Warren that "His tragic loneliness (partly self-obsession) wars with his liberal humanism" (185n).

But if we remember the context Warren gives this poem in the *Arcturus* sequence, we can understand that the brotherhood he is here evoking is that of the "Brotherhood in Pain" that has been the subject of the last three poems, and that it has everything to do with suffering and death, particularly in the most recent of the three, "Season Opens on Wild Boar in Chianti." Like the boar, the "Brother, Rebuker" confronts death first, setting an example for the poet to follow. Along with the hunters, Warren was "wondering who will be able / To choose his own ground when the adversary / Encounters him." That "when" is significantly paralleled by the same word in "Brother, . . . will you be with me when / I arrive . . . to fumble / My way to a place to lie down," as that "place to lie down" parallels one's "own ground" that one hopes to be able to choose at the end.

In the last part of the poem, the poet reflects, decades later, on what he recounted in the earlier section, how as a drunken youth one Louisiana summer he almost ran his car into an old black man whom he claimed was on the "ass-hole wrong side of / The road, naturally." In that conclusion, he awakens one snowy night and imagines the man returning home after the incident. He "Unhitches the mule. / Stakes it out. Between cart and shack, / Pauses to make water, and while / The soft, plopping sound in deep dust continues, his face / Is lifted into starlight, calm as prayer." Who is this "Brother, Rebuker" and why is he pissing as he gazes at the stars? As Randy Hendricks suggests, he "may be likened to Warren's many fictional father figures" (119).[6] Certainly as a man who can teach him how to die he could qualify for that honor. But he also qualifies as an equivalent of the strange father figure Warren was writing about at the same time as this poem in *A Place to Come To.* I alluded in an earlier chapter to the ambiguity cast on Buck Tewksbury's final gesture by what his son overhears from the mourners at his funeral (was he "tryen to jack off" or just "standen up to piss" [7]?). The narrator also recalls another occasion, one he witnessed himself, when his father relieved himself while standing on the same mule wagon from which he fell to his death:

> [H]e was standing up, fumbling at the front of his overalls to extract his member. He stood there steady enough, it seemed, his noble head again thrown back to glare at the stars, clutching his great member, with a force that must have been painful, waving it at the stars, crying out in manic glee: "Got the biggest dong in Claxford County—and what the hell good does it do me!"
>
> He began to laugh. . . . And now, in the midst of the wild mirth, he was relieving himself on the hindquarter of the near mule, playing the stream on that target, a gleaming arc in starlight. (15)

Though more discreet, the black man's act takes place in similar starlight. He drives a mule cart, while Tewksbury drives a mule wagon; he almost dies on the cart, as Tewksbury did die in a fall from the wagon.

The poet's near-accident bears an intriguing resemblance to another classical encounter between a father and his son, when Oedipus was blocked on the road by the man who turned out to be his father. The closer we look, the greater the resemblance becomes. Like Oedipus, the poet (1) meets an "old man" (*presbus;* 805)[7] on the road (2) riding in a mule-drawn vehicle (*apênê;* 753, 803)[8] (3) who blocks his path[9] and (4) turns out to be his father.

Then there is the matter of the stars. "Warned by the oracle" that he would slay his father and sleep with his mother, Oedipus recounts, "I turned and fled,— / And Corinth henceforth was to me unknown / Save as I knew its region by the stars" (*kagô pakousas tauta tên Korinthian, / astrois to loipon ekmetroumenos, xthona / epheugon* [794–95]).[10] To avoid fulfilling the oracle's prophecy, he keeps his distance from his native soil (and from Polybus and Merope, whom he thinks are his parents) by means of the stars. But later in the play another star will serve to confirm that he has indeed fulfilled the prophecy, and that star is Arcturus: a messenger arrives from Corinth to announce that Polybus has died and that the Corinthians want Oedipus to replace him as king; in the ensuing conversation he reveals to Oedipus that Polybus was never his father, and that he, the messenger, had brought him to Corinth as a foundling. Oedipus summons the herdsman who gave the messenger the child. The herdsman claims not to know the messenger, but the latter tells Oedipus he knows how to make him remember:

> MESSENGER: I will revive
> His blunted memories. Sure he can recall
> What time together both we drove our flocks,
> He two, I one, on the Cithaeron range,
> For three long summers; I his mate from spring
> Till rose Arcturus; then in winter time
> I led mine home, he his to Laïus' folds.
> Did these things happen as I say, or no?
>
> HERDSMAN: 'Tis long ago, but all thou say'st is true. (1132–41)

This acknowledged recollection leads to another: that the herdsman had on one of those summers given an infant boy to the messenger to raise as his own, that it was Laius's and Jocasta's offspring, that they were afraid of a prophecy concerning it, and that he had been told to kill the child. It is at this point that Oedipus realizes the truth and expresses the wish never to see light again.

"Can I see Arcturus from where I stand?" is not, then, an idle question. The star is not always visible. The messenger was alluding to the fact that until mid-September—the beginning of fall and the end of sheep-grazing season—it is hidden below the horizon.[11] Thus the "where" in Warren's question is to some extent a matter of "when." It is when the star becomes visible in the messenger's discourse that the herdsman's memory is awakened and the dreadful truth comes out. Its appearance in the play (and this is its only appearance in Sophocles) provokes the final revelation of the truth. Could this be what Warren means—that one can see Arcturus when one is about to discover the truth about what one has done to one's parents?

"Season Opens on Wild Boar in Chianti," like "Old Nigger," concludes with a look at the stars. The hunters pass the poet's door, carrying the boar on a pole, his "great head swinging down, tusks star-gleaming. / The constellations are steady." Those stars would have included Arcturus, for the boar hunt takes place when the "Gold light of October falls over / The vineyards."

That tusk-gleam (of "tusks star-gleaming") insists, for we can see it earlier in the poem as well, when the boar was still alive: "He is full of years, and now waits where / His tusks gleam white in the dark air." Like the man on the cart, the boar is old, and like the "Philosopher past all / Casuistry," he is wise: "the great head swings weighty and thoughtful / While eyes blank in wisdom stare hard." And the boar's tusk-gleam is answered by a glow from the old man's nail: "The last glow" of a match struck in the shack just before retiring "is reflected on the petal-pink / And dark horn-crust of the thumbnail."

In a letter to Warren on April 3, 1975, Cleanth Brooks wrote that he had difficulty making sense of its beginning: "I like very much indeed "Old Nigger" etc. I think the final section is superb. It repeats one of your big themes but does so in its own way and with a special richness of tonality. . . . The preceding sections of the poem are vintage Warren. I don't quite connect up the first section of the poem with what follows—but that is probably simply my own density—my difficulty in connecting the nameless dancer with the rest of the experience" (*Cleanth Brooks and Robert Penn Warren* 377). The first section describes the party in the back country Warren was driving home from when he met the old man on the road:

> Flesh, of a sudden, gone nameless in music, flesh
> Of the dancer, under your hand, flowing to music, girl-
> Flesh sliding, flesh flowing, sweeter than
> Honey, slicker than Essolube, over
> The music-swayed, delicate trellis of bone
> That is white in secret flesh-darkness. What
> The music, it says: *no name, no name!* —only
> That movement under your hand, what
> It is, and no name, and you shut your eyes, but
> The music, it stops. O.K. Silence
> Rages, it ranges the world, it will
> Devour us, for
> That sound I do now hear is not external, is
> Simply the crinkle and crepitation,
> Like crickets gone nuts, of
> Booze in the blood. (italics in the poem)

Without realizing it, Brooks put his finger on a connection between this part of the poem and its conclusion, for the namelessness of "the dancer, under your hand" is answered by the hope the poet there expresses that what he holds in his hand will not be nameless:

Entering into that darkness to fumble
My way to a place to lie down, but holding,
I trust, in my hand, a name—
Like a shell, a dry flower, a worn stone, a toy—merely
A hard-won something that may, while Time
Backward unblooms out of time toward peace, utter
Its small, sober, and inestimable
Glow, trophy of truth.

If Time unblooms backward, Warren's sequences tend, when read retrospectively, to bloom, unfolding hidden depths as the reader retraces steps backward from the end, with the result that the section that Brooks may have found a little out of place in the poem finds ample justification in the sequence. For the "delicate trellis of bone / That is white in secret flesh-darkness" curiously recalls the boar, whose "tusks gleam white in the dark air" and whose feet are "delicate, razor-sharp" (themselves recalling "the most delicate Hellenistic chisel-work" left by a tooth in "Brotherhood in Pain"). In seeing the skeleton beneath the skin, turning the young woman into a memento mori at the feast, Warren connects her to the old man on the cart who will show him how to die. An intermediate connection is provided by the mule attached to his cart, which comes into view before he does:

And the mule-head
Thrusts at us, and ablaze in our headlights,
Outstaring from primal bone-blankness and the arrogant
Stupidity of skull snatched there
From darkness and the saurian stew of pre-Time,
For an instant—the eyes. The eyes,
They blaze from the incandescent magma
Of mule-brain. Thus mule-eyes. Then
Man-eyes, not blazing, white-bulging
In black face. . . .

This encounter with blazing eyes recalls one with red ones, when the poet imagines the boar's final stand: "To choose his own ground when the adversary / Encounters him, red eye to red eye." And the mule's blank stare—"Outstaring from primal bone-blankness"—recalls the dead boar's, whose "eyes blank in wisdom stare hard." But what he sees of the mule, the "bone-blankness" and "skull" emerging "From darkness," is also a reiteration of the "bone / That is white in . . . -darkness" he imagined beneath the flesh of the dancer, as Warren plays upon "blank" as both "empty" and, in its root sense, "white."

In another connection between the slain prey and the girl, the boar, strange to say, was a dancer too. In fact, what was delicate about him was precisely what danced—just as it was the "delicate trellis of bone" in the girl that was "music-swayed": the boar's "delicate, razor-sharp feet, not / Now dancing, now dancing, point starward." Of course, at the party the poet was dancing, too, and in at least one other respect he too has something in common with the hunters' prey, for he has "Booze in the blood," while the boar has the fruit of the vine in his: "The blood of the great boar has thickened / With grapes."

"Season Opens" opens, as does "Old Nigger," with music. The hunters' "voices in distance are music. / Now hounds have the scent, they make music. / The world is all music, we listen." Then suddenly, in both poems, there is silence:

> The music, it stops. O.K. Silence
> Rages. ("Old Nigger")

> Since sunrise the halloo and music
> Has filled all the vineyards, and wild ground.
> Music echoed among the high pine boughs.
> It was heard where the oak leaf cast shadow.
> Now where the rushes are trampled, is no sound.
> Dead too, at the tusk-point, the best hound. ("Season Opens")

And after the silence, panting:

> . . . The night pants hot like a dog. . . . ("Old Nigger")

> In the twilight and silence, now passing
> Our door, men pant with the heavi-
> ness of their destiny's burden. . . . ("Season Opens")

Arcturus, like many of Warren's sequences, yields more meaning when read as a single poem, with particular attention to the ways each poem within it reworks elements from its immediate predecessor. But, perhaps uniquely among those sequences, it can also be read another way, with an eye to how the poems (in this collection at least) reach farther back than that, the last to the first, the penultimate to the second, the antepenultimate to the third, and the seventh to the fourth.

In "Old Nigger," Warren asks his reader, "Have you ever / Had the impulse to stretch forth your hand over / The bulge of forest and seize trees like the hair / Of a head you would master?" As I have said, this strangely echoes the moment in "A Way to Love God" "when, by the hair, the headsman held up the head / Of Mary of Scots." It is oddly self-referential as well, for it would be by stretching forth his hand in a similar gesture from the end to the beginning of the sequence that the reader of these lines could touch the head held by the hair in the first poem. Mary's suspended head is also recalled when "I wake to see / Floating in darkness above the bed the / Black face, eyes white-bulging, mouth shaped like an O." And that her "lips kept on moving, / But without sound" anticipates her counterpart's failed attempt to communicate: "man-mouth / Wide open, the shape of an O, for the scream / That does not come."

The sheep whose "eyes / Stared" and "Were stupid" are recalled by the mule's eyes "Outstaring" with "arrogant / Stupidity," while the "stone white in darkness" of their natural setting is paralleled by the "bone / That is white in secret flesh-darkness" of the girl, the slickness of whose flesh ("flesh flowing . . . slicker than Essolube") is strangely anticipated by that of a "slug's white belly . . . sick-slick and soft."

The second and ninth poems pair two images of the father, the evening hawk and the boar. Both have wisdom: "His wisdom / Is ancient, too, and immense," Warren says of the bat, meaning by that "too" that the hawk's wisdom is ancient, while the boar's eyes "in wisdom stare." Both have wielded a sharp weapon: "the honed steel-edge" of a wing and the "razor-sharp feet." The "stalks of Time" cut by that wing reappear as "rushes . . . trampled" by those razor-sharp feet. "The constellations are steady" in "Season Opens" as "The star / Is steady" in "Evening Hawk."

The poet's "heart bleeds" in the third poem, "Loss, of Perhaps Love," as the matrix from which the object on which you fix your stare in "Brotherhood in Pain," the eighth, "is torn / Bleeds profusely." One of those chance objects could be the sock you left "on the bathroom tiles," while in the other poem the play of sunlight "on the bathroom floor" is proposed as a possible place to begin. In both poems, Warren invites the reader to begin anywhere, eyes shut: "Shut your eyes, think hard, it doesn't really / Matter which end you start from—forward from / The earliest thing you remember . . . or backward from just now" ("Loss, of Perhaps Love"); "Fix your eyes on any chance object. . . . / Whirl around three times like a child, or a dervish, with eyes shut, / then fix on the first thing seen when they open" ("Brotherhood in Pain").

Finally (since the fifth and sixth are already connected through the sequential structure), in "Answer to Prayer," the fourth poem, the poet is left standing "Alone" in the snow when the woman disappears into a church, somewhat like the oak that "stands alone in a world of snowy whiteness" in the seventh poem, "Trying to Tell You Something." But also like himself in that poem as well: "some December night, / You stand on a hill, in a world of whiteness, and // Stare into the crackling absoluteness of the sky." In "Answer to Prayer," he stares at a winter sky less absolute:

Alone,

As often before in a night-street, I raised eyes
To pierce what membrane remotely enclosed the great bubble of light that now
The city inflated against the dark hover of infinities,
And saw how a first frail wavering stipple of shadow

Emerged high in that spectral concavity of light, and drew down to be,
In the end, only snow.

The prayer was answered but "later, and . . . long out / Of phase." The implied question is, did Cinina mean for him to be happy in the way that he turned out to be? "In such a world, then, one must be pretty careful how one prays." The symmetrically matching seventh poem concludes, with a certain rhyming similarity in spite of the contextual difference (not about answered prayer but about what happens when the "cables will sing" in one's own head), "no one can predict the consequences."

AFTERWORD

AFTER *ARCTURUS*

Warren arranged his last four volumes of poems in webs as tightly woven as the eight that preceded them. I wrote of their intricacy in *The Braided Dream: Robert Penn Warren's Late Poetry* in 1990, though at that time I mistakenly thought that it was *only* in those sequences that he had arranged his poems with such care. I invite readers to consult that study for an account of the interlockings connecting the poems of *Now and Then: Poems 1976–1978, Being Here: Poetry 1997–1980, Rumor Verified: Poems 1979–1980,* and *Altitudes and Extensions 1980–1984.*

One thing I had not considered in my reading of *Now and Then* is the way its first poem, "American Portrait: Old Style," recycles elements from "Old Nigger," the last poem in *Can I See Arcturus from Where I Stand?* I will follow that connective tissue here, together with some of the threads that connect the first poems of *Now and Then,* to give some sense of how Warren continued to weave the fabric of his poems past the point where the present study ends.

In "American Portrait," Warren recalls as a boy finding two traces from the pioneer past in the countryside near his Kentucky hometown. One is an "old skull . . . all nameless / And cracked in star-shape from a stone-smack," the other a "trench, six feet long, / And wide enough for a man to lie down in, / In comfort, if comfort was still any object. No sign there / Of any ruined cabin or well, so Pap must have died of camp fever, / And the others pushed on, God knows where." He found the skull in a marsh and the grave on a hill farther up the path. Young Warren and his friend K (for Kent Greenfield) played war games there, pretending to be Confederates firing at "Bluebellies / Who came charging our trench." Sixty years later, the poet revisited the site and "saw the trench of our valor, now nothing / But a ditch full of late-season weed-growth. . . . I / Just lie in the trench on my back . . . and I wonder / What it would be like to die, / Like the nameless old skull in the swamp."

The "nameless" skull recalls the "Flesh, of a sudden, gone *nameless* in music" that belonged to the girl Warren was dancing with at the party at the beginning of "Old Nigger." For he sees the skeleton beneath that nameless flesh: "The music-swayed, delicate trellis of bone / That is white in secret flesh-darkness. . . . / The music, it says: *no name, no name!*" I argued in the previous chapter that this trellis of bone is connected within that poem to the mule skull that the poet sees (or imagines seeing beneath the mule-flesh) in the headlights of his car as he suddenly confronts the man driving his "death-trap" of a mule cart: "the mule-head / Thrusts at us . . . / Outstaring from primal bone-blankness and the arrogant / Stupidity of skull snatched there / From darkness." For the "bone-blankness" recalls the white-ness of the dancer's "delicate trellis of bone / That is white in secret flesh-darkness," and the "darkness" from which the skull emerged recalls that "flesh-darkness"; thirdly, with both the girl and the mule the poet imagines the bone beneath the skin. And of course the mule parallels its driver, as Warren considers first one and then the other in his headlights: "The eyes, / They blaze from the incandescent magma / Of mule-brain. Thus mule-eyes. Then / Man-eyes . . . white-bulging / In black face." The black man on the mule cart, as I argued, is Warren's mythic father, both the Laius that Warren as Oedipus encounters on the highway and the Zeus who fathered Warren as Perseus. Thus it is fitting that Warren should give the name "Pap" to the man whose grave the ditch was, and in which the poet would lie down at the end of "American Portrait." At the end of the other poem, he does the same thing, seeing himself with "my own cart of junk / Unfended from the storm of starlight" and entering a shack like the black man's, "Entering into that darkness to fumble / My way to a place to lie down." That shack is his "grave," as Warren has noted (quoted in Szczesiul 169). Thus both poems end with the poet lying down in a grave, and that grave is a father's.

The ditch in which he lies down at the end of "American Portrait," practic-ing for death like the lovers in "Bearded Oaks," was anticipated by a ditch in which he could have died, in his brush with death: "A death-trap. But / I snatch the wheel left in a dust-skid, / Smack into the ditch." That "Smack" returns in the description of the nameless skull: "cracked in star-shape from a stone-smack." In one poem, the poet is smacked into a ditch; in the other, he lies in a ditch thinking of a smacked skull. The latter's starlike shape is no more an accident than the echoing smacks, for the first of these two poems is all about stars. The near-accident on the road takes place "under the high stars"; the man on the cart when he returns to his shack (and urinates, like father Zeus) lifts his face "into starlight, calm as prayer"; the poet can see himself leaving his own cart of junk "Unfended from the storm of starlight" and is moved to ask if a certain star is visible: "Can I see Arcturus from where I stand?" As I argued in the last chapter, whether Arcturus can be seen, and its becoming visible again in recollection (in the recollection of the herdsman the messenger interrogates in Sophocles' play) is part of the discovery process that leads Oedipus to the truth.

That the skull was smacked into a certain pattern of fault lines has yet another resonance in "Old Nigger," in a pattern provoked by a snap: "by what magnet, I demand, / Are the iron and out-flung filings of our lives, on / A sheet of paper, blind-blank as Time, snapped / Into a polarized pattern"? In this fine instance of self-reference, two patterns themselves align themselves in a pattern that emerges when we realize their co-presence in these two poems. Like a magnet, each appears to exert a force upon the other. The connection between stone and star persists in the setting Warren gives the events of the second poem in *Now and Then,* "Amazing Grace in the Back Country": "In the season of late August star-fall." For those are in fact not stars but stones, the meteors of the—how appropriately named!—Perseid shower. A stone smacked the skull in "American Portrait" into star-shape; stones are now stars.

Like the trench that was first a burial site and later a place for K and RPW to reenact the Civil War, the tent that housed the late August revival may have previously been the site of a carnival complete with gold-toothed whores: "Here no carnival now—the tabernacle / To the glory of God the Most High." Warren's poems in sequence are each likewise a site for more than one event, as they invite being read in conjunction first with their predecessors and then their successors. In the case of "Amazing Grace," after the tent meeting the worshippers went home, "Found bed *and lay down* . . . / Until that morning they would not rise, not ever," while in the other half of the intertext this poem forms with its successor, "Boy Wandering in Simms' Valley," young Warren visits an abandoned house where a man nursed his sick wife until she died, then picked up his shotgun "*and* simply *lay down* by her side" before taking his own life. In "Amazing Grace," young Warren, after thinking about those who went home and lay down and would do so repeatedly until they died, lay down too, by a star-reflecting spring in the woods outside the tent, "lay / Wondering and wondering how many / A morning would I rise up." This conclusion to the poem on the one hand parallels his lying down at the end of "American Portrait" in Pap's grave for a foretaste of death, and on the other is echoed by the wondering in which he engages at the conclusion of "Boy Wandering": "wondering what life is, and love."

What set him to wondering in "Boy Wandering" was what had caught his eye just before he was about to leave the abandoned house: "*Then suddenly* / [I] Saw the old enameled bedpan," a tangible sign of the care Simms had given his wife in her illness. Warren sets us to wondering about why he would choose to follow this with a recognition introduced by an identical expression in the next poem, "Old Flame": "who was that pile of age-litter? / 'Don't you know me?' it wailed. *Then suddenly*, by Christ, I did." What is the connection, or the parallel, between one sudden perception and the other? The old flame of the title was once a girl whose twin black braids had fascinated young Warren as he walked behind her to school. Their "bewitching twitch" left him "tongue-tied." Now, fifty years on, she is "a grisly old dame," a "pile of age-litter," like the detritus of time he had beheld in the bedroom of the abandoned house just before he had his sudden realization from the bed-pan: "sheets hang spiderweb-rotten, and blankets a mass / Of what weather and leaves from the broken window had done, / Not to mention the rats."

As a "grisly old dame," she calls to mind the "old-fool dame" in the tent revival in "Amazing Grace" who crouched by the poet's knees and "tugged me to kneel / And save my pore twelve-year-ole soul." Within that poem, she forms a parallel to the other old women who lay in wait to entice male visitors to the carnival in what may have been the same tent, "whores to whom menopause now / Was barely a memory, one with gold teeth and one / With game gam, but both / With aperture ready to serve / Any late-lingerers." Together the golden-toothed whores and the pious old woman evoke the figure of Medusa, familiar to readers of Warren from "Myth on Mediterranean Beach: Aphrodite as Logos" in *Incarnations*. Medusa turned the men who gazed on her to stone; the old woman at the revival had a similar effect on Warren: "But the Pore Little Lamb, he hardened his heart, / Like a flint nigger-head rounded slick in a creek-bed" and, running down the aisle, fled the tent. The grisly old dame whose hair Warren once found "bewitching" exerted, if not a stiffening effect, a paralyzing one: "I followed, drifting, tongue-tied, / Gaze fixed" on those black braids. "Tongue-tied," he repeats, "—why, yes." As Perseus never gazed on Medusa directly, but only through a mirror, young Warren, it seems, only saw the back of her head: "When her name escapes, I can usually call to mind / . . . some kind of braids. Never, never, a face."

He never spoke to her: "in nine years no word ever passed, certainly not conversation. / Then I was gone, and as far as I cared, she could moulder, / Braids and all, in the grave, life carved in compressed notation." In "Evening Hour," we find him, again as a boy, at a graveyard outside of town looking for arrowheads, oblivious to the dead around him—as he and K turned the ditch of Pap's grave into the trench of their valor with nary a thought for the repose of its original inhabitant. "Not thinking of flesh and its nature, but *suddenly* still / For maybe two minutes." That "suddenly" leads us to expect a sudden realization, along the lines of the ones in "Old Flame" and "Boy Wandering in Simms' Valley" that were each prefaced by a "suddenly." And one almost comes, but not quite. The poet does not achieve a full realization of the reality of death: "Not morbid, nor putting two and two together / To make any mystic, or fumblingly philosophical, / Four." Yet he "more than once felt the crazy impulse grow / To lay ear to earth for what voices beneath might say." Putting two and two together is what he at first did not do in "Old Flame," and then did. That poem begins: "I never then noticed the rather sausage-like trotters / That toted incomparable glory down the street / Schoolward . . . / That glory then being twin braids plaited plump and neat." The two he noticed were the braids; the two he did not were the legs. What happens in the poem, when he sees the girl become an elderly woman, leads to his noticing both pairs in its conclusion: "When her name escapes, I can usually call to mind / Sausage-legs, maybe some kind of braids. Never, never, a face." The rather unappetizing legs were there at the beginning, when she had the braids, but all he saw then was her hair. Only now does he see the whole picture. In a self-referential way "Old Flame" and "Evening Hour" invite the reader to put two and two together, the two and two of one poem with the two and two of the other, to see what one could never see within only one.

The next poem in the sequence brings the reality of death to the boy who didn't quite see it in the graveyard. In "Orphanage Boy," an orphan who came to work on Warren's uncle's farm became attached to Bob, the farm's dog. Al and Bob would sit together after supper watching the sun go down. But one day a snake bit the dog, and though it did not kill him outright, he never quite recovered. The uncle "handed a / Twelve-gauge to Al, and said, 'Be sure / You do it right back of the head.' / He never named Bob's name." Al dutifully performs the task. Young Warren tags along and afterward sees the boy weeping. The orphan subsequently runs away from the farm, but not before making a grave for the dog, complete with a wooden cross, which Warren discovers six months later when he revisits the spot. "He must have come back to the / Barn for the shovel and hammer, / And back again to hang them up."

Warren chose to follow this poem about a boy who shoots a dog with "Red-Tail Hawk and Pyre of Youth," in which another boy—Warren himself—shoots a hawk. Like Al, Warren weeps afterward: "in / Eyes tears past definition . . . the bloody / Body already to my bare flesh embraced, cuddled / Like babe to heart, and my heart beating like love." Yet his heart was at the same time "leaping in joy," for shooting the hawk at such a range had been quite a feat of prowess. He carried it home: "Like a secret, I wrapped it in newspaper quickly / And hid it deep / In the ice chest."

That the uncle "never named Bob's name" finds resonance in "Red-Tail Hawk," for, seen at a distance, the hawk, too, was "nameless." When it got closer, "suddenly

I knew the name." But what was that name, exactly? Thinking of the hawk's eyes, which the boy sees as "unforgiving, for they, like God, see all," Calvin Bedient argues that the hawk is the father: "As the unforgiving father-god falls, as the winged phallus plummets, the boy's heart leaps in joy" (190). We know from Warren's *Portrait of a Father* (55) that Robert Franklin Warren was called "Bob" by Warren's mother (and I know from Warren's sister Mary that the children called him "Daddy-Bob").[1] No wonder the uncle never named that name, for it would have come too close to the truth. Though we can come close to the truth by reading the poems in sequence.

THE PERSONAL MYTHOLOGY

The primary focus of this study has been the way Warren put together his poetic volumes, with a secondary focus on the personal myth he constructed for himself involving Perseus, Danae, and Medusa. Because allusions to the myth are dispersed throughout the poems, I thought it would be useful to gather them in one place, together with some additional allusions in works not previously discussed.

The myth as Warren makes use of it comprises two principal episodes, Danae's insemination by Zeus in the form of a golden shower and Perseus's confrontation with Medusa. The golden shower is variously light, leaves, money, a pocket watch, pollen, urine, blood, water, and gold-tinted hair. Elements of the Medusa story that appear in Warren include her dangerous gaze, its petrifying power, its ability to excite sexual arousal in the male beholder, the mirror through which Perseus gazed on her in safety, her decapitation, and the purse in which he placed the head. In addition to these two events, Warren also alludes to Perseus killing his grandfather Acrisius and freeing Andromeda from a sea-lashed rock.

An early reference to Medusa appears in 1925 in "Dawn: The Gorgon's Head" (19). The Gorgon in the title (the word does not appear in the poem) is what the speaker imagines seeing in his mirror reflection: "go to the mirror on the wall. / See what you are—the eyes and there behind / Grey cells rotting in thought which are the brain." Warren will rework this scene in "Clearly about You" (145), in *You, Emperors, and Others,* though without reference to a Gorgon: "You won't look in the mirror? Well—but your face in there / Like a face drowned deep under water, mouth askew, / And tongue in that mouth tastes cold water, not sweet air, / And if it could scream in that medium, the scream would be you."

But the term "Gorgon" does return in "Goodbye" (29), which appeared in *American Prefaces* in 1941, and which Warren published nowhere else:

> And you have felt the live locks lift
> And coil, upon your crimeless head,

And fled your own un-Gorgoning gift,
As some young Gorgon might have fled
Who, kindly yet and new in horror,
By the dawn's first light had leaned to peer
At love, and learned her mortifying power:
In his sculptured eye, the sculptured tear.
You flee, and by your treacherous foot create
Yourself, who fleeing, yet all motion hate.

The "live locks" that "lift / And coil" are clearly a reference to the writhing serpents that form Medusa's hair. What is surprising is the speaker's intense identification with the Gorgon. He is both the slayer and the slain, feeling the serpents on his own head and yet having his "own un-Gorgoning gift"—the ability to undo the monster. He compares that gift to Medusa's "mortifying power" to turn men to stone. She "leaned to peer / At love," casting, apparently without meaning to in this instance, her deadly gaze on a male onlooker who was looking at her with love. For though hideous, she was nevertheless an object of lust; it is the paradoxical combination of those qualities that make her such a haunting figure. The lover turns to stone: a sculptured eye, a sculptured tear.

The "sculptured eye" likely bears an additional meaning, referring to Warren's own sculptured eye, the glass one he acquired in 1934 after the surgical removal of his left eye, injured in 1921. Thus the poet, in addition to seeing himself as both Medusa and Perseus, is the lover turned to stone for having lusted after Medusa and suffered the mortifying power of her gaze, and the petrification process has already begun—in his eye. His glass eye is the mark of Medusa, the lasting effect of his confrontation with the Gorgon.

Warren's 1924 suicide attempt was prompted by his fear of going blind as a result of the injury, as he revealed in a 1978 letter to Allan Tate in which he alluded to "the fits of depression that led up to my foolish try at suicide when the fear of blindness got the better of me" (Blotner 439). He had confronted death, saved only by the alert response of a friend who found him unconscious from the effects of a chloroform-soaked towel. Having tried to take his own life, Warren, by the time he wrote "Dawn: The Gorgon's Head," was a dead man walking. Like Perseus, who alone among mortals had the courage and ability to confront the death-dealing Gorgon and survive, Warren too had faced death and lived to tell the tale. Perseus looked in a mirror and saw the Gorgon; so too did Warren, but with the difference that Perseus was not looking at himself.

In "Dawn: The Gorgon's Head," the speaker looks in the mirror and sees himself as that head, the image of death, his brain cells "rotting," as in "Clearly about You" the face reflected is a dead one, having drowned. This identification of himself with Medusa, pursued as well in "Goodbye," is somewhat puzzling, but can I think be explained by the realization that in his confrontation with death he played both roles, the slayer and the slain. It may also find an explanation in the identification between mother and son evident in "Letter of a Mother." In that poem, the speaker is trying to escape from the claims of that flesh that was once his own: "By now this woman's milk is out of me. . . . / The mother flesh that cannot summon back // The tired child it would again possess / As shall a womb more tender than her own." The mother in Warren, as we have by how had ample occasion to learn, is Medusa (though she is also Danae, and sometimes—as in "Myth on Mediterranean Beach," *Audubon*, and "Internal Injuries"—both). So that if she is Medusa, and he and she are one flesh, then he too is the Gorgon. We catch yet another glimpse of the mother as Medusa in "The Return: An Elegy" (33), when the poet, returning home on the occasion of her death, anticipates his gaze being locked in hers as were Medusa's victims: "I am not blind. / Eyes, not blind, press to the Pullman pane. . . . / What will I find . . . ? / O eyes locked blind in death's immaculate design / Shall fix their last distrust in mine." In these lines we also find him denying his own partial blindness, for the plural in "*Eyes,* not blind, press to the Pullman pane" is, to the extent that he is writing himself into the poem, false. It is a denial that by its insistence proclaims the truth, and reveals as well a further identification between mother and son. He suffers from blindness, and so, thanks to her death, does she, her "eyes locked blind in death's immaculate design."

In "Letter of a Mother" (41), he speaks as well of "gratitude / For the worthier gift of her mortality," a turn of phrase that is worth considering in light of the "un-Gorgoning gift" of which he speaks in "Goodbye." The "gift of her mortality" can be interpreted in two ways, as we saw in the chapter on *Thirty-Six Poems.* First, she gave him, in giving birth, mortality, which is to say both life and death, for to be born in the world is to be condemned to die. Second, she gave him her own mortality: her death is her gift, which in the context of "Letter of a Mother" is impossible because she is not yet dead, yet in that poem he does yearn to be free of her, a release her death would give at least the illusion of providing. Yet we know that, in the context of Warren's own life, when he wrote that poem his mother was already dead, and that in "The Return: An Elegy" (when she was not yet dead), he expresses what could be read as a sigh of relief: "the old bitch is dead." By either interpretation, the "gift" in "Letter of a Mother," like the "gift" in "Goodbye," is associated with death. By either interpretation, it is the same gift as the "un-Gorgoning" one. By the first, his own death is the gift in "Letter," and his own death is what he chooses by his suicide to use his un-Gorgoning gift to achieve, since by killing himself he is killing the Gorgon and confronting death as fearlessly as Perseus. By the second, because his mother is Medusa, her death is the aim to which to the un-Gorgoning gift in "Goodbye" is applied.

By a chain of events both biographical and poetic, the injury to his eye in 1921, which led to his suicide attempt in 1924, is at the origin of the presence of the Perseus myth in Warren's work, for once he realized he had confronted the Gorgon in his suicide attempt, he had to acknowledge the rest of the story: identifying himself as Perseus, tracing his origin to Zeus's coupling with Danae. Yet equally at the origin, in fact prior, is Warren's difficult relationship with his mother, which would have made the myth of Medusa a tempting one to incorporate into his own personal poetic myth in any event. In "Goodbye," "The Return: An Elegy," and "Letter of a Mother," we see him making poetry out of the material of his life. He would continue to do so throughout his career, speaking in the "Afterthought" to *Being Here* of "a shadowy narrative, a shadowy autobiography" within his poems, "an autobiography which represents a fusion of fiction and fact in varying degrees and perspectives. . . . Indeed, it may be said that our lives are our own supreme fiction" (441).

Other allusions to the Perseus myth—part of the fiction Warren fused with the facts of his existence—appear in each of the eight poetic sequences discussed in this book, as well as in *Brother to Dragons, Audubon,* and several of the novels. I will take them up here in chronological order, occasionally jumping ahead in time to follow later developments of a particular image.

By 1931, when he began writing "The Return: An Elegy"—or between that year and 1934, when it was first published—Warren had seen the relevance of Perseus's origin to what may have started out as an interest in Medusa. For here we find the first of the many allusions to urination that will grace his work: "good lord he's wet the bed come bring a light" (34). The yellowed bed anticipates the one in "I Am Dreaming of a White Christmas: The Natural History of a Vision" (275) in *Or Else:* "the mattress / Bare but for old newspapers spread. / Curled edges. Yellow. On yellow paper dust, / The dust yellow. No! do not. // Do not lean to / Look at that date. Do not touch / That silken and yellow perfection of Time that / Dust is." This is the bed on which he was conceived; in addition to its connection to Time, that yellow residue presents itself as the trace of his Perseid origins. In "Genealogy" (42) in *Thirty-Six Poems,* an ancestral coupling takes place in a liquid yellow light: "Grandfather Gabriel rode from town / With Grandmother Martha in a white wedding gown. / Wine-Yellow was sunshine then on the corn."

Though the predominant classical allusion in *Night Rider* (1939), his first published novel, is to Oedipus,[2] Warren names his Oedipal protagonist *Percy* Munn; his friends call him *Perse,* a name that by itself evokes the Gorgon slayer. He was to return to variations on this name in his last novel, *A Place to Come To* (1977): *Perry* Gerald was protagonist Jed Tewksbury's rival for the affections of Agnes Andresen, his first wife; similarly *Perk* Simms, his stepfather, is a rival for those of his mother (*The Taciturn Text* 239–40). Both the wife and the mother had eyes Warren describes alternately as seductive and dangerous. Perk told his stepson about the way his mother would "just for a second give you a look that made you feel you and her had a wonderful secret. Sometimes . . . she'd give me a wink, and then pretend she hadn't never" (*A Place to Come To* 393). Tewksbury was similarly susceptible to the eyes of his mistress Rozelle, which reminded him "of the biblical words 'she taketh thee with her eyelids'" (129). Agnes Andresen made use of her eyeglasses to get Jed to propose marriage: "She still had the horn-rims on and drove the sharp corner through fabric and flesh . . . while she twisted the spikelike corner of the horn-rims into the bleeding wound, I was taking a deep breath, and saying, 'Listen . . . what about marrying me and just forgetting the hell out of this little Perry?'" (90–91).

The first three of the *Eleven Poems* (1942) feature something golden descending from the sky. In "Monologue at Midnight" (65): "How soundlessly / The maple shed its pollen in the sun." Warren does not give the color of maple pollen in that poem, but in "A Vision: Circa 1880" (159) in *You, Emperors, and Others* he will: "Out of the woods where pollen is a powder of gold / Shaken from pistil of oak minutely, and of maple." In "Bearded Oaks" (65), "The storm of noon above us rolled, / Of light the fury, furious gold."[3] In "Picnic Remembered" (66), there is an "amber light" that "laved" the trees above the lovers' heads, "and us."

Medusa makes an explicit appearance in *All the King's Men* (1946) in the person of Sadie Burke: "Her hair was flying with distinct life and her face was chalk-white with the pock marks making it look like riddled plaster, like, say, a plaster-of-Paris mask of Medusa which some kid has been using as a target for a BB gun" (141). There is also a mirror, though this Medusa sees her own reflection, of which Jack sees nothing: "Then she went past me to the wall, where a mirror hung, and stared into the mirror, putting her face up close to the mirror. . . . I couldn't see what was in the mirror, just the back of her head" (143)—as he would focus his attention on the back of the head of the girl with twin braids in "Old Flame." As the mistress of Willie Stark, a father figure to Jack, Sadie Burke plays to some degree the mother's role.[4]

The urination motif unites father and son in *Brother to Dragons* (1953). On the drive to Smithfield, Warren and his father "stopped just once to void the bladder. . . . / The sunlight screamed, while urine spattered the parched soil" (15). This could be interpreted as the son showing that he has the power to become a father (which Warren at this point had become).

In "Gold Glade" (113) in *Promises* (1957), the father is figured as a "Gold-massy" beech tree from which descends "that bright gold of leaf-fall." Warren has taken the falling gold from the Danae myth and joined it with a thematic thread of his own design in which the father is seen as a beech tree. The protagonist in *World Enough and Time* has a mystical vision of a beech tree one winter's morning in which he takes an icicle from the tree, puts it in his mouth, and finds that "my own strength seemed to pass away through my fingers into the very tree. I seemed to become the tree" (29). Later, crouching outside Cassius Fort's house just before murdering that object of his oedipal hatred, Jeremiah Beaumont recalls that moment with the beech: "That memory was important to him now, for it seemed to verify him, to say that all his past was one thing . . . that all had moved to this moment" (238). He becomes a beech tree in order to have the strength to murder the father, for the father in Warren, certainly in "Gold Glade," is a beech. Beaumont once had a dream in which he saw trees but could not remember their name, and the fact that he could not "was terrible to him" (188); later, in the same western Kentucky landscape as the one of which he had dreamed, he would recognize certain trees, despite the darkness, as beeches (417).

Beaumont as a boy loved to hide out in caves, "And while I lay there I thought how . . . my father might at the moment be standing in a field full of sun to call my name wildly . . . to no avail" (315). This scene, with the son hidden in the womb while the father is pictured above him bathed in gold light, will return in "Vision Under the October Mountain" (301) in *Or Else:* "did we / once in the womb, dream / a gold mountain in gold / air floating . . . ?" The mountain, as the father, is "the image of authority." Warren would spin an entire narrative out of this in *The Cave,* in which a son is trapped in a cave while his father, outside, expresses the hope that he be rescued (though he secretly desires that he not be). The entrance to the cave is beneath "the great humping gray roots of the biggest beech" (208) on Beecham's Bluff. That place name is an allusion, within Warren but outside the frame of the novel, to the name of the historical personage on which the protagonist of *World Enough and Time* is based, Jereboam Beauchamp (pronounced Beecham). Another visitor to the cave found when he leaned against a stalagmite that it had a "funny sort of smoothness" that made it feel "like a beech." Thus the father's presence is inescapable even in the cave, this beech trunk–like column looking (or feeling) remarkably like his sexual organ within the mother's.

In the year following publication of *The Cave,* Warren would picture his father with his "brow bearing a smudge of gold pollen" in "A Vision: Circa 1880" (159) in *You, Emperors, and Others.* In 1961, he would have the protagonist of his novel *Wilderness* confront a bronze statue "of Perseus meditatively holding the head of Medusa" (67) and would reincarnate her as Molly the camp follower, her naked buttocks under the lash taking the place of the face that in the myth is too terrible to be gazed at directly. The protagonist "carefully looked at the faces of the other men. They were all staring at the woman. . . . [T]he eyes of all were fixed there where he, Adam Rosenzweig, did not dare to look" (206). Seeing her through their eyes, he imitated Perseus eyeing Medusa through the reflecting surface of Athena's shield.

Tale of Time (1966) is particularly rich in such allusions. There is the visit to the substitute mother in "Tale of Time," where "light / Lay gold on the roofs of Squiggtown . . . and / The room smelled of urine" (188, 189), designating the old black mammy as an avatar of Danae. And then in the next poem, "Homage to Emerson," he again encounters an old African American, who advises him, "You quit that jack-off, and that thing go way" (194), alluding to the wart on the boy's right forefinger. The closeness between urine and semen that these parallel passages suggest will be confirmed a decade later by the opening scene of *A Place to Come To.* "Elijah on Mount Carmel" refers to the golden shower in two different ways: "the spilled gold of storm" by which the Deity displays his power, and the prophet's mocking question to the priests of Baal, "Has your god turned aside to make pee-pee?" (208) Making pee-pee is precisely what Warren has Jehovah do in "the spilled gold of storm."

In *Incarnations* (1968) more allusions appear. In "Where the Slow Fig's Purple Sloth," the fig plays the role of Danae succumbing in erotic bliss in a golden light. In "Myth on Mediterranean Beach: Aphrodite as Logos" (228), the "old / Robot with pince-nez and hair dyed gold" is not only Aphrodite but Danae and Medusa too, the former from her golden stain, the latter from her ability to interfere with a young man's sexual "interest" (in the poem as published; his "erection" in a manuscript version). In "Internal Injuries" the black woman is Medusa in seven ways: (1) the narrator fears that her gaze would be sharp and paralyzing, turning him into "a piece of white paper filed for eternity on the sharp point of a filing spindle" (245); (2) consequently he takes the precaution, as did Adam Rosenzweig in *Wilderness,* of looking at her through the reflecting surface of onlookers' eyes; (3) he tells her to look in a mirror (as if to turn her basilisk's gaze back upon herself); (4) "in your inward darkness" (recalling the fig's "Hot darkness" in "Where the Slow Fig's Purple Sloth" in the same volume) her sex threatens to become visible; (5) the Gorgon's decapitation is alluded to in her detached hat, about to be crushed by a truck wheel; (6) she is wet with urine; and (7) she prefigures the old woman who will be victimized on a street in *A Place to Come To* by a robber explicitly likened to Bellini's statue of Perseus. In "The Faring," also in *Incarnations,* Warren's wife is cast as Andromeda awaiting the arrival of her Perseus.

In Warren's next poetic volume, *Audubon* (1969) he again presents a woman who is both Danae and Medusa. As Danae, the woman to whom Audubon almost loses his life is fascinated by the "gleam" of his gold watch (256), which seems to bring her back to her past; we will not be able to fully grasp the allusion until Warren repeats it in "Natural History" in *Or Else,* where the woman is explicitly his mother and the gold that fascinates her is explicitly both money (an allusion to the tradition that interprets the shower as constituted of gold coins) and sex: "The money the naked old mother counts is her golden memories of love" (272). As Medusa, the woman gives Audubon an erection when he sees her hanging by the neck, her "face . . . beautiful as stone" "Under / The tumbled darkness of hair."

As just noted, in *Or Else* (1974) the narrator's mother, paralleling the woman in *Audubon,* is made to remember her past by gold coins that evoke her memories of love. This collection also contains "I Am Dreaming of a White Christmas" (275), where the narrator's parents' marriage bed is covered with yellow dust, and "Vision Under the October Mountain" (301), where he takes refuge in his mother's womb while the mountain, embodying the father's "authority," floats above in golden light.

Can I See Arcturus from Where I Stand? (1976) begins, in "A Way to Love God" (325), with a woman's decapitated head. It belongs to Mary, Queen of Scots, but evokes the Gorgon's, particularly in light of the paralysis that follows. In "Loss, of Perhaps Love, in Our World of Contingency" (326), Warren reveals that his first memory was of "the dapple // Of sunlight on the bathroom floor while your mother / Bathed you," an evocation of the golden sunlight he elsewhere associates with the original shower; here, he is the infant Perseus with his mother Danae. The pissing father (seen in *Brother to Dragons*) returns in "Old Nigger on One-Mule Cart" (333), who reveals himself to be Laius as well, with the poet reprising the oedipal role he had his fictional protagonist play in *Night Rider.* A father is engaged in what is variously interpreted as either the same activity or masturbation in the opening scene of *A Place to Come To* (1977), Warren's last novel. Either way, it leads to his death: "he ends up like tryen to jack off," says one mourner at the funeral; "naw, he must of been standen up to piss" (7), says another. The ultimate indeterminability of Buck Tewksbury's final act is the essence of the golden shower. The novel also features a statue of the Discobolos (61), an allusion to the way Perseus accidentally killed his grandfather Acrisius. Another pertinent statue is evoked near the end of the novel, when the protagonist sees a young man poised in flight, holding the purse he has just stolen from a woman who parallels the black woman in "Internal Injuries": "he leaped . . . to the hood of the nearest halted automobile, to stand beautifully balanced there with the purse—like Medusa's head hanging from the hand of Cellini's Perseus in Florence. . . . I remember thinking how beautiful, how redemptive, all seemed. It was as though I loved him. I thought how beautifully he had moved, like Ephraim, like a hawk in sunset flight" (187). Ephraim is Jed Tewksbury's son; the hawk in sunset flight is one of Warren's favorite images for the father. The reason Warren has this modern Perseus stand beautifully balanced on the hood of an automobile—a gesture somewhat lacking in verisimilitude on the part of a thief whose chief concern ought to have been to make a clean getaway—is to set up a parallel with the first page of the novel, where he had Tewksbury's father "standing up in the front of his wagon" (3), not so beautifully balanced, "to piss on the hindquarters of one of a span of mules and, being drunk, pitching forward on his head, still hanging on to his dong, and hitting the pike in such a position and condition that both the left front and the left rear wheels of the wagon rolled, with perfect precision, over his unconscious neck" and he died. The father was reenacting, or parodying, Zeus's insemination of Danae, which would make his son Perseus, though that son would see his own son Ephraim in the reenactment of Perseus holding the head of Medusa in the thief beautifully balanced on the hood of the car. Evidently being Perseus is an inherited trait.

Finally, Danae, explicitly named as such, makes her first and only appearance in the late poem "No Bird Does Call" (416) in *Being Here* (1980). As in "Gold Glade," and in accord with the symbolism that connects that tree to the father both there and in *World Enough and Time* and *The Cave,* the gold in her lap comes from beeches:

> Bowl-hollow of woodland, beech-bounded, beech-shrouded,
> With roots of great gray boles crook'd airward, then down
> To grapple again, like claws, in the breathless perimeter
> Of moss, as in cave-shadow darker and deeper than velvet.
>
> And even at noon just a flicker of light,
> In summer green glint on darkness of green,
> In autumn gold glint on a carpet of gold, for then
> The hollow is Danae's lap lavished with gold by the god. (416).

Jeremiah Beaumont in *World Enough and Time* sought refuge in caves; the speaker in the poem sought it in the "cave-shadow" of Danae's lap. "I, in despair, fled deeper and deeper, / To avoid the sight of mankind and the bustle of men." He lay back "With closed eyes," and "one noon-ray strayed through the labyrinths of leaves, / Revealing to me the redness of blood in eyelids, / And in that stillness my heart beat. The ray // Wandered on." Touched by this paternal golden ray, warmed back to life, his eye is healed, perhaps, from Medusa's freezing effect (in "Goodbye"), that had made it a "sculptured eye."

THE LYRIC POETIC SEQUENCE AND ITS AVATARS

Warren is not the only writer to have exploited the possibilities of sequential structure. Evidence is now emerging that this and other structuring principles (such as symmetry) are widespread in literary collections, whether they be of poems, short stories, essays, or letters in an epistolary novel. The Groupe de Recherche sur le Recueil, based at the Université de Laval and the Université de Rennes 2, was formed in 2000 to further the investigation of such phenomena.[5] In *Reading Raymond Carver,* I analyze a writer who has the reputation of being a minimalist but was in fact a self-reflexive metafictionalist who made use of sequential echoes in his collections to allow his stories to talk about each other. In *In La Fontaine's Labyrinth,* I explore how the French fabulist arranged his poems in such a way that each echoes its predecessor, and in particular how he added and subtracted elements from his sources in order to create those echoes. In "La séquence et la symétrie comme principes d'organisation chez Montesquieu, La Fontaine et Montaigne," I argue that Montesquieu's *Persian Letters* and La Fontaine's *Contes* display a similar organization and that Montaigne's *Essays* likewise have an echoing structure, but based on symmetry. I am currently writing a study of the sequentially echoing structure undergirding Boccaccio's *Decameron,* the *Heptameron* of Marguerite de Navarre, and La Fontaine's *Contes,* as part of a tradition in which the latter two consciously imitated the first.[6] The tradition of writing a large-scale work composed of self-referentially echoing smaller units goes back at least to Ovid's *Metamorphoses,* in which one tale metamorphoses into the next in ways that parallel the transformations recounted therein.

Though not alone in practicing such an art, Warren was particularly suited by temperament and personal history to become a writer who throughout his long career would insistently re-create the textual equivalent of the stereoscopic vision he had lost. His lyric poetic sequences are at the same time the very incarnation of his epistemology as expressed in "Knowledge and Image of Man." We find ourselves, he writes, in a "world with continual and intimate interpenetration, an inevitable osmosis of being. . . . [a] texture of relations."[7] How better to describe his poetry than by likening it to such a world? In fact, Warren in that essay goes on to speak of poetry as a form of knowledge and of the essential role of *form* (and here I am thinking of the particular form Warren so consistently chose for his poems: interpenetrating sequences):

> If knowledge by report and knowledge by symptom, however valuable and interesting such knowledge may be, are not characteristic and differentiating, then what kind of knowledge am I talking about? I should say: knowledge by form. No, knowledge *of* form.

> By this I mean . . . the organic relation among all the elements of the work, including, *most emphatically*, those elements drawn from the actual world and charged with all the urgencies of actuality, urgencies not to be denied but transmuted. . . . The form is a vision of experience, but of experience fulfilled and redeemed in knowledge, the ugly with the beautiful, the slayer with the slain, what was known as shape now known as time, what was known in time now known as shape, a new knowledge. It is not a thing detached from the world but a thing springing from the deep engagement of spirit with the world. (245)

Through the complex network of relations I have traced in these pages, involving such elements drawn from the actual world as Warren's eye injury, his difficult relation to his mother, and the Perseid myth (which, like the elements of his personal experience, is drawn from the actual world), Warren has pursued knowledge through, by, and of form. It is the form of the lyric poetic sequence in which elements interflow and the individual poems are continually engaged in "repetition and congruence" (in the language of "Elijah on Mount Carmel") with each other. In a larger sense, the same organic interpenetration informs his entire work, as his fiction and nonfiction prose and poetry are all part of the same texture of relations. His work, in its osmosis, both reenacts and incorporates the world.

NOTES

INTRODUCTION

1. Robert Penn Warren's literary reputation, far from going into eclipse after his death in 1989, just keeps rising. Book-length studies by Hugh Ruppersburg (1990), William Bedford Clark (1991), Robert Koppelman (1995), Leonard Casper (1997), Lucy Ferriss (1997), Lesa Corrigan (1999), Cecilia Donohue (1999), Jonathan Cullick (2000), Randy Hendricks (2000), James A. Grimshaw Jr. (2001), and Anthony Szczesiul (2002) attest to the interest his diverse body of work continues to inspire. Joseph Blotner's *Biography* (1997) invites us to read Warren's work in the context of his life, for which a wealth of new information is now available in the volumes of his *Letters* (1998, 2000, 2001) under the editorship of Grimshaw and Clark. In addition, there have been three collections of essays on Warren, edited by Joseph R. Millichap (1992), Dennis L. Weeks (1992), and David Madden (2000). Most important for Warren's reputation as a poet, and for the purposes of this study, John Burt's edition of the *Collected Poems* (1998) allows readers to see entire sequences that had been unavailable for decades, especially the *Thirty-Six Poems* and *Eleven Poems*. No sequence was ever reprinted whole in any of the *Selected Poems* (*Selected Poems 1923–1943; Selected Poems, New and Old 1923–1966; Selected Poems 1923–1975;* and *New and Selected Poems 1923–1985*)—except for *Eleven Poems* in 1943, but even then out of order and with other poems interspersed. The sequences *Tale of Time, Can I See Arcturus from Where I Stand?,* and *Altitudes and Extensions* made their first appearances in the *Selected Poems* of 1966, 1976, and 1985, respectively.

2. "Foreword," Robert Penn Warren, *The Collected Poems of Robert Penn Warren,* ed. John Burt (Baton Rouge: Louisiana State UP, 1998) xxiii.

3. Brooks to Warren, Nov. 3, 1966, in Robert Penn Warren, *Cleanth Brooks and Robert Penn Warren: A Literary Correspondence,* ed. James A. Grimshaw Jr. (Columbia: U of Missouri P, 1998) 276.

4. Victor Strandberg, *A Colder Fire: The Poetry of Robert Penn Warren* (Lexington: UP of Kentucky, 1965) 207.

5. Dave Smith, "Notes on a Form to Be Lived," *Homage to Robert Penn Warren,* ed. Frank Graziano (Durango, CO: Logbridge-Rhodes, 1981) 46–57.

6. A. J. Clements, "Sacramental Vision: The Poetry of Robert Penn Warren," *Critical Essays on Robert Penn Warren,* ed. William Bedford Clark (Boston: G. K. Hall, 1981) 226.

7. Daniel Hoffman, "Poetry: After Modernism," *Harvard Guide to Contemporary American Writing,* ed. Daniel Hoffman (Cambridge: Harvard UP, 1979) 463.

8. Robert S. Koppelman, *Robert Penn Warren's Modernist Spirituality* (Columbia: U of Missouri P, 1995) 98.

9. John Burt, *Robert Penn Warren and American Idealism* (New Haven: Yale UP, 1988) 111.

10. Robert Penn Warren, "Notes on the Poetry of John Crowe Ransom at His Eightieth Birthday," *New and Selected Essays* (New York: Random, 1989) 322, 323, 324n.

11. Robert Penn Warren, "John Crowe Ransom: A Study in Irony," *Virginia Quarterly Review* 11 (Jan. 1935): 93–112.

12. Quotations from Warren's poems are taken from John Burt's edition of *The Collected Poems of Robert Penn Warren,* with page numbers indicated parenthetically in the text.

CHAPTER 1. "TWO BY TWO": *THIRTY-SIX POEMS*

1. Robert Penn Warren, *Selected Letters of Robert Penn Warren,* vol. 2, *The Southern Review Years 1935–1942,* ed. William Bedford Clark (Baton Rouge: Louisiana State UP, 2001).

2. Roland Barthes evokes the practice of the Roman augurs in *S/Z,* trans. Richard Miller (New York: Hill and Wang, 1974), in which he breaks up a short story by Balzac into short fragments which he calls "lexias," treating them as the augurs did the rectangle in the sky: "The text, in its mass, is comparable to a sky, at once flat and smooth, deep, without edges and without landmarks; like the soothsayer drawing on it with the tip of his staff an imaginary rectangle wherein to consult, according to certain principles, the flight of birds, the commentator traces through the text certain zones of reading, in order to observe therein the migration of meanings, the outcropping of codes, the passage of citations" (14). My lexias are any two contiguous poems in a sequence; Barthes's are more arbitrary (and, since he was analyzing a work of fiction, have nothing to do with sequential elements): "[A]ll we require is that each lexia should have at most three or four meanings to be enumerated" (13–14). In practice, they range in length from a single word to several sentences.

3. John Burt writes that the poem "was apparently begun in California immediately before Warren learned of the seriousness of the illness that was to kill his mother but after he had received some suggestion that she was unwell" (*Robert Penn Warren and American Idealism* 76). In his notes to the *Collected Poems,* Burt cites an early prose draft in which Warren wrote that "the matter is, roughly, this: I have been summoned to the funeral of my mother (a fine woman if I do say it myself) and have departed, dutifully and at considerable expense, the eastern city, where I am engaged in the pursuit of happiness and profit, and now rest, troubled by insomnia, in lower berth, number five" (648n).

4. For more information on Allen, as well as an illuminating meditation on "The Return: An Elegy" and other poems Warren wrote about his mother, see William Bedford Clark's "Letters from Home: Filial Guilt in Robert Penn Warren," *Sewanee Review* 110.3 (Summer 2002): 385–405.

5. The Lamartine and Thomas poems may be found on pages 907–9 and 826–28, respectively, in Bernard Delvaille, ed., *Mille et cent ans de poésie française* (Paris: Robert Laffont, 1991).

6. Actually, he might have gone out to check on the cattle, but he had made a dangerous habit of going out in the cold to answer "the call of nature, and once out" would "See snowflakes falling, falling, and ponder on it a half-hour, / Making no move, sunk deep in the world, like a part / Of God's own world, a post, a bare tree, dung heap, or stone." A half-hour of immobility in cold as intense as it was that night would have been fatal. He had just been recalling how when "Old Ma" was dying, he carried her into the kitchen so she wouldn't freeze "Between the sheets." This linkage between the mother's death and urination repeats that found in "The Return: An Elegy." The urination theme in "Minnesota Recollection" carries over from the poem before, where it is connected with sexual potency. In "The First Time," a "great bull" elk in "Gal season" who is "Rounden up his take"—that is, assembling his harem—is admired in these terms: "Now ain't he a pisser!" (533).

7. "Rank has shown in a number of papers that certain arousal dreams produced by organic stimuli (dreams with a urinary stimulus and dreams of emission or orgasm) are especially suited to demonstrate the struggle between the need to sleep and the claims of organic needs, as well as the influence of the latter upon the content of dreams" (Sigmund Freud, *The Interpretation of Dreams,* ed. James Strachey [New York: Avon, 1965] 271n). "[I]t not infrequently happens that a stimulus awakens a dreamer after a vain attempt has been made to deal with it in a dream under a symbolic disguise" (438).

8. Indeed, Warren records that at the time of his mother's death, in 1931, after he had just written "The Return: An Elegy," "I do remember that the poem (in which I had felt, or hoped, that I had made some sort of break-through) seemed a thing of evil omen, tangled with all sorts of emotions and crazily with some sense of nameless complicity and guilt" (Warren's commentary on "The Return: An Elegy," *Thirtieth Year to Heaven* [Winston-Salem: Jackpine, 1980] 15).

9. For a recent discussion of the controversy, see Anthony Szczesiul, *Racial Politics and Robert Penn Warren's Poetry* (Gainesville: UP of Florida, 2002) 8–25. African American poet Sterling Brown responded with, "Cracker, your breed ain't exegetical" (quoted in Szczesiul 9). Randy Hendricks maintains that it is "an objectionable line only if readers take it as a direct statement from Warren and reduce Warren to a twentieth-century Confederate writing a metaphysical poem; such a reading fails to understand the significance of the buzzards" (*Lonelier than God: Robert Penn Warren and the Southern Exile* [Athens: U of Georgia P, 2000] 108). The buzzards, according to Hendricks, represent upper-class southern Brahmins oblivious to the plight of their

fellow men. "Warren gave such high-caste groups rhetorical hell—whether as Southerners as in 'Pondy Woods' or New Englanders as in *John Brown: The Making of a Martyr*" (110). Szczesiul takes issue with Hendricks on this point (221–22n), seeing as most damning Warren's use of the word in "Tryst on Vinegar Hill": "Niggers are the damnedest breed" (23; Szczesiul 18–21).

10. Lesa Carnes Corrigan detects in Warren's line an allusion to the "fractured atoms" to which humans are reduced after death in T. S. Eliot's "Gerontion" (*Poems of Pure Imagination: Robert Penn Warren and the Romantic Tradition* [Baton Rouge: Louisiana State UP, 1999] 53).

11. Joseph Blotner, *Robert Penn Warren: A Biography* (New York: Random, 1997) 558. Future references given parenthetically in the text.

12. William Bedford Clark maintains, "These lines recall the Agrarians' indictment of the fruits of industrial capitalism in the days before the Great Crash" (*The American Vision of Robert Penn Warren* [Lexington: UP of Kentucky, 1991] 51–52).

13. Herodotus, *The History*, trans. George Rawlinson (Chicago: Encyclopedia Britannica/Great Books, 1952) 222. Future references given parenthetically in the text.

14. Warren will again write of time as a glacier in "Reading Late at Night, Thermometer Falling" in *Or Else*: "the past, great / Eater of dreams, secrets, and random date, and / Refrigerator of truth, moved / Down what green valley at a glacier's / Massive pace" (314).

15. Abhorson is particularly comic in act 4, scene 2, when he sets out to prove that the executioner's trade is a "mystery."

16. In a letter written from Guthrie in 1924, Warren makes mention of "the village Croesus, who is gruff and who rides by our place every day" (Warren to Donald Davidson, July 1924, in Robert Penn Warren, *Selected Letters of Robert Penn Warren*, vol. 1, *The Apprentice Years, 1924–1934*, ed. William Bedford Clark [Baton Rouge: Louisiana State UP, 2000] 57). William Bedford Clark notes that he "may have been any one of several wealthy men living in or around Guthrie at the time" (*Selected Letters* 1: 57n). It is interesting that in the poem, first published in 1927, the Croesus is still "gruff."

17. Strandberg calls her a "girl" (*A Colder Fire* 51), but I am not sure on what basis. All we know is that she is wearing a blue dress and is thus presumably female. He also concludes, from the evidence of the line "So frost astounds the summer calyxes," that she has died—a tempting conclusion, but not, I believe, a necessary one. James A. Grimshaw Jr. reads the poem as being about an actual painting (*Understanding Robert Penn Warren* [Columbia: U of South Carolina P, 2001] 116).

18. Yet it is not yet late autumn, for she was "sustained in the green translucence that resides / all afternoon under the maple trees." Red-winged blackbirds leave Kentucky and Tennessee in September, when maples are still green.

19. As Socrates was accused of doing in "The Apology": "There is a wise man called Socrates who . . . can make the weaker argument defeat the stronger" (translated by Hugh Tredennick in Plato, *The Collected Dialogues*, ed. Edith Hamilton and Huntington Cairns [Princeton: Princeton UP, 1961] 4–5). I am indebted to John Burt for pointing this out to me.

20. Which itself repeats the "no tone" of Keats's "Ode on a Grecian Urn": "Heard melodies are sweet, but those unheard / Are sweeter; therefore, ye soft pipes, play on,— / Not to the sensual ear, but, more endear'd, / Pipe to the spirit ditties of no tone."

CHAPTER 2. "IN MIRRORED-MIRRORED-MIRROR-WISE": *ELEVEN POEMS ON THE SAME THEME*

1. John Burt, "Introduction," *Selected Poems of Robert Penn Warren,* ed. John Burt (Baton Rouge: Louisiana State UP, 2001) xiv.

2. "I can't get with music. . . . I'm indifferent to it" (interview with Dick Cavett, in Robert Penn Warren, *Robert Penn Warren Talking: Interviews, 1950–1978,* ed. Floyd C. Watkins and John T. Hiers [New York: Random, 1980] 282).

3. Strandberg interprets the greater smallness of the image in the heart as evidence that these two persons are "meaningless" to each other (*A Colder Fire* 76), but that would be to denigrate smallness and ignore the value Warren places on intricacy. When he made that comment, Warren had not yet praised the "sunlit, intricate rhythm" of sea-foam's "Arabic scrawl" in "Aspen Leaf in Windless World" (430).

4. Sunlit pollen will again descend in Warren's vision of his father as a boy, "A Vision: Circa 1880" (159): "Out of the woods where pollen is a powder of gold / Shaken from pistil of oak minutely, and of maple, / . . . the boy comes."

5. Not just the jewel in the toad but also the "use" that "you" no longer have for it form a probable allusion to *As You Like It,* 2.1: "Sweet are the uses of adversity which, like the toad, ugly and venomous, wears yet a precious jewel in his head."

CHAPTER 3. "THIS COLLOCATION / OF MEMORIES": *PROMISES: POEMS 1954–1956*

1. I am grateful to John Burt for supplying me with a computer file of his text of *Promises* for the *Collected Poems.* My statements about the occurrences of particular words are based on that.

2. The "hole now filled" announces his mother's death, which is the fulfillment it prophesies: "we, too, now go . . . / My mother and I, the hole now filled. / . . . / As we pass from what is, toward what will be, fulfilled." In "Grackles, Goodbye" (*Being Here*), the hole filled is her grave: "once my mother's hand / Held mine while I kicked the piled yellow leaves on the lawn / And laughed, not knowing some yellow-leaf season I'd stand / And see the hole filled. How they spread their obscene fake lawn" (391).

3. The "volcanic black boulders" along the old woman's path suggest that the Italian shore of the Rosanna poems is the setting, for "black lava-chunks" appear in "The Flower."

4. That it is the moon that is paying the respect is evident from the way Warren revised this line in later *Selected Poems:* "Yes, to even a puddle you've been known to pay some respect" (671n).

5. In "Kentucky Mountain Farm," Warren attributes a power greater than merely causing tides to "the obscene moon whose pull / Disturbs the sod, the rabbit, the lank fox, / Moving the waters, the boar's dull blood, / And the acrid sap of the ironwood" (35).

6. His lethal thoughts are directed against his older brother, the one who will inherit the title.

7. He is quoted as saying, "I don't believe in God" and "I take Christianity as a myth" (from correspondence cited by Blotner 450).

8. As opposed to the kind worn on a finger (in "Founding Fathers") or the verb meaning to resonate (elsewhere in "Boy's Will").

CHAPTER 4. "THE LOGIC OF DREAM": *YOU, EMPERORS, AND OTHERS: POEMS 1957–1960*

1. Interview in 1969 with Robert Sale, in Warren, *Robert Penn Warren Talking* 119–20.

CHAPTER 5. "THE HEART CRIES OUT FOR COHERENCE": *TALE OF TIME: NEW POEMS 1960–1966*

1. Because some of the poems in *Tale of Time* extend over several pages, I will give page numbers from *The Collected Poems* for most citations.

2. Though John Burt, reading the passage in light of Warren's saying a few lines earlier that he had thought "of copulation," interprets it as "memories of what seems to be the scene of an early assignation, a sun-dappled wood rather like that of 'Bearded Oaks'" (*Robert Penn Warren and American Idealism* 79).

3. Floyd Watkins, *Then and Now: The Personal Past in the Poetry of Robert Penn Warren* (Lexington: UP of Kentucky, 1982) 54.

4. Though difficulty in walking was itself anticipated by an episode in "Homage to Emerson," in which at 2:00 A.M. in front of a bar in New Orleans "a drunk // Crip slipped, and the air was full of flying crutches." The poet recalls having "managed to reassemble everything and prop it // Against a lamp post" (195), but the man fell flat on his backside once more and politely declined further assistance, saying that that was as good a place as any to watch the stars.

5. Emerson's toes, by contrast, turned outward: "He walked lightly, his toes out" (194). Saul's successor David, when Saul in a moment of insanity throws a spear at him, will slip away, "his foot / Leaving no print among rocks" (211). Perhaps David was more like Emerson.

6. The full text from "Into Broad Daylight" is "Your will, nor hand, can never seize on / Delight" (215). In "Mediterranean Beach," "delight" is not named as such, but what the speaker invites his listener to participate in—"instant joy"—is clearly another name for the "Delight" that "comes like surprise" in "Into Broad Daylight."

7. The titles according to the two ways of counting them: 1. "Into Broad Delight," 2. "Mediterranean Beach, Day after Storm," 3. "Deciduous Spring," 4. "Something Is Going to Happen," 5. "Dream of a Dream the Small Boy Had," 6. "Dawn," 7. "Intuition," 8. "Not to Be Trusted," 9. "Finisterre"; "I. Into Broad Daylight," "II. Love: Two Vignettes," "III. Something Is Going to Happen," "IV. Dream of a Dream the Small Boy Had," "V. Two Poems About Suddenly and a Rose," "VI. Not to Be Trusted," "VII. Finisterre."

8. Or nearly each, for the "Dream of a Dream the Small Boy Had" may be an exception, alluding to joy but not to suddenness.

CHAPTER 6. "ALL // ONE FLESH": *INCARNATIONS: POEMS 1966–1968*

1. Cleanth Brooks to Robert Penn Warren, Nov. 3, 1966, Warren, *Cleanth Brooks and Robert Penn Warren* 276.
2. Letter from RPW to Albert Erskine (quoted by Blotner 366).
3. Sigmund Freud, "The Infantile Genital Organization of the Libido," trans. Joan Riviere, *Sexuality and the Psychology of Love,* ed. Philip Rieff (New York: Collier, 1963) 174n4.
4. Sigmund Freud, "The Medusa's Head," trans. James Strachey, *Sexuality and the Psychology of Love,* ed. Philip Rieff (New York: Collier, 1963) 212. Future references given parenthetically in the text.
5. James Justus reads the words about meaning blooming like a begonia as coming from the woman, not the narrator (86). In a rejected poem for the sequence (untitled, it would have come between poems 5 and 6), Warren did conceive of a blooming taking place in the woman: "Tell me, tell me, does there come / A point past the point where the pain goes numb, / And numbness at last blooms into bliss / . . . ?" (I am grateful to Anthony Szczesiul for communicating to me a copy of this poem, from the Warren Papers at the Beinecke Library at Yale University).
6. Like Jake's sweat drops, her screams are multiple: "as regular / As a metronome. Twelve beats / For a period of scream, twelve / For a period of non-scream" ("The Scream").
7. As do those of the Union soldiers staring at the exposed buttocks of a woman being flogged in *Wilderness: A Tale of the Civil War* (New York: Random, 1961): "He carefully looked at the faces of other men. They were all staring at the woman. . . . [T]he eyes of all were fixed there where he, Adam Rosenzweig, did not dare to look" (206). Earlier in the novel, Adam had already encountered, in Aaron Blaustein's study, a "great bronze of Perseus meditatively holding the head of Medusa" (67).
8. In the section alluded to in note 5.
9. Old Jack Harrick in *The Cave* (New York: Random, 1959) recalled committing the same offense: "He could remember . . . how once when he was a boy . . . he had climbed up the Sumpter Ridge, and had gone swimming in the pool below the falls, and then he had climbed on up to the glade where the big beeches were . . . and had wondered if the sun would dry his hair enough so his mother wouldn't give him a whaling for getting in the creek" (376).
10. I suspect this poem has contributed to the misapprehension that Jake is scheduled for execution. The narrator is staying at the same "cheap motel" where relatives of a convict about to be electrocuted wait to claim the body, and his thoughts turn to the convict he glimpsed in the can: "But referring to Jake, how / Could they schedule delivery, it might be next week, / Or might, if things broke right, be even tomorrow." In the context of the motel's associations, one might be misled into thinking that scheduling "delivery" in Jake's case means scheduling his execution. But executions are not

scheduled as capriciously as that (and it's impossible that Jake would have been on death row for "nigh forty years"). The uncertainty as to whether the event would occur the next day or the following week is due to the nature of that event, which is his death from cancer. As to how the narrator can imagine Jake in the car with him— "I'm due to blow / At half-past, but if he'd be checked out and ready, / If that's not too early for him, he can go // With me, and we roll, and his eyes stare moody / Down a road all different from the last time he passed"—we should bear in mind the poem's subtitle: "A Ghost Story." The shift from the past to the present tense ("we roll, and his eyes stare") signals a leap into unreality. Until then, the narrator was referring to taking Jake's body home after the cancer claims him; beginning with his description of a wide-awake and living Jake in the car, it is his ghost.

11. Ovid, *Metamorphoses,* trans. Samuel Garth et al. (Amsterdam, 1732; New York: Garland, 1976) 142.

CHAPTER 7. "THE WORLD / IN WHICH ALL THINGS ARE CONTINUOUS": *OR ELSE: POEM/POEMS 1968–1974*

1. Smith 40, 46–47. Future references given parenthetically in the text.
2. I write "sequences" in the plural, for there will turn out to be two structured sequences, the arabic-numeraled one and the one that results from the intertwining of both—in other words, the sequence of each poem in *Or Else* regardless of which of the two sequences it appears in. As far as I can tell, the roman-numeraled poems do not refer to one another in this way.
3. Robert Graves, *The Greek Myths* (London: Folio Society, 1996) 225.
4. I can make this claim thanks to the kind assistance of John Burt, editor of *The Collected Poems,* who has provided me a zip disk containing all the poems in that volume.
5. It was not Bellevue but a hospital in White Plains, New York.

CHAPTER 8. "EVERYTHING SEEMS AN ECHO": *CAN I SEE ARCTURUS FROM WHERE I STAND? POEMS 1975*

1. The only other instance I know of occurs in "End of Season" (*Eleven Poems*): "Leave beach, *spiagga, playa, plage* or *spa*" (70).
2. Warren was surely aware that the executioner did not realize that Mary was wearing a wig, and that when he held up the head, the wig came off. The head fell to the floor and to the onlookers' surprise her actual hair was revealed to be "as grey as one of threescore and ten years old, polled very short" (eyewitness account by Robert Wynkfield, <http://tudorhistory.org/primary/exmary.html>).
3. The sheep, which as it happens are French sheep (Warren recalls seeing them "on the Sarré"), may, on the other hand, recall those on which Doctor Guillotin tried out and perfected the invention that would have made Mary Queen of Scots' death easier, for the headsman needed more than one stroke to carry it off.

4. Citing a personal interview with Warren, Joseph Blotner records that it was indeed "his earliest memory." Though she had hired a nurse, "one task Ruth Warren especially enjoyed was bathing the baby." The infant Warren "looked down at the bright pattern of the tile floor. Years later when he returned to test the accuracy of the memory, the pattern was there just as he recalled it" (9).

5. John Burt notes of "Midnight Outcry" that "[i]f this poem is rooted in autobiography, it revisits some of the scenes of 'To a Little Girl, One Year Old, in a Ruined Fortress'" (812n). That would situate it in 1954, when mother, father, and infant daughter spent the summer at La Rocca, a medieval fortress on the Italian coast.

6. Hendricks is actually making the point that although he may be a father figure, he is also something else: "one of a type in the Warren canon often represented by a black, Jew, European exile, tramp, or military deserter—an Other who becomes paradoxically representative of the self's experience" (119). On this black man as "Other," T. R. Hummer writes: "For all the 'improvement' in the thought of the narrator over the undivulged distances of the leap at the center of the poem, there are still deep problems presented by this text's projection of what we have come in such facile fashion to label 'the other.' The man at the end of the poem, after all, is unreal—only a memory construct, arguably a sentimentalized one, arguably invoked to aggrandize the narrator, to redeem him. The real man on the real mule cart remains as unknown and unrepresented as ever" ("Christ, Start Again: Robert Penn Warren, a Poet of the South?" Madden, *Legacy of Robert Penn Warren* 43). Hummer's complaint resembles Bedient's in that he objects to the politics he sees in the poem: "[I]n all honesty, I have to say that I dislike this poem—very likely because I discover in it too many painful traces of my own experience as a white Southerner" (43). I will argue here that what the man really represents is neither a southern black nor an Other like the vagrant in "Blackberry Winter" but the father in Warren's personal mythology: the Zeus who creates the golden stream to which the poet as Perseus traces his origin as well as the Laius this Oedipus meets on the road. A writer's personal mythology trumps both politics and tramps in my book.

7. References are to line numbers in the Greek text; translated passages are from the facing page.

8. "Laïus in a mule-car (*apênê*) rode" (753) (*apênê d'êge Laion* [753]), according to Jocasta; "In a car (*apênê*) drawn by colts" (*kapi pôlikês / anêr apênês embebôs* [802–3]), as Oedipus recalled it (in the Storr translation [Cambridge: Harvard UP/Loeb Library, 1913]). An *apênê* was a "four-wheeled wagon, drawn by mules" (Henry George Liddell and Robert Scott, *A Greek-English Lexicon* [Oxford: Oxford UP, 1996]), a "Vehiculum mulare, vehiculum quod muli juncti trahebant, ut Pausan. [Pausanias] docet, sic scribens in Eliacis 5, 9, 2" (Stephanus, *Thesaurus Graecae Linguae* [Graz: Akademische Druck–u. Verlagsanstalt, 1954]), vol. 2: 1312. The Pausanias reference (*Description of Greece,* trans. W. H. S. Jones and H. A. Ormerod [Cambridge: Harvard UP/Loeb Library, 1918] bk. 9, chap. 5, sec. 2) is: "[E]ach cart (*apênê*) was drawn by a pair of mules, not horses (*ên gar dê apênê kata tên sunôrida hêmionous anti hippôn echousa*)," in a description of athletic contests. Within Sophocles's lifetime (495–406 B.C.E.) the *apênê* event was held in the Olympic Games with mules pulling the chariots.

9. "The man in front and the old man himself / Threatened to thrust me rudely from the path" (804–5). On the presence of Oedipus in Warren, see Victor Strandberg, "Robert Penn Warren and the Classical Tradition," *Mississippi Quarterly* 48.1 (Winter 1994–95): 24–25.

10. The Jebb translation is somewhat more literal: "When I heard this, I turned in flight from the land of *Corinth,* from then on thinking of it only by its position under the stars." Liddell and Scott translate the phrase *astrois ekmetroumenos xthona* as "calculating its position by the stars."

11. It is not, as Blotner writes (428), the Pole Star (which, of course, *is* always visible). In *Hesiod's Works and Days* (l. 610), it marks the beginning of the grape harvest: "When Orion and the dog star rise to the middle of the sky and rosy-fingered dawn looks upon Arcturus, then, Perses, gather your grapes and bring them home" (Hesiod, *Theogony, Works and Days, Shield,* trans. Apostolos N. Athanassakis [Baltimore: Johns Hopkins UP, 1983], 82).

AFTERWORD

1. As I learned in a conversation with Mrs. Mary Warren Barber on January 31, 1988.

2. Thebes, the city where Oedipus unwittingly took his father's place on the throne and in his mother's bed, is reincarnated as a town of the same name in Kentucky; the novel's protagonist tries to slay a father figure. See Randolph Paul Runyon, *The Taciturn Text: The Fiction of Robert Penn Warren* (Columbus: Ohio State UP, 1990) 9–36.

3. Anticipating the "spilled gold of storm" (208) in "Elijah at Mount Carmel."

4. I discuss Stark as the father in *The Taciturn Text* 60–81. For a different interpretation of Sadie Burke as Medusa, see Deborah Wilson, "Medusa, the Movies, and the King's Men," Madden, *Legacy of Robert Penn Warren.*

5. See their web site, <http://www.creliq.ulaval.ca/grr/activ.htm>.

6. Other writers in whom I have seen the phenomenon at work include Victor Hugo, Charles Baudelaire, Alphonse Daudet, Michel Tournier, and Albert Camus.

7. Robert Penn Warren, "Knowledge and the Image of Man," *Robert Penn Warren: A Collection of Critical Essays,* ed. John Lewis Longley Jr. (New York: New York UP, 1965) 241. Future references cited parenthetically in the text. Jack Burden put it a little differently in *All the King's Men:* "[T]he reality of an event . . . arises from other events which, likewise, in themselves are not real" (384). In "Pure and Impure Poetry," Warren says the same of poetry, that it "does not inhere in any particular element but depends upon the set of relationships, the structure, which we call the poem" (24).

WORKS CITED

Apollodorus. *The Library.* Trans. James George Frazer. Cambridge: Harvard UP, 1976.

Barthes, Roland. *S/Z.* Trans. Richard Miller. New York: Hill and Wang, 1974.

Bedient, Calvin. *In the Heart's Last Kingdom: Robert Penn Warren's Major Poetry.* Cambridge: Harvard UP, 1984.

Blotner, Joseph. *Robert Penn Warren: A Biography.* New York: Random, 1997.

Burt, John. *Robert Penn Warren and American Idealism.* New Haven: Yale UP, 1988.

Casper, Leonard. *The Blood-Marriage of Earth and Sky: Robert Penn Warren's Later Novels.* Baton Rouge: Louisiana State UP, 1997.

———. *Robert Penn Warren: The Dark and Bloody Ground.* Seattle: U of Washington P, 1960.

Clark, William Bedford. *The American Vision of Robert Penn Warren.* Lexington: UP of Kentucky, 1991.

———. "Letters from Home: Filial Guilt in Robert Penn Warren." *Sewanee Review* 110.3 (Summer 2002): 385–405.

Clements, A. J. "Sacramental Vision: The Poetry of Robert Penn Warren." *Critical Essays on Robert Penn Warren.* Ed. William Bedford Clark. Boston: G. K. Hall, 1981. 216–33.

Corrigan, Lesa Carnes. *Poems of Pure Imagination: Robert Penn Warren and the Romantic Tradition.* Baton Rouge: Louisiana State UP, 1999.

Cullick, Jonathan S. *Making History: The Biographical Narratives of Robert Penn Warren.* Baton Rouge: Louisiana State UP, 2000.

Delvaille, Bernard, ed. *Mille et cent ans de poésie française.* Paris: Robert Laffont, 1991.

Donohue, Cecilia S. *Robert Penn Warren's Novels: Feminine and Feminist Discourse.* New York: Peter Lang, 1999.

Freud, Sigmund. "The Infantile Genital Organization of the Libido." Trans. Joan Riviere. *Sexuality and the Psychology of Love.* Ed. Philip Rieff. New York: Collier, 1963. 71–75.

———. *The Interpretation of Dreams*. Ed. James Strachey. New York: Avon, 1965.

———. "Medusa's Head." Trans. James Strachey. *Sexuality and the Psychology of Love*. Ed. Philip Rieff. New York: Collier, 1963. 212–13.

Graves, Robert. *The Greek Myths*. London: Folio Society, 1996.

Grimshaw, James A., Jr. *Robert Penn Warren: A Descriptive Bibliography, 1922–1979*. Charlottesville: UP of Virginia, 1981.

———. *Understanding Robert Penn Warren*. Columbia: U of South Carolina P, 2001.

Hendricks, Randy. *Lonelier than God: Robert Penn Warren and the Southern Exile*. Athens: U of Georgia P, 2000.

Herodotus. *The History*. Trans. George Rawlinson. Chicago: Encyclopedia Britannica/Great Books, 1952.

Hesiod. *Theogony, Works and Days, Shield*. Trans. Apostolos N. Athanassakis. Baltimore: Johns Hopkins UP, 1983.

Hoffman, Daniel. "Poetry: After Modernism." *Harvard Guide to Contemporary American Writing*. Ed. Daniel Hoffman. Cambridge: Harvard UP, 1979. 439–95.

Hummer, T. R. "Christ, Start Again: Robert Penn Warren, a Poet of the South?" Madden, *Legacy of Robert Penn Warren* 32–44.

Justus, James. *The Achievement of Robert Penn Warren*. Baton Rouge: Louisiana State UP, 1981.

Koppelman, Robert S. *Robert Penn Warren's Modernist Spirituality*. Columbia: U of Missouri P, 1995.

Liddell, Henry George, and Robert Scott. *A Greek-English Lexicon*. Oxford: Oxford UP, 1996.

Madden, David, ed. *The Legacy of Robert Penn Warren*. Baton Rouge: Louisiana State UP, 2000.

Millichap, Joseph R., ed. *Robert Penn Warren: A Study of the Short Fiction*. Twayne Studies in Short Fiction 39. New York: Twayne, 1992.

Ovid. *Metamorphoses*. Trans. Samuel Garth et al. Amsterdam, 1732. New York: Garland, 1976.

Pausanias. *Description of Greece*. Trans. W. H. S. Jones and H. A. Ormerod. Cambridge: Harvard UP/Loeb Library, 1918.

Plato. *The Collected Dialogues*. Ed. Edith Hamilton and Huntington Cairns. Princeton: Princeton UP, 1961.

Runyon, Randolph Paul. *The Braided Dream: Robert Penn Warren's Late Poetry*. Lexington: UP of Kentucky, 1990.

———. *In La Fontaine's Labyrinth: A Thread through the Fables*. Charlottesville: Rookwood, 2000.

———. *Reading Raymond Carver*. Syracuse: Syracuse UP, 1992.

———. "La séquence et la symétrie comme principes d'organisation chez Montesquieu, La Fontaine et Montaigne." *Le Recueil littéraire: Pratiques et théorie d'une forme*. Rennes: Presses Universitaires de Rennes, 2003. 177–86.

———. *The Taciturn Text: The Fiction of Robert Penn Warren*. Columbus: Ohio State UP, 1990.

WORKS CITED

Ruppersburg, Hugh. *Robert Penn Warren and the American Imagination.* Athens: U of Georgia P, 1990.

Smith, Dave. "Notes on a Form to Be Lived." *Homage to Robert Penn Warren.* Ed. Frank Graziano. Durango, CO: Logbridge-Rhodes, 1981. 33–55.

Sophocles. *Oedipus the King.* Trans. F. Storr. Cambridge: Harvard UP/Loeb Library, 1913.

————. *The Oedipus Tyrannos of Sophocles.* Ed. Richard Jebb. Cambridge. Cambridge UP, 1887.

Stephanus. *Thesaurus Graecae Linguae.* Graz: Akademische Druck–u. Verlagsanstalt, 1954.

Strandberg, Victor. *A Colder Fire: The Poetry of Robert Penn Warren.* Lexington: UP of Kentucky, 1965.

————. *The Poetic Vision of Robert Penn Warren.* Lexington: UP of Kentucky, 1977.

————. "Robert Penn Warren and the Classical Tradition." *Mississippi Quarterly* 48.1 (Winter 1994–95): 17–28.

————. "Whatever Happened to 'You'?—A Poetic Odyssey." *RPW: An Annual of Robert Penn Warren Studies* 1 (2001): 143–61.

Szczesiul, Anthony. *Racial Politics and Robert Penn Warren's Poetry.* Gainesville: UP of Florida, 2002.

Walker, Marshall. *Robert Penn Warren: A Vision Earned.* Edinburgh: Paul Harris, 1979.

Warren, Robert Penn. *All the King's Men.* New York: Harcourt, Brace, 1946.

————. *Brother to Dragons: A Tale in Verse and Voices.* New York: Random, 1953.

————. *The Cave.* New York: Random, 1959.

————. *The Circus in the Attic and Other Stories.* New York: Harcourt, Brace, 1947.

————. *Cleanth Brooks and Robert Penn Warren: A Literary Correspondence.* Ed. James A. Grimshaw Jr. Columbia: U of Missouri P, 1998.

————. *The Collected Poems of Robert Penn Warren.* Ed. John Burt. Baton Rouge: Louisiana State UP, 1998.

————. Commentary on "The Return: An Elegy." *Thirtieth Year to Heaven.* Winston-Salem: Jackpine, 1980. 11–16.

————. *The Gods of Mount Olympus.* New York: Random, 1959.

————. *John Brown: The Making of a Martyr.* 1929. Nashville: J. S. Sanders, 1993.

————. "John Crowe Ransom: A Study in Irony." *Virginia Quarterly Review* 11 (Jan. 1935): 93–112.

————. "Knowledge and the Image of Man." *Robert Penn Warren: A Collection of Critical Essays.* Ed. John Lewis Longley Jr. New York: New York UP, 1965. 237–46. Orig. in *Southern Review,* Spring 1955.

————. *New and Selected Essays.* New York: Random, 1989.

————. *Night Rider.* New York: Random, 1939; New York: Vintage, 1979.

————. "Notes on the Poetry of John Crowe Ransom at His Eightieth Birthday." *New and Selected Essays,* 303–32. Orig. in *Kenyon Review,* June 1968.

————. *A Place to Come To.* New York: Random, 1977.

————. *Portrait of a Father.* Lexington: UP of Kentucky, 1988.

———. "Pure and Impure Poetry." *New and Selected Essays*, 3–28.

———. *Robert Penn Warren Talking: Interviews, 1950–1978*. Ed. Floyd C. Watkins and John T. Hiers. New York: Random, 1980.

———. *Selected Letters of Robert Penn Warren*. Vol. 1, *The Apprentice Years, 1924–1934*. Ed. William Bedford Clark. Baton Rouge: Louisiana State UP, 2000.

———. *Selected Letters of Robert Penn Warren*. Vol. 2, *The Southern Review Years, 1935–1942*. Ed. William Bedford Clark. Baton Rouge: Louisiana State UP, 2001.

———. *Selected Poems of Robert Penn Warren*. Ed. John Burt. Baton Rouge: Louisiana State UP, 2001.

———. *Wilderness: A Tale of the Civil War*. New York: Random, 1961.

———. *World Enough and Time*. New York: Random, 1950. New York: Vintage, 1979.

Watkins, Floyd. *Then and Now: The Personal Past in the Poetry of Robert Penn Warren*. Lexington: UP of Kentucky, 1982.

Weeks, Dennis L., ed. *"To Love So Well the World": A Festschrift in Honor of Robert Penn Warren*. New York: Peter Lang, 1992.

Wilson, Deborah. "Medusa, the Movies, and the King's Men." Madden, *Legacy of Robert Penn Warren*, 70–83.

INDEX
WARREN'S
WORKS

News Photo, 142, 163–64
Night: The Motel Down the Road from the Pen, 106
Night Is Personal, 106, 130, 132, 134, 141
Night Rider, 201, 205
Nightmare of Man, 78, 93
Nightmare of Mouse, 78, 92
No Bird Does Call, 13, 57, 144, 155, 177, 206
Nocturne, 59, 60, 79
Nocturne: Traveling Salesman in Hotel Bedroom, 78, 90
Not to Be Trusted, 94, 104–5, 214n7
Notes on the Poetry of John Crowe Ransom, 210n9
Now and Then, 1, 76, 121, 193–95
Nursery Rhymes, 78, 91–93

O
Obsession, 78
Old Nigger on One-Mule Cart Encountered Late at Night When Driving Home from Party in the Back Country, 174, 176, 184–85, 186, 187–90, 193–95, 205
One Drunk Allegory, 94
Only Trouble, The, 106
Or Else: Poem/Poems 1968–1974, 1, 95, 134, 137, 138, 143–74, 177, 201, 203, 205, 212n14, 216n2
Original Sin: A Short Story, 36, 40–42, 43, 153
Ornithology in a World of Flux, 78, 88–89

P
Pacific Gazer, 8, 10, 30–31
Paradox, 174, 180–81
Paul Valéry Stood on the Cliff and Confronted the Furious Energies of Nature, 106, 113–14, 122, 125

Penological Study: Southern Exposure, 106, 124, 128–29, 130, 132, 135–36, 137
Picnic Remembered, 36, 38, 40–41, 42, 45–46, 202
Place and Time, 94
Place to Come To, A, 4, 13, 97–98, 131–32, 134, 138–39, 144, 148, 154, 176, 177, 201–2, 204, 205
Place Where Nothing Is, A, 106, 123, 124, 136
Place Where the Boy Pointed, The, 94
Pondy Woods, 8, 9, 10–11, 16–18, 19, 25, 211–12n9
Portrait of a Father, 127–8, 135, 198
Problem in Spatial Composition, A, 142, 172
Problem of Knowledge, 8, 31–32, 33
Prognosis: A Short Story, the End of Which You Will Know Soon Enough, 78, 79, 91
Promises: Poems 1954–1956 (1957), 1, 2, 3, 48–78, 79, 116–18, 132, 138, 203, 213n1
Psychological Profile, 142
Pure and Impure Poetry, 218n7
Pursuit, 36, 43–45, 180

Q
Question and Answer, 36, 43–44, 45–46

R
Ransom, 8, 11, 22–23
Rattlesnake Country, 142, 156–59
Reading Late at Night, Thermometer Falling, 142, 166–68, 169, 173, 212n14
Real Question Calling for Solution, A, 78, 82–83
Rebuke of the Rocks, 8, 16–18

INDEX

GENERAL
ENTRIES

Freud, Sigmund: "The Infantile Genital Organization of the Libido," 116, 215n3; *The Interpretation of Dreams*, 15, 169, 211n7; "Medusa's Head," 116–18, 132, 145, 215n4

G
grandfather, 19–21, 41–43, 55–58, 60, 142, 165–66, 198, 201, 205
Graves, Robert, 176, 216n2
Grimshaw, James A., Jr., 37, 98, 209n1, 209n3, 212n17

H
Hardy, Thomas, 3, 14
Hendricks, Randy, 97, 185, 209n1, 211–12n9, 217n6
Herodotus, 23, 212n13
Hesiod, 218n11
Hoffman, Daniel, 2, 210n7
Hugo, Victor, 218n6
Hummer, T. R., 217n6

I
insemination, 97, 103, 117, 126, 134, 146, 177, 198, 206

J
Justus, James, 13, 108, 143, 215n5

K
Koppelman, Robert, 2, 209n1, 210n8

L
Lamartine, Alphonse de, 12–13, 211n5
Latimer, Ronald Lane, 10

M
Medusa, 4–7, 13, 67, 115–19, 123, 130–35, 139, 145–46, 148, 150, 196, 198–206, 215n4, 215n7, 218n4

mirror, 4, 6, 44–47, 84, 118, 131, 142–44, 146, 152, 162, 198–99, 202, 204
mother, 4, 11–16, 19–21, 42–43, 57, 61–62, 70, 92–98, 103, 105, 116–17, 123, 126, 132–33, 135–38, 144–46, 148, 151, 161, 165–66, 177–78, 200–205, 208, 210n3, 210n4, 211n6, 211n8, 213n2, 215n9, 218n2
music, 18–19, 37, 85, 92, 186, 189, 194, 213n2

O
Oedipus, 116, 185–86, 194–95, 201, 217n6, 217n8, 217n9, 218n2
Orpheus, 24–25, 31–33
Ovid, 6–7, 32–33, 139, 207, 216n11

P
parents, 20, 51–52, 54–55, 67, 70, 116, 126, 134, 150, 154, 161, 186, 205
Pausanias, 217n8
Perseus, 4–7, 13, 67, 97, 100, 115–18, 130–34, 139, 145–48, 176–77, 194–99, 201–6, 215n7, 217n6
Pound, Ezra, 2, 158

R
Ransom, John Crowe, 2, 3, 8, 11, 22–23, 210n10, 210n11
Runyon, Randolph Paul: *The Braided Dream*, 1, 13, 124, 176, 193; *The Taciturn Text*, 13, 116, 202, 218n2, 218n4
Ruppersburg, Hugh, 133, 209n1

S
Shakespeare, 23, 24
Smith, Dave, 1, 143, 149, 209n5, 216n1
Sophocles, 186, 195, 217n8
Strandberg, Victor, 1, 2, 132; *A Colder Fire*, 13, 15–16, 17–18, 23–25, 27–28, 37, 41, 44, 46, 49–54, 58, 62, 73, 76, 79–80,

92, 209n4, 212n17, 213n3; *The Poetic Vision,* 26, 58–59, 108, 126, 129, 169, 178, 181; "Robert Penn Warren and the Classical Tradition, 217–18n9; "Whatever Happened to 'You'?—A Poetic Odyssey," 83

suicide, 83, 105, 199–201

Szczesiul, Anthony, 184, 194, 209n1, 211–12n9, 215n5

T

Tate, Allen, 9–10, 129, 199

Thomas, Antoine-Léonard, 13, 211n5

V

Virgil, 42, 83

W

Walker, Marshall, 127

Warren, Robert Franklin (father), 85, 135, 198

Watkins, Floyd, 98, 214

Wilson, Deborah, 218n4

X

Xerxes, 23–26

Ghostly Parallels was designed and typeset on a Macintosh computer system using QuarkXPress software. The body text is set in 10/13 Adobe Garamond and display type is set in Granjon. This book was designed and typeset by Kelly Gray and manufactured by Thomson-Shore, Inc.